The Austraflora A-Z ot
Australian Plants

Bill Molyneux and Sue Forrester

Published in Australia in 2002 by Reed New Holland
an imprint of New Holland Publishers (Australia) Pty Ltd
Sydney • Auckland • London • Cape Town

14 Aquatic Drive Frenchs Forest NSW 2086 Australia
218 Lake Road Northcote Auckland New Zealand
86 Edgware Road London W2 2EA United Kingdom
80 McKenzie Street Cape Town 8001 South Africa

This edition first published in 1997 by Reed Books
Reprinted in 2002 and 2003 by Reed New Holland

National Library of Australia Cataloguing-in-Publication Data:

Molyneux, Bill.
The Austraflora A–Z of Australian plants.

Bibliography.
ISBN 1 876334 84 3.

1. Native plant gardening - Australia. 2. Wild flower
gardening - Australia. 3. Plants - Australia -
Identification. 4. Plants - Identification. 5. Botany -
Australia. I. Forrester, Susan Glen. II. Molyneux, Bill.
Austraflora guide to choosing and growing Australian plants.
III. Austraflora Nursery. IV. Title. V. Title : A–Z of
Australian plants. VI. Title : A to Z of Australian plants.

635.95194

Formatting and paging by Melbourne Media Services
Printed in China and produced by Phoenix Offset

The name Austraflora and its logo are protected by Trade Mark
and Copyright.

Website: www.austraflora.com
Email: info@austraflora.com

Foreword

ill Molyneux and Sue Forrester have produced a valuable upgrade
to their *Austraflora Handbook* with the 1997 edition. Their guide to
hoosing and growing Australian Plants is a timely addition to the
ollective knowledge of the day.

There is a worldwide trend to cultivate local area plants. In WA this
as been fostered by groups such as Greening Western Australia and
ie State Water Utility. Adopting this philosophy aids in reducing the
raw on our precious and increasingly threatened water resources and
arries many other benefits. Local animals and even insects are often
ependent on certain plants for habitat, food, shelter and even repro-
uctive support.

As Local Authorities and community groups struggle to reverse the
egradation of previous years and encourage home owners to replant
ie local species one ingredient that is often missing is plant knowl-
dge. This book, with its highly detailed yet easily accessible style, will
ring information about many varieties within easy reach of home gar-
eners and professionals alike.

Australian Plant Breeders Rights legislation has given real encour-
gement to breeders to look seriously at our plant heritage. It is now
orthwhile for them to develop or find variations in our wonderfully
iverse and unique plants so the world's gardeners can enjoy these cul-
vars.

While Bill and Sue have been responsible for more than a few such
itroductions their book strives to keep pace with the new additions to
ur plant lexicon. With the rapidly widening selection of new cultivars
: is imperative that the *Austraflora A-Z of Australian Plants* is con-
tantly updated.

I commend this handbook to you. It is a compact mine of plant
escriptions and information that can be carried on visits to garden cen-
es, walks through Botanical gardens or strolls through the bush. I
ope you will find it as informative and easy to use as I have.

Neville Passmore

*Neville Passmore is a regular member of the
"Gardening Australia" Team – presenting on ABC TV and
contributing to the* Gardening Australia Magazine.

Contents

Introduction

This revised edition represents thirty years of continuous production of *The Austraflora A–Z of Australian Plants*. Over 1600 plants are listed, more than 100 of which are new inclusions.

You can select for climatic conditions Australia-wide — and overseas, where many Australian plants are now being grown. This is not just a single-nursery catalogue, but one in which the plants described are regularly available through nurseries and garden centres across Australia It's like having a dozen nursery catalogues rolled into one.

So no matter where you live, you'll find plants suitable for your garden in this extensive collection. And the sections on climates, soil and design will help you to prepare your garden better for the plants you select.

Gardening should be a pleasure, with the energy and thought expended resulting in a pleasing environment in which to relax and entertain.

New Plant Developments

Some plants take the world by storm, and a dwarf *Banksia* called 'Birthday Candles', which we at Austraflora developed and introduced some years ago, is such a plant. Have a look at the photograph opposite page 32 and you'll see what we mean.

In Japan it is called the 'Bonsai Banksia', and it's just as popular in other Asian countries, as well as New Zealand. Another Austraflora plant, 'Mozzie Blocker', a soft, attractive shrub with the ability to keep mosquitoes at bay, has been launched on both Australian and overseas markets.

To celebrate the life and work of Mary MacKillop, also known as The People's Saint, a superb new bottlebrush has been released. *Callistemon* 'Mary MacKillop' is available Australia-wide, with sales supporting the continuation of her work.

How to use *The Austraflora A–Z of Australian Plants*

The following information is relevant to the many people wishing to create a new garden or to add to the one they have, as well as those involved in design on a broader scale, such as landscape architects and designers, and directors of civic parks and gardens. People on the land will find the right trees and shrubs for stock shade and shelter belts.

In addition to the alphabetical **Plant Selection List** (pp. 30-156), numerous **Quick-pick Mini-lists** (pp. 157-171) have been compiled to provide you with information on plants for specific purposes; for example, there are mini-lists of plants for narrow, confined areas and plants suitable for hedges and screening. Once you have found the plants that meet your particular requirements in the relevant mini-list you can consult the **Plant Selection List** for detailed information on their size, structure, flowering time and growing needs.

If you live in a temperate zone, you may be surprised by the range of beautiful northern rainforest species listed in *The Austraflora A–Z of Australian Plants* which can thrive in cool, drier climates. Similarly, if you live in the northern regions of Australia, you will be delighted to find that a considerable number of southern plants are able to adapt quite well to your conditions.

Pleasure and Fulfilment in Your Garden

The section on **The Basics of Good Gardening** covers recognition of soil types and how to overcome deficiencies, as well as planting, staking, fertilising, maintenance and design. Our decades of experience in designing and installing countless gardens, both private and industrial, have given us a clear understanding of what it takes to create a garden of pleasure, fulfilment and permanence.

We believe sharing our knowledge with you will help make your own gardening experiences even more satisfying.

We have even tossed in a bit of botany to help you understand why plants are named the way they are.

Name Changes in Plants

Talking of botany, since our last edition of *The Austraflora A–Z of Australian Plants* there has been a major change in the status of the 'bloodwood' group of eucalypts. These species now have the generic name of *Corymbia*. For example, using perhaps the most popular member of this group, the Lemon-scented Gum, it is now known as *Corymbia citriodora*, not *Eucalyptus citriodora*. You will find those 'bloodwoods' included in *The Austraflora A–Z of Australian Plants* listed as *Corymbia* in the relevant section on page 175.

An Overview

While garden fashions seem to be as changeable as clothing or art, one thing remains constant; that is, quality — if the fashion is to survive. In the world of gardening, the quality of fashion is often dubious.

The more time spent on the initial planning of a garden, the fewer ongoing problems there should be. And less doubts about whether you've done the right thing'.

Design and build a garden for your needs, taking into account the available time you may have for its maintenance. Look at all plants, whether Australian or introduced, and choose and blend to create your preferred garden. Most importantly, do your own thing, don't just copy someone else's ideas. It will be so much more satisfying this way, and much more fun.

The Name of Edna Walling

Amongst the plants detailed in the New and Recent Introductions (page 172) you will notice a number of plants bearing the cultivar name 'Edna Walling', honouring Australia's best known landscape and garden designer. Sue, who has personal connections both with Edna Walling and with Bickleigh Vale, the village Walling created over several decades from the 1920s, has been selecting forms of Australian plants which are appropriate to the Edna Walling style of garden. This range of plants will increase with time, and fulfill the wishes of Edna Walling's executors that her name be perpetuated in a meaningful and honourable way.

Austraflora Plants — A Tradition Continued

Whilst Austraflora Nursery, the acknowledged leader in the development and introduction of Australian plants, no longer has a retail division, Austraflora-bred plants are now becoming widely available through retail nurseries and garden centres around Australia. The Austraflora Collection, presenting more than fifty registered varieties, encapsulates the best of our thirty years of selecting, developing and introducing to horticulture some of Australia's rich flora. Enquire at your own local nursery for this range of plants, which carry the distinctive Austraflora label.

Planning Your Garden

Gardens should be places of beauty and relaxation in which you find respite from the pressures of life. They should be structured to suit your way of life and the amount of time you have available for their upkeep. Unfortunately, too many gardens just 'happen'.

These days a garden is no longer an area occupied simply by trees, shrubs, grass, a clotheslines and a toolshed: even a confined suburban block may have, in addition, a double garage, a swimming pool, a spa, a hot tub, a barbecue, a trampoline or even a boat tucked away in a corner. Just as the allotment of space is critical inside the home, so is it outside, if one or several of these items are to be accommodated within the limited area available. It does not matter whether you live in tropical Cairns or the drier southern temperate regions, you must establish your outdoor needs before you start planting. Ask yourself the following questions:

- Have we determined what permanent fixtures will be built in the garden?
- Do we want hard surfaces or lawns or a combination of both?
- When the children are old enough to have their own cars, where will they park them?
- Do we want a formal garden, an Australian cottage garden or a combination of styles?
- What is the direction of the prevailing wind?
- Where is the sun's path in relation to our block?
- Are there buildings or neighbouring houses to be screened?
- Are there animals to be allowed for?

Once you know your requirements, sketch a basic plan. You should plan your garden as you would, say, a kitchen, where efficient use of space is vital. Set out on paper all the items you feel may need to be incorporated (now and in the future) and where they would be most appropriately placed.

As part of your planning you should also take time to visit other gardens. Try to isolate the factors that make certain gardens appealing. Remember that simplicity and uncluttered lines will result in a harmonious garden — a jumbled collection of plants chosen at random will always be just that. If you feel uncertain about your ability to handle the task yourself, use a professional landscape planner, just as you would engage an architect or draughtsman to assist in planning a house.

Whether you are embarking on a new garden or renovating an old one, first spend time grasping the basic principles and practices of good gardening. Understanding your soil and what may be required to condition it correctly is vital to success. Most gardeners completely overlook the need to consider the structure and deficiencies of their soil when they plan a new landscape. If plants are the furnishings of a garden, soils are the foundations; and we all know what happens to houses with poor footings. (The following section, The Basics of Good Gardening, provides information on how to prepare your soil before you begin planting.)

The selection of plants and their placement can make or break a garden — and sometimes foundations and a few roof tiles! Most gardens have space for one or two medium to large trees. Trees are not only aesthetically pleasing: they also assist in conditioning the atmosphere around the home. A good leafy canopy, in addition to keeping summer temperatures down by casting shade and shedding moisture, reduces winter radiation of heat from the earth and buildings.

Ensure, however, that the tree you choose is not planted too close to your house, particularly if you have older or unprotected foundations. It does not take many years for the roots of a vigorous tree to spread beyond the line of its canopy in search of nutrients and anchorage. In doing so the roots often disturb and damage foundations or drainage pipes. The roots of some trees actually enter pipes in their search for water.

People often think it is necessary to use deciduous trees on the northern or western sides of houses to allow winter sun to penetrate. This may be true in some instances, but a deciduous tree allows more heat to escape from a house on a winter night than it helps that building gain during the day. A fully foliaged tree, on the other hand, as we have pointed out, assists heat retention on winter nights. With correct selection, placement and pruning, an evergreen tree can be more effective in allowing winter sun under its canopy than a many branched, low, spreading deciduous tree.

Many trees which are planted in small suburban allotments are more suited to open parklands: either people don't recognise just how big they will grow, even in a relatively short time, or they are seeking a quick effect. So balance and scale are important aspects to consider, otherwise that bare block can easily become an over-planted forest in just a few years.

Unfortunately the reverse is true of many northern Australian gardens. People in tropical regions are often resistant to planting even medium-sized trees, perhaps because they are frightened that trees might fall on their houses if a cyclone occurred. It seems a pity to allow such a very remote possibility to limit the shade and comfort of a property. The residents of Darwin, however, have not let one of the worst cyclones in recent Australian history prevent them from planting trees in their restored gardens, and the advantages are already apparent.

Screening for privacy is an aspect of gardening requiring a lot of thought. Because few people can picture a small plant in a pot as a fully grown shrub, many shrubs are planted in areas too narrow or confined for their eventual size. Narrow walkways between the house and fenceline can become so overgrown that they become impossible to use. Just as effective a screen can be achieved, without loss of space, by growing climbing plants on a wire frame. For an area approximately 1.5 metres wide, privacy and beauty can be attained with a width loss of perhaps only 20 centimetres.

The height of your wire fence should be determined by your requirements. If the house next door and your own have only low windows facing each other, you may not need to construct a wire frame higher than 2.5 metres. On the other hand, if the house next door has a second storey, your screen may need to be higher. We have included a mini-list on climbing plants (p. 158) to help you select the correct climbers for your needs.

In summing up the principles of establishing a garden, we cannot over-emphasise the need for long-term planning, rather than short-term, stop-gap alternatives that may prove to be quite unsuited to your needs. Remember that a garden represents a large financial investment. Sympathetically created it will add greatly to the value of your property. More than that, a successful garden is a place of relaxation where you may enjoy peace and solitude or the company of family and friends. It should never be a constant source of work or frustration.

The Basics of Good Gardening

Soil Preparation

If your soil is sandy you have the advantage of being able to work it at any time of the year: it is seldom so wet that turning it over is impossible. However, most sandy soils lack humus, which must be added to create a satisfactory growing medium. Up to 100 per cent by volume of humus may be added. Humus and its application are discussed later in the section.

1   2

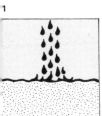 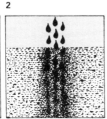

1 Some sandy soils, especially those low in humus, resist the penetration of water.

2 Adding humus allows the water to penetrate and be held in the soil. The inclusion of a water saturation aid, such as Debco SaturAid, assists this effect even more.

If you live in a clay area you are not so fortunate: attempting to turn over and break up clay when it is in a wet, plastic state can be frustrating. You will achieve far more in those times of the year when the soil is drier. Clay soils require the addition of gypsum (to floculate the soil particles) and humus (to open up the soil) to make them friable.

1   2

1 This soil is dry clay loam low in humus. Water poured into a hole in it will not drain away, a sure indication of the soil's structural deficiency.

2 After an hour only the top centimetre of soil has absorbed any water. It is sticky and unworkable, while the soil below is still dry.

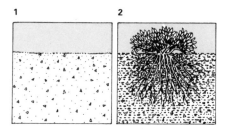

1 Gypsum gives clay soil a more open structure.

2 Clay with added gypsum and humus becomes friable and allows roots to penetrate freely.

Gypsum

You will find that breaking up clay to the point where gypsum may be added is a lengthy job. The largest lumps should be no bigger than a golf ball: if they are any larger than this in diameter the chemical action of the gypsum will not be effective. Medium clay requires the application of 1 kilogram of gypsum per square metre. Worms will also further help to break down the lumps of clay.

1 Clay soils should be thoroughly dug or rotary hoed to a depth of approximatley 15 centimetres.

2 Broadcast half the gypsum evenly over the broken-up surface.

3 Dig or rotary hoe the clay again to mix the gypsum in deeply. Add the remaining gypsum and work through thoroughly.

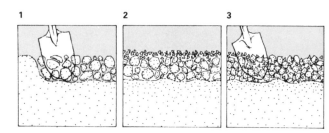

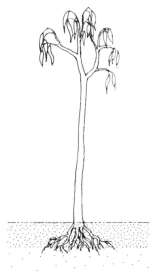

Spindly top growth and instability result from poor root development in heavy clay soil.

The long-term results of less than thorough soil preparation are quite unsatisfactory. A popular practice in clay soil areas is first to pick at the surface of the heavy soil with a fork and then to 'ice the cake' by adding a 50:50 mixture of 'sandy loam' (often high in salt and low in humus) and 'mountain soil' (generally a rich red colour, but with a high clay content). This mixture is spread over the planting surfaces, often to a minimal depth. Inevitably, when a hole is dug for a plant, the heavy clay is encountered again below the 'icing'. So remember that if you are placing soil over clay that has not previously been worked, the latter should be turned and supplied with gypsum beforehand.

Humus

The word humus describes all organic matter in the soil structure. Humus is comprised of plant remains, such as roots, stems and spent leaves, together with animal and insect excretions. In simple terms, it is that part of the soil that holds the elements important to plant growth and supplies them in dilute form. Water. the diluting agent in this process, is also vital, and humus has the ability to retain it for plant needs.

1 Humus is essential to good soil structure. It retains moisture in open, sandy soil and makes dense, compacted clay more friable.

2 Humus has been worked through this calcareous sand at a ratio of 50:50. The soil is now capable of supporting young, fibrous-rooted plants, even in times of heat stress.

Healthy root development occurs in open soils with a good humus level; this in turn increases the plant's ability to take up and use nutrients for growth. Root development and therefore plant growth are retarded in soils such as clay which are so fine that they compact and cement or in soils like leached sand which have a low humus content.

The addition of humus to clay is beneficial. If compost is not to hand, shredded pinebark (pinepeat), which is generally available, can be used.

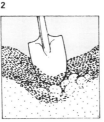
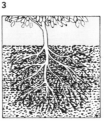

1 Add humus to the soil surface to a depth of 8–10 centimetres.

2 Work the humus evenly through the clay.

3 The resulting friable soil allows good root development.

A layer of humus to the suggested depth of 8–10 centimetres will support a range of plants from greatly differing natural habitats. When this amount of humus is worked through the clay, it provides a well-drained and aerated planting depth of 18–20 centimetres. Coarse river sand may also be added to assist drainage. Remember, too, that the gypsum previously worked in is working on the soil below this level, further improving air and water movement. Your plants will therefore have nearly 30 centimetres in which to grow, and the top 30 centimetres are the critical zone for many of the small, fibrous-rooted heathland and sandplain plants that are so horticulturally desirable. Epacris, dryandras, small banksias, verticordias and lechenaultias will thrive in these conditions.

Planting Out

Cutting-grown Plants

A young cutting-grown plant develops a fibrous root system. In many cases the roots are not sufficiently developed to bind the soil ball together so no preparation is needed before planting; in other cases the roots may require just the lightest teasing with your fingertips to loosen them prior to planting. However, as a cutting-grown plant ages it develops a dense root mass at the bottom of the pot. It may be necessary to loosen and lightly prune these roots before planting. This will promote vigorous new root growth.

1 A cutting-grown plant has a fibrous root system.

2 If its roots are tightly matted, soak the root ball and gently tease the roots out a little.

1

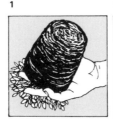

2

Seedling-grown Plants

A plant grown from seed develops a thick primary or 'tap' root and many, slightly thinner, secondary roots. These may only need to be gently uncoiled and spread a little, so that can move away from the pot soil and into the prepared ground once the plant has been planted. In a very old plant, the tap root may become so tightly coiled that it is referred to as pot or root bound. However, careful root pruning will help such a plant develop into a healthy shrub or tree.

1 A seedling-grown plant develops a robust root system.

2 Its roots may require light pruning and gentle teasing out.

1

2

Positioning the Plant

When positioning the plant in the ground, ensure that it is neither too low nor too high. If the plant is too low, its stem may be so constantly wet that it rots; if the plant is too high, its roots may be exposed to hot, drying sun and wind as soil washes away. Positioning the plant a fraction below the ground surface does not matter as the surrounding soil will slightly subside.

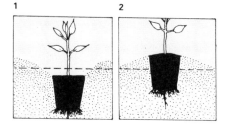

1 A shrub which has been planted too low.

2 A shrub which has been planted too high.

Fertilising

Fertiliser can be applied at the time of planting or be included in the soil preparation beforehand. A number of fertilisers with different methods and rates of nutrient release are available. The coated, slow-release pellets are popular and convenient, and again there is a choice of release rates.

Australian plants in general prefer low levels of phosphorus, so select your fertiliser accordingly. Fertilisers are rated by their NPK content, that is, by their nitrogen (N), phosphorus (P) and potash (K) levels. Select a fertiliser that has a low level of phosphorus and use it according to the manufacturer's directions. Fertilisers with higher levels of phosphorus are suitable for plants originating in the wet northern rainforests of Queensland and New South Wales, but are not suitable for plants from the leached soils of heathlands and sandplains.

Blood-and-bone and hoof-and-horn are two commonly used fertilisers in powdered form. Their main disadvantage is that their odour attracts dogs, cats and even foxes. Fortunately, it repels rabbits.

The most practical way of applying fertiliser is to thoroughly mix the prescribed amount through the soil into which a plant is to go. This ensures that the roots will find this food source as they spread out and that large concentrations of fertiliser do not occur in patches. After planting, thoroughly water both the plant and the surrounding soil. Any firming down of the soil should be done prior to this and not when the soil is very wet. Over-working wet soil drives out air and can cause water logging.

On-going Fertilising

Regular fertilising, like pruning, is essential for healthy, vigorous plants. It is best to apply fertilisers beyond the plants' perimeters to encourage their roots to grow outward.

Adding a saturation aid such as Debco SaturAid will enhance the effect of your fertiliser and, if regular watering is not possible, Debco Raindrops or a similar product which assists water retention can also be helpful.

Granulated nitrogen, available as Easi-green, is recommended for top dressing in early spring. The fine, white grains start dissolving as soon as water is applied to them, providing a ready supply of nutrients for plants hungry after winter.

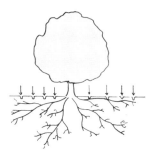

When feeding established plants, apply fertiliser mainly beyond the canopy, in holes made with a fork.

These fertilising methods are also effective for plants growing in pots, tubs or hanging baskets.

A Caution

Although aged stable straw may be used as a mulching material or even as a source of humus when dug into the soil, care should be exercised with animal manures. Fowl, pig and cow manures are potentially harmful to Australian plants even after lengthy aging. You should confine the use of such materials to the gross-feeding plants of the vegetable garden which can cope with high nutrient levels.

Staking

Sometimes, large plants require support while their root systems are developing. However, bad staking can only impede healthy plant growth.

The worst method is to drive a heavy stake into the ground close to the trunk, which is then lashed to it. The action often damages roots and the rigidity of the stake hinders further root development. As well, the trunk develops an attenuated, spindly habit when it is prevented from moving freely.

Two or three stakes with a flexible tie running between them should be used instead. The flexible tie gives support in windy weather, but allows sufficient movement for the trunk and root to grow strongly.

1 The correct support for a large plant.

2 An incorrectly staked plant.

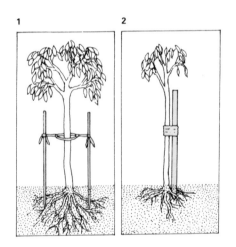

OPPOSITE PAGE:
The tall, smooth-trunked trees impart a parkland effect to this secluded, mud-brick walled garden. Light screening provides privacy as one sits and enjoys the numerous delicate plants at close quarters.

TOP LEFT AND LEFT:
Archirhodomyrtus beckleri
'Rose Myrtle'

A pretty glossy-leaved small shrub with perfumed 'mini rose' flowers in spring and summer, followed by juicy berries which can be made into a delicious sticky conserve. 'Rose Myrtle' may be successfully used in mixed plantings, and is a lovely container plant.

BELOW:
Goodenia ovata
'Austraflora Coverup'

The Australian answer to ivy with none of its vices. Drought-tolerant, its layering habit assists in soil binding, and its flowers will brighten gardens large or small in winter–spring and late summer–autumn.

Tie material should not be abrasive. Thick, plastic-covered wire is suitable, as are old tights or ties made from similar material. Rope, while strong, should be wrapped in a softer material if it is to be in contact with the plant.

Stakes should not be used to hold up trees which have fallen over. The failure of these trees to establish a good hold on the soil is almost always due to inadequate soil preparation or incorrect staking in the first place. The addition of a stake will accentuate rather than solve this problem, and eventually the tree will have to be replaced.

Rocks may be used as a form of support for trees such as *Eucalyptus caesia*. Partly buried in the soil covering the tree roots, the rocks look like a natural outcrop and provide an attractive feature in the landscape. This method of support is most effective in very windy areas where it is difficult to establish even small shrubs.

Fences and Tree Guards

In rural or broad-acre plantings, where rabbits, hares, goats or stock may cause damage to young plants, protection must be provided. A wire-mesh fence erected around planted areas is the best method of preventing rabbits and hares from getting to the plants. The netting can be obtained in large rolls, and a width of 1 metre provides sufficient height for the fence; the openings in the mesh should be 5 centimetres in diameter.

The fencing is easily constructed by driving star pickets into the ground at 5 metre intervals and fastening the netting to these. Approximately 30 centimetres of the netting is turned out at the bottom and covered with soil, held in place with rocks or secured with wire pegs. Rabbits and hares attempt to dig at the foot of a fence, and this method prevents them from getting in. For additional strength and rigidity after the base has been secured, the netting can be fixed to wire which has been run all the way around the fence through an upper hole in the star pickets. No tree guards are required with this method of fencing. However, for stock such as cattle or sheep a sturdier fence will be necessary.

Tree guards with stakes can be used to discourage small predators such as rabbits and hares, particularly where it may be difficult to erect a fence. Guards are available in a range of materials, including open-weave cloth and clear plastic, and are usually held in place by three wooden stakes. The woven material is generally preferable, as it holds in place better on the stakes and does not cause the heat stress that trees have experienced with plastic.

Mulching

The materials that provide a mulch on the ground are, firstly, the plants themselves; secondly, leaves and twigs that have been collected together and perhaps shredded; and thirdly, rocks, with gravel and sand which derive from the rock.

While unmulched plants are not necessarily under more stress than mulched plants from lack of water, the use of mulching materials over the soil performs two very important functions. The soil surface does not dry out, thereby preventing the caking effect that makes penetration of water into the soil very difficult. As well, plant roots are operating in a more even temperature and damage to those close to the surface is avoided.

Rocks serve a number of functions. They are used to change levels on a gently sloping bed; as a visual aspect of the landscape; and to provide a moist, cool position for roots that venture under them.

Twigs, leaves, wood chips, sand, gravel, well-aged lawn clippings and stable straw are regularly used as mulches. So too are some of the porous woven materials which can be used under any of the above to assist in weed control while still allowing water and air through to the soil.

Plants, leaves, twigs, rocks, gravel and sand all contribute to the mulching process.

Dense, ground-covering plants, some of which sucker or layer, provide the most visually pleasing mulch. They protect not only their own roots, but also those of taller, more upright shrubs growing among them.

Avoid using powdery sawdust from sanding machines as mulching material: it packs hard and is almost impervious to water. Remember too that as uncomposted (or fresh) organic mulches break down they take nitrogen from the soil; it is therefore necessary to apply a nitrogenous fertiliser, such as blood and-bone or Easi-green, to the soil beneath the mulch each year during the warmer months.

Pruning

Pruning is a necessary discipline to develop plant shape and to maintain plant vigour in an established garden. You will find that it is seldom difficult and often rewarding because it brings you into closer contact with your plants.

On windy sites, regular pruning will reduce the amount of whipping experienced by tall, slim plants that have developed in response to excessive water and fertiliser. The removal of part of the growth evenly over plants encourages lateral and lower growth, which helps to stabilise trees and shrubs.

Some plants, such as boronias, croweas, baeckeas, tetra-thecas and a host of other small shrubs, need only regular tip pruning to encourage a dense, compact habit. Other plants, such as callistemons and many grevilleas, require considerable cutting back.

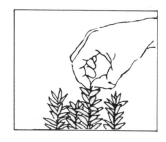

Tip prune all shrubs, using secateurs or finger and thumb.

1 This callistemon has become too open because it has not been pruned. The seed heads that followed previous flowers are still on the stems, with the current flowers above.

2 Prune behind the spent flower, sacrificing new growth.

3 Lush new growth will sprout from this point.

4 A dense shrub results from regular pruning, and each new stem can produce a flower.

Watering Your Garden

Many people water their gardens for relaxation. This probably means that the waterer is deriving more benefit than the garden. Certainly, washing the dust and grime from the foliage is sensible, but it is deep down in the soil that plants most require the water.

A myth prevails that Australian plants do not need watering. This is an extraordinary idea when you consider, for instance, that the natural habitat of *Callistemon viminalis* is northern creek sides and waterways or that boronias and a host of other small shrubs grow with a mass of fibrous roots close to the soil surface. All plants need water: they may differ in the amounts they need and in the stages of development at which they need it, but need it they do.

A group of established, twenty-year-old trees may require no direct watering because their roots have penetrated deeply, but much smaller plants, many of which are cutting-grown, need

regular deep watering in warm to hot weather. Water encourage
the main roots of shrubs to develop in the deeper, cooler soi
layers, rather than at the surface where temperature and moistur
levels can fluctuate too severely. As well, it encourages them to radi
ate down and away so that the plants function over a wider are
and become stabilised. Watering therefore should be concentrate
on the area outside the canopy line of established plants, rather tha
around the stem or trunk.

With newly installed plants, however, it is essential to keep th
immediate soil around them moist until their roots start growing awa
from the root ball. It is easy to forget that this was the area of con
centrated watering while the plants were still in pots. This is th
main cause of post-planting fatalities.

Sprinkler and trickle irrigation systems are now so sophisticat
ed and so relatively cheap, in view of the benefits they supply, tha
they probably provide the best method of applying the right amount
of water at the most needed points. For the majority of plants, water
ing at ground level is best; for ferns and rainforest plants, overhea
watering is preferred because it simulates the humid atmosphere o
their natural habitat, although, of course, their soil still needs to b
kept moist.

Water should be applied when needed, not simply as a habit; i
in doubt, test your soil's moisture level with your fingers or a prob
meter. Your plants will usually tell you when they are dry by exhibit
ing tip wilt, although lush new growth may wilt on a hot, dryin
day without the plant being short of water.

Water wastage occurs in one main area of the garden: large lawns
which are constantly watered in hot weather. While we all appre
ciate a cool, green swathe of grass, the area allotted to lawn is ofte
greater than is necessary. With so many outdoor living activities i
seems more practical to make the areas of constant traffic (around
for example, barbecues and swimming pools) hard or paved sur
faces. Certainly 'think green' in your garden, but 'think green
wisely.

Watering can be substantially reduced on lawns and gardens by
using a product such as Debco Saturaid. Newly installed plants ben
efit from the application of products which help disperse or stor
water, like Debco SaturAid or Debco Raindrops.

Predators

Most plants suffer occasional damage from infestation or predation
and while some damage is easily treated, it can require the remova
of part or all of the affected plant.

Borers
Without a doubt, the most physically damaging predators are bor
ers. These are the larvae of beetles or moths which, as their name
implies, bore into the stems and branches of a wide range of shrub
and trees. This action may not only ringbark a plant, but also severe
ly weaken it if the borer tunnels down the centre of the stem or
branch. Sometimes, as a result, a badly affected section of the plan
will need to be cut off. The main times of infestation are summe
and autumn.

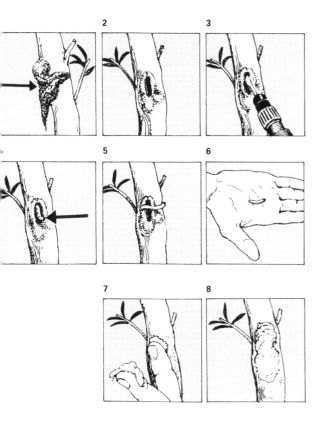

1 Webby sawdust on the outside of the stem indicates the presence of borer.

2 A tunnel, pencil-sized in diameter, is revealed when the sawdust is cleared away. Look for a secondary hole above or below.

3 Use a pyrethrum spray to thoroughly saturate the borer tunnel.

4 If present, the borer will quickly show itself.

5 It will then exit from the tunnel.

6 While not large, these active larvae of beetles or moths cause considerable damage if undetected.

7 After thoroughly clearing the entrance, block it with tree-wound dressing or similar material such as grafting wax.

8 Filling the hole prevents the plant becoming infected and the wound should heal as the stem grows.

Chewing Grubs

One of the most unattractive grubs found on trees, particularly eucalypts, is the spitfire or sawfly larvae. Spitfires cluster together during the day. When disturbed they wave their tails, at the same time spitting out an unpleasant liquid. During the night they wander around their temporary home, feeding on leaves. Their tail-waving and spitting is a means of frightening off predators, mainly birds, although some are not put off by these antics.

Spitfires are easily controlled by removing the cluster and squashing it beneath your boot. If this offends you, however, you can spray with Dipel, which is a safe, larvae-specific pesticide.

All caterpillars can also be treated with Dipel, but please remember that few, if any, will cause other than temporary damage to trees and many become beautiful butterflies and moths.

There are many other sucking, chewing and infesting insects. You will often dig up cockchafer grubs when you are working your soil. They are mistakenly called witchetty grubs, but bear only a passing resemblance to these much larger larvae. Cockchafers are approximately 3 centimetres long, with creamy bodies and black heads. They are frequently found in moist clay loam soils; the soggier the soil the more common they seem to be. The adult is a large, clumsy beetle, commonly seen around outside lights in summertime.

Cockchafers damage not only lawns and pasture, but also the roots of plants. Unless you intend growing only species of plants that tolerate 'wet feet', you should take the presence of cockchafer grubs as an indication that work is needed to make your soil more friable and free draining. Cockchafers are not easy to control, but proper drainage will help to discourage them.

Aphids collect in large numbers and suck the sap from new leaves. They are soft insects, only 1 or 2 millimetres in length. They often leave a sticky exudation on the leaves. Spray them with pyrethrum during spring, the main period of infestation.

Thrips are also small and often difficult to see with the naked eye. They suck sap from the leaves, which usually turn an unsightly grey. Thrips do most damage in summer. Often a potent spray is needed to control them fully: we recommend a combination of horticultural Clensel and White Oil, applied according to the manufacturer's instructions. This suffocates them.

Leaf hoppers, unlike many sucking insects, take evasive action by hopping or flying away when disturbed. They quickly return to the area where they were feeding once the danger is over. They, too, appear in summer and should be sprayed with pyrethrum.

Scale insects are common pests. They can often be detected along plant stems, hiding in their light or dark coloured shells which look like waxy lumps. Ladybird beetles are a natural predator of scale, but often scale insects occur in such large numbers that even these voracious hunters cannot control them.

Spray scale over a month with equal parts of White Oil and horticultural Clensel in warm water, following the manufacturer's instructions. To test the effectiveness of the treatment squash a few shells: if the scale are alive they will exude a bright red liquid.

Ants feed on the honeydew of scale and other insects, and it is to their advantage to ensure these insects survive. They will often carry the young of scale to non-sprayed areas to keep their food supply going.

Psyllids attack a range of native plants, members of the Myrtaceae family often being the most susceptible. They usually attach themselves to the underside of leaves. They are protected by their scaly, often fringed, covering. A bad infestation will leave a tree's foliage with many 'sucked out', dry patches. Similar damage is caused by a myrtle bug, which is freer in its movement. Myrtle bugs often attack large trees, so spraying can be difficult, but pyrethrum is effective if you are able to reach them.

Factors Affecting Plant Selection

No guide to plant selection can be perfect because there are so many variables and combinations of climate, soil, elevation and drainage that it is impossible to make any definitive statement about the needs of particular plants. However, the Plant Selection List we have devised is an extension of a system we have employed successfully for more than two decades.

Several major factors control the natural distribution of plants: altitude, temperature, moisture, soil, light, coastal proximity and frost. It is these factors, either singly or in combination, which will determine the successful growth of the plants you wish to introduce from other zones. Therefore, in the Plant Selection List we provide information on the specific requirements of plants.

It is often incorrectly said that 'if it's an Australian plant, it will grow anywhere'. When you have read through the Plant Selection List and found listed in it plants from such diverse habitats as rainforests, deserts, alpine areas, swamps, sand plains and coastal headlands, you will see how inaccurate this statement is.

Plants have evolved in, or have adapted to, particular conditions over many millions of years, and some will struggle or die in any other conditions. Others are more adaptable and tolerate a range of soils and climates. It is, however, possible to recreate the growing conditions of 'difficult' species in your own garden by giving particular attention to the structure and depth of the soil. For example, you can build a raised planter box and fill it with a top quality soil mix, or create a broad, deep sand mound.

Height and Width of Plants

The dimensions for trees and large shrubs given in the Plant Selection List indicate the mature but not necessarily ultimate size. For smaller shrubs the dimensions given indicate the size they will attain in the short to mid term and the one at which pruning will maintain a healthy, vigorous appearance. You need to remember that growing conditions will affect height and width. Many trees of the densely shaded rainforests grow very large in their natural 'twilight' environment, being constantly drawn to the top of the canopy in search of light. In open, sunnier situations, even in the tropics, most of these develop a squatter shape and a broader canopy.

Height is the first dimension given in the Plant Selection List, as this is always of major concern, but bear in mind that width, too, will determine whether a plant is suitable for your requirements.

Our perceptions of trees and shrubs are determined not only by their height and width, but also by their habit and density. It is not unusual, therefore, to find plants of the same height variously referred to in the Plant Selection List; for example, a plant with a height of 7 metres may be described as a large shrub or a small tree or, as in the case of *Acacia cognata*, both. Generally, we categorise a plant as a shrub or a tree according to whether it has a trunk or not. In the case of *A. cognata* there are two forms, one with a trunk, and one with a low, branching habit and foliage sweeping down to the ground.

The descriptions accompanying each entry in the Plant Selection List are designed to give you a quick picture of the plant. If a description suggests a plant which may answer your needs, it is then simply a matter of checking that the plant's growing requirements, as given in the list, accord with your garden conditions.

Climatic Zones

One glance at the map, Climatic Zones of Australia, will make it clear why Australia's population is concentrated in the eastern, south-eastern and south-western coastal sections of the continent. Approximately 50 per cent of the land mass, consisting of the vast central area extending to the Great Australian Bight in the south and the Indian Ocean on the west coast, is arid.

The map will give you some understanding of climatic variations within Australia. However, you need to keep in mind that lines on a map do not indicate that a weather pattern occurs on one side of a division and not on the other; rather, they mark points of pattern convergence. The climatic zones themselves represent broad categories within which are to be found considerable differences of temperature and rainfall. For example, most mainland temperate areas are classified as warm temperate, whereas Tasmania is mainly cool temperate, but even within these sub-categories there are variations. While the northern half of Tasmania has predominantly winter precipitation, the southern half has rain evenly distributed throughout the year. And in warm temperate zones local conditions, in particular frost, have to be taken into consideration in deciding on a plant's suitability. Obviously altitude is another important factor because of its modifying influence on temperature. Therefore, we cannot emphasise too strongly that an understanding of your local conditions is your best guide to the specific climate of your area and vital to successful planting.

We have assigned specific climatic zones to plants in the Plant Selection List on the basis of their broadest needs. However, we are aware that even in the same area micro-climatic variations can occur from garden to garden (and even within gardens). For instance, one garden may be on a high site and have a shady canopy and dense shrubbery, while a property lower down may have no canopy, consist mainly of open, grassed space and be more frost prone.

You will notice that we often specify more than one climatic zone for a plant. Plants may originate from one zone only, such as tropical or sub-tropical (both having high summer temperatures and primarily summer rainfall), but will often grow in a cooler more temperate region if given protection from the cold and extra summer watering if in a dry situation. Plants from the semi-arid zone will often, with additional water and mulching, adapt to more arid conditions because it is the lack of water in arid areas, and not only the heat, which is stressful to plants.

If only temperate is indicated for a plant in the Plant Selection List it will grow in both warm and cool temperate zones. Where a doubt exists about a plant's ability to handle cool temperate conditions, it is listed as warm temperate only.

Specialised knowledge of plants in a particular group will often allow you to extend their growing range. The genus *Eremophila* illustrates this well. While we specify that the majority of eremophilas need a warm temperate to arid climate, no doubt specialists will be able to grow a number of them in cool temperate zones.

Certain entries in the Plant Selection List may appear contradictory. For example, *Macadamia tetraphylla* is from northern rainforest regions, but grows well in open, moist (though frost-free) areas of Melbourne. However, whether it would grow successfully in similar but cooler sites in, say, Hobart, is not certain. And, coming from a zone with predominantly summer rainfall, *M. tetraphylla* would need additional water to reach its full potential in hot, dry zones.

Climatic Zones of Australia

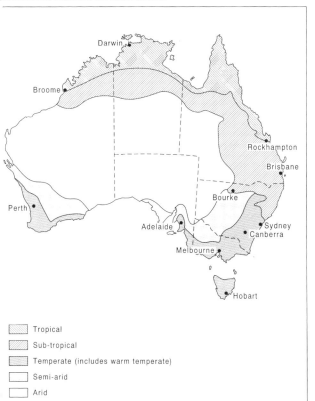

- Tropical
- Sub-tropical
- Temperate (includes warm temperate)
- Semi-arid
- Arid

Climatic Zones of Australia

Tropical

Summer
Heavy periodic rains (especially in highland and coastal areas)
Hot, high humidity

Winter
Generally rainless
Mild to warm, with less humidity

Sub-tropical

Summer
Heavy periodic rains (especially in highland and coastal areas)
Hot (humid in highland and coastal areas of eastern Australia)

Winter
Some rainfall
Mild to warm

Warm temperate

Summer
Mainly reliable rain
Warm to hot

Winter
Mainly reliable rain
Cool to mild

Temperate

Summer
Irregular rain
 (moderate to heavy)
Warm to hot

Winter
Reliable rain
 (moderate to heavy)
Cold, or cool to mild

Arid

Summer
Very dry
Warm to very hot

Winter
Irregular light rain
Mild to warm

Semi-arid

Summer
Very irregular rain
Warm to hot

Winter
Variable light rain
Cool to mild

Soil

The Plant Selection List also classifies plants according to their soil requirements. The main soil types are as follows.

Moist, well-drained
These soils include sand, sandy gravel or even clay gravel. They are soils through which moisture travels freely, with sufficient being retained for plant use. The free movement of water also indicates a soil that aerates satisfactorily.

Wet
This term refers to permanently wet soils which can be either clay, clay loam or the sand of, for example, swamp margins. We have not included sandy soils that may be wet after rain for an extended period, but then dry out. There is a mini-list of plants for seasonally wet sands (page 169).

Dry
Dry soils are often hydrophobic (water repellent). Working a saturation aid, such as Debco SaturAid, into these soils will improve their moisture-holding capacity.

Dry limy
These are soils derived from limestone; they can be found extensively around Perth, Adelaide and many coastal or near-coastal areas, as well as inland. The high alkalinity of such soils locks in essential elements for many plants. Unless a lot of humus is added, these plants struggle to survive. Stunting and yellowing are signs of plants that are unhappy in limy soils.

Light

Plants have certain light and shade requirements, but they are surprisingly adaptable when other conditions are at an optimum.

Full Sun
Where we have specified full sun in the Plant Selection List this means that the plant needs no shade at all.

Filtered Sun
This category includes plants that either tolerate or require filtered sun. Those listed under filtered sun only will not tolerate full sun, but generally may be assumed to tolerate full shade.

Coastal Proximity

If you live near the coast you will need to grow plants that tolerate salt-laden, strong winds, and we have specified plants for either first or second line planting. First line plants are those that will bear the full brunt of coastal conditions. Second line plants are those that need more protection: they must be planted behind the first line plants or further away from the coast.

Frost

The severity or otherwise of frost influences plant selection and growth. While the accompanying map, Number and Season of Frost Days in Australia, shows in general terms where and to what extent frosts occur, local conditions can modify the picture quite dramatically. To realise this one only needs to stand on a timbered rise, where warmth has been trapped, and look down on the frost that has collected on a broad, open river flat. If your garden were up on the edge of the timber, it would not suffer the degree of exposure experienced by one on the lower flats.

In the Plant Selection List we have used letters to signify frost tolerance: L for light frost, H for heavy frost. It is not only the number of frost days which cause plant damage, but the severity of the frost itself: some frosts are of such a low temperature that they can actually destroy the inner cellular structure of plants by freezing the sap, which then expands.

People often assume that because a plant comes from an area known for heavy frosts it will tolerate severe frost in a garden. This is by no means so. Within a heavy frost region particular plants may habitually benefit from the protection of trees or grow on a higher area offering greater protection.

Number and Season of Frost Days in Australia

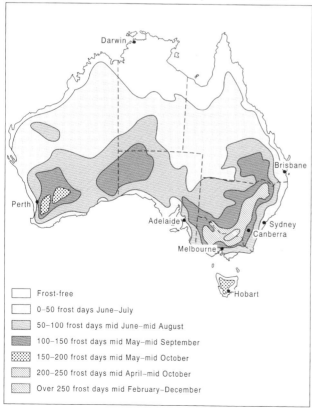

Frost-free

0–50 frost days June–July

50–100 frost days mid June–mid August

100–150 frost days mid May–mid September

150–200 frost days mid May–mid October

200–250 frost days mid April–mid October

Over 250 frost days mid February–December

What can be done to reduce the damage caused by consecutive severe frosts? While many stop-gap methods, such as suspending hessian covers or sheets of newspaper over individual plants, may be used, it is difficult and unsatisfactory to try to cover a whole garden.

Commercial crop growers operating in regions of heavy frost usually employ one of three methods. The first method is to place a series of burners throughout the crops to raise the temperature around foliage. The second method is to mount large-bladed fans on towers. These are used to mix the rising warm air, radiated from the soil, with the cold air moving down to replace it. While both these methods are commercially satisfactory, they are fairly expensive and mostly not applicable to small gardens.

The third method, which has proven very satisfactory, involves using a simple system of flexible pipe with risers, on the top of which are misting heads operated by a temperature-control mechanism. Mist is released when ambient temperature drops toward freezing point. The mist films the plants and freezes, thereby insulating them against colder, more damaging frosts. The water then turns off automatically and the control resets itself. Several companies supply kits of pipework and sprinklers, and timing devices are also readily available.

A Note on Plant Names

The easiest and least confusing way to refer to a plant is by its correct or botanical name. Therefore, in the Plant Selection List, all plants are listed alphabetically according to their botanical names. Common names are included occasionally, if they are particularly well known or frequently used.

Common names undoubtedly have charm and very often an historical link with the early years of white settlement. Who would not find pleasure in the name of Eggs-and-bacon given to some of the *Pultenaea* species or Chocolate Lily for *Dichopogon strictus*? So there is certainly a place for common names in our Australian horticultural history; it would be a great pity if we were to discard them, for in doing so we would be denying our relationship with the bush, its simplicity and its wildflower qualities, that are implied in so many of the old traditional names.

However, the use of common names often leads to confusion. For instance, *Acacia doratoxylon*, which is commonly called Spear Wood, is listed in *Plants of Western New South Wales* as having eight common names. So also has *A. pendula*. And to add to the confusion, the same common name may sometimes be applied to two different plants. Common names are therefore better avoided if you are seeking a specific plant in a nursery.

Botanical names consist of two parts: the genus and the species. A genus name is like a family surname. A species (or specific) name is similar to a given name used to distinguish one family member from another. So we may have *Grevillea lanigera*, as we would Smith, John. (It is standard scientific practice to use the 'surname' first, followed by the 'given name'.)

In addition to botanical and common names, plants may also have cultivar names. A cultivar plant may either be a hybrid, that is, the product of natural or artificially induced cross-pollination between two species, or a specially selected form of a species, such as a prostrate form of a normally large, upright shrub. For instance, *Melaleuca hypericifolia* 'Ulladulla Beacon' is a prostrate form of *M. hypericifolia*, normally a medium shrub 2.5–4 metres high by 2.5–4 metres wide. Habit (the way a plant grows) is not the only way in which a plant may differ from its normal form. Colour or size of flower or leaf may also render the selected form sufficiently different to warrant special attention. Cultivar plants are generally registered in Canberra, with the Australian Cultivar Registration Authority, to record for horticultural purposes their origins and other important factors.

Renaming

Constant revisionary work is occurring in the naming of Australian plants, so you may suddenly find that a familiar group of plants has a new name: for instance, most of the genus *Eugenia* (the Lilly Pillies) are now known as *Syzygium*. Other genera, such as *Eucalyptus* and *Casuarina*, are in the process of changing names but, as there is not yet universal agreement about the changes, we have retained their familiar names.

In 1987 the first total botanical revision of the large and horticulturally important genus *Grevillea* was released. Numerous new species have been named but, as well, a number of previously well-known names have disappeared.

It has been found that plants thought to be separate species are, in fact, tribal variations of another species. For example, two previously separate species, *G. dimorpha* from the Grampian Ranges in Victoria and *G. oleoides* from the Sydney region have become sub-species under *G. speciosa* (and are listed as such in the Plant Selection List).

In some instances, names have been incorrectly applied to certain plants. For example, *G. biternata* and *G. tridentifera* have been used to refer to the same plant, a popular ground-covering species. Neither of these names is relevant to that plant, which is now known as *G. curviloba*.

Unfortunately, lack of space has prevented us from cross-referencing all the old and new *Grevillea* names, and for this we apologise.

Plant Selection List

The Plant Selection List will enable you to choose the right plants with a minimum of difficulty even if you have not planted a garden before. The categories in the list have been designed to provide you with the information essential to the successful growing of particular plants. For a more detailed discussion of the areas covered by the categories of the Plant Selection List see the preceding pages on Factors Affecting Plant Selection.

Key

Height and Width

The dimensions given indicate mature, though not necessarily ultimate, sizes.

Shrub heights
Dwarf   30–60cm
Small   60cm–1.5m
Medium   1.5–3m
Large   3–5m

Tree heights
Small   5–8m
Medium   8–13m
Large   13m or more

Groundcover spreads
Small: to approximately 1m
Large: to more than 1m

Climber spreads
Light: to approximately 1m
Medium: 1–3m
Vigorous: 6m or more

Climatic Zones

See the key at top left of Plant Selection List and the map Climatic Zones of Australia (page 24) for the distribution and characteristics of the zones and to ascertain the one in which you live.

Soil Types

The type specified indicates the soil requirements of the particular plant.

Moist, well drained: soils which retain some moisture, but drain and aerate readily.

Wet: permanently saturated or spongy soils.

Dry: soils with low humus content, retaining little moisture even after rain.

Dry limy: dry soils with low humus content and high alkaline levels.

Light Requirements

Full Sun: plant prefers no shade at all.

Filtered Sun: plant requires dappled shade or morning sun only; full shade is also generally tolerated.

Coastal Regions

1   1st line (plant will take full brunt of conditions)
2   2nd line (plant requires more protection, either behind 1st line or further away from coast)

Frosty Regions

H = heavy frost
L = light frost
Many plants are not frost tolerant at all, so receive no rating.

Bird Attraction

F   attracts fruit (or berry) eating birds
N   attracts nectar-feeding birds
S   attracts seed-eating birds
Many plants also attract insects, thereby attracting insect-eating birds. Numerous fruits and seeds are also suitable for human consumption.

mp — temperate	L — light
te — warm temperate	H — heavy
op — tropical	N — nectar-feeding
tr — sub-tropical	S — seed-eating
ar — semi-arid	F — fruit-eating

		Height	Width	Climatic zones	Soil types				full sun	filtered sun	coastal regions	frosty regions	bird attraction
					moist, well drained	wet	dry	dry limy					
acia acinacea	Small to medium compact shrub, small neat crowded leaves, massed rich yellow flowers in spring. Useful for screening and low hedges.	60cm–2m	1–2m	Temp S. ar	•		•		•	•		H	S
acia uleatissima	Open ground-covering plant, fine needle foliage, pale yellow flowers in spring. Suitable for rockeries.	prostrate	1–2m	Temp S. ar	•	•			•	•		H	S
acia acuminata spberry Jam Tree	Small to medium tree, long fine leaves, yellow rod flowers in spring. Hardy, long-lived, borer resistant. Wood sweetly fragrant when cut.	6–10m	3–5m	Temp S. ar	•		•	•	•	•		H	S
acia adunca	Large shrub or small tree, fine foliage, vivid yellow flowers in winter. Very showy and graceful.	4–8m	3–5m	Temp S. tr	•		•		•	•		L	S
acia alata	Small open shrub, unusual winged foliage, deep yellow flowers in spring. Very hardy; useful in shady areas.	1–2m	1–2m	Temp S. tr	•		•			•		L	S
acia amblygona ustraflora Winter old'	Low cascading plant, dense small triangular leaves, deep yellow flowers in winter. Attractive for rockeries or large containers. Prune lightly.	30–60cm	90cm–1m	Temp S. tr	•		•		•	•		L	S
acia anceps	Medium to large dense shrub, silver-grey foliage, bright yellow ball flowers spring–summer. Tolerates periods of extended dryness.	3–4m	3–4m	Temp S. tr Arid S. ar	•		•	•	•	•	1		S
acia aneura lga	Small to medium, very dense tree; grey drooping leaves, golden yellow rod flowers winter–spring. Useful for shade and fodder; borer resistant.	4–10m	2–6m	W. te Arid S. ar	•		•	•	•	•		H	S
acia argyrophylla	Large spreading shrub, silver-grey foliage, golden flowers in spring. Hardy in dry areas; useful for windbreak planting.	3–4m	4–6m	W. te S. ar	•		•	•	•	•		H	S
acia ausfeldii	Medium to large arching shrub, fine curved leaves, yellow flowers in spring. Attractive and useful for dry areas.	2–4m	2–3m	Temp S. ar	•		•		•	•		H	S
acia baileyana otamundra attle	Small dense tree, grey feathery foliage, masses of bright yellow flowers in winter. Hardy and long-lived.	5–6m	4–5m	Temp S. tr S. ar	•		•		•	•	2	H	S
acia baileyana r. purpurea rple-tipped ootamundra attle	As for the above, except that new growth is rich purple. Seed pods on both forms are showy and decorative.	5–6m	4–5m	Temp S. tr S. ar	•		•		•	•	2	H	S

		Height	Width	Climatic zones	Soil types							
Temp — temperate W. te — warm temperate Trop — tropical S. tr — sub-tropical S. ar — semi-arid	L — light H — heavy N — nectar-feeding S — seed-eating F — fruit-eating				moist, well drained	wet	dry	dry limy	full sun	filtered sun	coastal regions	frosty regions
Acacia beckleri	Medium to large upright open shrub, broad leathery leaves, large individual bright gold flowers in winter. Showy and adaptable.	2–4m	1–3m	W. te S. ar	•		•		•	•		H
Acacia bidentata	Low arching shrub, crowded tiny leaves, showy bright yellow flowers in winter. Useful for rockeries.	30–60cm	60cm	Temp S. ar	•		•		•	•		L
Acacia boormanii Snowy River Wattle	Medium to large shrub, soft fine grey foliage, massed bright yellow flowers in winter. Very showy; useful for light screening. May sucker lightly.	3–4m	2–3m	Temp	•		•		•	•		H
Acacia brachybotrya	Large shrub, furry grey rounded leaves, golden ball flowers winter–late spring. Showy; attractive in dry areas.	2–5m	3–6m	W. te S. ar	•		•		•	•		H
Acacia buxifolia Box-leaf Wattle	Upright medium shrub, smooth grey foliage, bright yellow flowers in early spring. Useful as a light screen in dry areas.	2–4m	2–3m	W. te S. ar	•		•		•	•		H
Acacia calamifolia	Large shrub, fine hooked foliage, masses of bright yellow flowers late winter–spring. Graceful; useful in dry areas.	2–5m	2–4m	W. te S. ar	•		•	•	•	•		H
Acacia cardiophylla Wyalong Wattle	Weeping medium shrub, soft feathery foliage, small rounded heads of golden flowers spring–summer. Hardy, graceful and attractive.	2–3m	2–3m	Temp S. ar	•		•		•	•		H
Acacia chinchillensis	Small to medium shrub, fine ferny leaves, very decorative long racemes of golden yellow flowers winter–spring.	50cm–2m	1–2m	W. te S. tr S. ar	•		•		•	•		L
Acacia cognata	Large shrub or small tree, fine perfumed weeping leaves to the ground, pale yellow globular flowers in spring. Beautiful wattle for well-drained sites.	5–7m	3–4m	Temp S. tr	•				•	•		H
Acacia colletioides	Rounded medium shrub, spiny leaves, rounded golden flower clusters in spring. Very drought resistant.	2–3m	2–3m	W. te S. ar	•		•	•	•	•		H
Acacia cometes	Low spreading shrub, short flat narrow leaves, yellow globular flowers in spring. Ornamental and drought resistant.	20–40cm	50–90cm	W. te S. ar	•		•		•	•		H
Acacia conferta	Upright medium shrub, small crowded foliage, clusters of globular golden yellow flowers held out from the branches autumn–winter–spring.	2–4m	2–4m	Temp S. tr S. ar	•		•		•	•		H

'Birthday Candles'

A dwarf form of *Banksia spinulosa* which has attracted attention world-wide; no surprise to anyone. While 'Birthday Candles' is stunning in a range of containers, it does just as well in the garden.

No matter what the scale of your garden, there is always room for water. While there may be only enough for a small pond or some bowls, owners of larger areas of land have the opportunity for developing broad, shallow pools or waterfalls, either in association with simulations of sandstone (right) or with natural rock shelving (below).

Legend:

- mp — temperate
- te — warm temperate
- p — tropical
- r — sub-tropical
- ar — semi-arid

- L — light
- H — heavy
- N — nectar-feeding
- S — seed-eating
- F — fruit-eating

Name	Description	Height	Width	Climatic zones	moist, well drained	wet	dry	dry limy	full sun	filtered sun	coastal regions	frosty regions	bird attraction
...acia coriacea	Medium shrub to small tree, pendulous leathery grey-green leaves, cream or yellow ball flowers summer–autumn–winter. Useful fodder tree.	3–10m	2–5m	W. te Arid S. ar	•		•		•	•	2		S
...acia cultriformis / Knife-leaf Wattle	Dense weeping medium shrub, grey triangular foliage, short bright yellow rod flowers in spring.	2–3m	2–3m	Temp S. tr	•		•		•	•		H	S
...acia cultriformis 'Austraflora Cascade'	As for the above, but with a prostrate spreading habit. Ornamental plant for banks, walls or in tall pipes, from which it cascades dramatically.	15–30cm	2–4m	Temp S. tr	•		•		•	•		H	S
...acia cyclops	Medium to large dense shrub, long flat leaves, yellow globular flowers in spring. Useful coastal windbreak; excellent for erosion control.	2–4m	2–4m	Temp S. ar	•	•	•	•	•	•	1		S
...acia dealbata / Silver Wattle	Large shrub or medium to large tree, grey pinnate leaves, racemes of bright yellow flowers winter–spring. Fast growing; used for revegetating barren ground.	6–18m	5–8m	Temp S. tr	•		•		•	•		H	S
...acia deanei	Large shrub or medium tree, pinnate leaves, yellow racemes of flowers in summer. Useful for quick shade or erosion control.	5–10m	3–6m	Temp	•		•		•	•		H	S
...acia decora	Medium to large dense shrub, grey foliage, golden new shoots and stems, golden flowers in spring. Drought resistant, adaptable and ornamental.	2–5m	3–4m	W. te S. tr S. ar	•		•		•	•		H	S
...acia decurrens / Early Black Wattle	Large shrub to spreading tree, pinnate leaves, spectacular racemes of perfumed golden flowers winter–spring. Fast-growing, useful shelter tree.	5–15m	5–8m	Temp S. tr	•		•		•	•			S
...acia denticulosa	Large open shrub, coarsely toothed rough large leaves, brilliant golden catkin flowers in spring. Rangy habit is oddly attractive.	3–6m	3–4m	Temp S. ar	•		•		•			H	S
...acia doratoxylon / Spear Wood	Usually a small tree, curved linear leaves, golden rod flowers in spring. The fine straight branches were used as spears by Aborigines.	5–10m	3–6m	Temp S. tr S. ar	•		•		•	•		H	S
...acia drewiana	Small to medium shrub, arching zig-zag stems, hairy ferny foliage, yellow ball flowers winter–spring.	1–2m	1.5–2m	Temp	•				•	•			S
...acia drummondii	Variable in habit but usually a small shrub, pinnate foliage, golden yellow rod flowers late winter–spring. Showy; several forms in cultivation.	1–1.5m	1–1.5m	Temp S. tr	•				•	•			S

		Height	Width	Climatic zones	moist, well drained	wet	dry	dry limy	full sun	filtered sun	coastal regions	frosty regions
Temp — temperate W. te — warm temperate Trop — tropical S. tr — sub-tropical S. ar — semi-arid	L — light H — heavy N — nectar-feeding S — seed-eating F — fruit-eating											
Acacia elata	Medium to large spreading tree, handsome pinnate foliage, masses of perfumed yellow flowers late summer–autumn.	9–15m	7–9m	Temp S. tr	•				•	•	2	L
Acacia elongata	Upright medium shrub, stiff linear foliage, bright yellow flowers winter–spring. Decorative; will tolerate periods of inundation.	1.5–2m	1.5–2m	Temp S. tr	•	•			•	•		L
Acacia farinosa Mealy Wattle	Low spreading shrub, blunt linear leaves, massed yellow ball flowers late winter–spring. Useful as low hedge or screen.	30cm–1.5m	2–3m	Temp S. ar	•		•	•	•	•		H
Acacia fimbriata Fringed Wattle	Weeping large shrub or small tree, crowded short narrow leaves, perfumed golden flowers late winter–spring. Adaptable and ornamental.	4–8m	3–5m	Temp S. tr	•		•		•	•		L
Acacia flexifolia	Small to medium shrub, silver-grey foliage, lemon ball flowers winter–spring. Ideal low hedge plant.	1–2m	1–2m	Temp S. ar	•		•		•	•		H
Acacia floribunda	Dense large shrub or small tree, fine foliage, yellow rod flowers winter–spring. Fast growing; for moist or sandy soils. Very suitable for screening.	5–7m	4–6m	Temp S. tr	•		•		•	•	2	H
Acacia genistifolia	Open medium shrub, short rigid leaves; globular yellow to golden flowers spring–early summer, and again late summer–early winter, bright and extremely showy.	1–3m	1–2m	Temp S. tr	•		•		•	•		H
Acacia glandulicarpa	Small to medium spreading shrub, crowded leaves, masses of golden ball flowers in spring. Suitable for dry banks requiring cover.	1–2m	2–4m	W. te S. ar	•		•	•	•	•		H
Acacia glaucoptera	Small, generally compact shrub; grey, lobed strap leaves and plum new growth, golden flowers in spring. One of the most ornamental wattles.	1–1.5m	2–2.5m	Temp S. ar	•		•	•	•	•		H
Acacia gracilifolia	Medium to large shrub, fine drooping foliage, profuse golden yellow flowers in spring. Very graceful and ornamental.	3–5m	2–3m	Temp S. tr	•		•		•	•		H
Acacia grandifolia	Large shrub or small tree, long hairy decorative foliage, golden yellow rod flowers in spring. Ornamental.	5–8m	3–4m	Temp S. tr S. ar	•		•		•	•		
Acacia guinetii	Small to medium spreading shrub, hairy branches, ferny hairy leaves, globular yellow flowers winter–spring.	1–2.5m	2–3m	Temp S. ar	•		•		•	•		L

p — temperate	L — light
e — warm temperate	H — heavy
tropical	N — nectar-feeding
sub-tropical	S — seed-eating
semi-arid	F — fruit-eating

		Height	Width	Climatic zones	moist, well drained	wet	dry	dry limy	full sun	filtered sun	coastal regions	frosty regions	bird attraction
cia gunnii	Open spreading dwarf shrub, small rigid triangular leaves, yellow ball flowers winter–spring. Attractive groundcover.	prostrate–50cm	50cm–2m	Temp S.ar	•		•		•	•		H	S
cia howittii	Dense large shrub or small tree, small sticky leaves, pale yellow flowers in spring. Exudes pleasant perfume on warm or wet days. Widely planted.	4–8m	3–6m	Temp S.tr	•		•		•	•		L	S
cia imbricata	Dense medium shrub, fine foliage, massed bright yellow ball flowers along the stems winter–spring. Particularly showy.	2–3m	2–4m	Temp S.ar	•		•	•	•	•		H	S
cia implexa twood	Large shrub or small tree, long pendulous leaves, cream ball flowers in summer. Useful shade tree for harsh rocky soils.	5–13m	4–10m	Temp S.ar	•		•		•	•		H	S
cia iteaphylla ders Range ttle	Medium to large shrub, dense pendulous grey foliage with plum coloured tips, bright yellow flowers autumn–winter–spring. Showy, hardy; excellent screen.	3–5m	3–5m	Temp S.ar	•		•		•	•	2	H	S
cia lanigera	Small to medium shrub, woolly grey-green foliage, many bright yellow ball flowers autumn–winter–spring. Hardy and adaptable.	50cm–2m	1–3m	Temp	•		•		•	•		H	S
cia lanuginosa	Small to medium shrub, very woolly grey foliage, yellow ball flowers in spring. Ornamental and drought resistant.	1.5–2m	2–3m	W.te S.ar	•		•		•	•		H	S
cia lasiocalyx	Medium to large open shrub, widely spaced long fine foliage, bright yellow rod flowers in spring.	3–5m	4–6m	W.te S.ar	•		•		•	•			S
cia lasiocarpa	Variable small to medium shrub, small pinnate foliage, masses of bright yellow ball flowers winter–spring.	50cm–2m	1–3m	Temp	•		•		•	•			S
cia leprosa amon Wattle	Dense large shrub or small tree, perfumed weeping foliage, lemon yellow flowers in spring. Widely grown ornamental plant for shaded sites; useful for screening.	5–8m	3–4m	Temp S.tr	•		•		•	•		L	S
cia ospermoides	Small spreading shrub, succulent grey linear leaves, profuse deep yellow ball flowers late winter–spring. Very decorative.	50cm–1m	2–3m	Temp S.tr	•		•		•	•		H	S
cia leucoclada	Large shrub or small tree, pinnate foliage covered in a white bloom, yellow racemes of flowers winter–spring. Borer resistant.	4–10m	3–6m	Temp S.ar	•		•		•	•	2	L	S

		Height	Width	Climatic zones	Soil types							
					moist, well drained	wet	dry	dry limy	full sun	filtered sun	coastal regions	frosty regions
Acacia lineata	Small to medium shrub, small hooked foliage, bright yellow ball flowers in spring. Hardy shrub for dry conditions.	1–3m	1–3m	Temp S. ar	•		•		•	•		H
Acacia littorea	Small to medium dense shrub, large triangular leaves, yellow ball flowers in spring. Used for sand stabilising in coastal areas.	1–3m	2–3m	Temp S. tr	•		•		•	•	1	
Acacia longifolia Sallow Wattle	Medium to large shrub or small tree, dense long flat leaves, bright yellow rod flowers winter–spring. Fast growing and useful for screening.	3–8m	3–5m	Temp S. tr	•		•		•	•		H
Acacia longissima	Small to medium dainty open shrub, fine foliage, creamy yellow loose ball flowers in all seasons but mainly late summer.	2–4m	1–2m	Temp S. tr	•		•		•	•	2	
Acacia macradenia	Medium to large shrub, zig-zag branchlets, long leathery drooping leaves, yellow ball flowers in long racemes winter–spring. Useful in hot dry areas.	3–4m	2–3m	W. te S. tr S. ar	•		•		•			L
Acacia mearnsii Black Wattle	Medium to large tree, ferny foliage, racemes of pale yellow flowers in spring. Fast growing; useful for shade and shelter.	8–25m	6–10m	Temp S. tr	•		•		•	•		H
Acacia melanoxylon Blackwood	Small to large tree, leathery dark leaves, showy pale yellow flowers winter–spring. Beautiful timber for furniture. Handsome tree for moist sites.	5–30m	4–15m	Temp S. tr	•				•	•		H
Acacia merinthophora	Medium to large shrub, fine wispy foliage, rich yellow rod flowers autumn–winter–spring. Very graceful; suitable for very dry conditions.	3–4m	3–4m	W. te Arid S. ar	•		•		•			L
Acacia muellerana	Large shrub or small tree, open ferny foliage, pale yellow flowers spring–summer. A decorative soft appearance.	4–6m	2–4m	Temp S. tr	•		•		•	•		L
Acacia myrtifolia	Small to medium shrub, smooth short flat leaves, cream to yellow flowers winter–spring. Hardy and adaptable.	1–2m	1–2m	Temp S. tr	•		•	•	•	•	2	H
Acacia papyrocarpa Western Myall (syn. *A. sowdenii*)	Large shrub to tall tree, silvery foliage, creamy yellow flowers spring–summer. Borer resistant; useful shade tree.	5–10m	4–6m	W. te Arid S. ar	•		•	•	•			H
Acacia pendula Weeping Myall	Small to medium tree, dense weeping grey foliage, pale yellow flowers winter–spring. Particularly ornamental; useful inland shade, fodder and timber tree.	6–12m	6–8m	W. te Arid S. ar	•		•		•			H

		Height	Width	Climatic zones	Soil types				full sun	filtered sun	coastal regions	frosty regions	bird attraction
					moist, well drained	wet	dry	dry limy					

Legend:

p — temperate	L — light
e — warm temperate	H — heavy
o — tropical	N — nectar-feeding
— sub-tropical	S — seed-eating
— semi-arid	F — fruit-eating

Name	Description	Height	Width	Climatic zones	moist, well drained	wet	dry	dry limy	full sun	filtered sun	coastal regions	frosty regions	bird attraction
cia pentadenia i Wattle	Medium to large shrub, soft ferny foliage, pale yellow perfumed flowers winter–spring.	2–4m	3–4m	Temp	•				•	•			S
cia perangusta	Large shrub to small tree, fine dark foliage, racemes of lemon to golden flowers winter–spring. Hardy and graceful.	5–8m	3–5m	W. te S. tr	•		•		•	•			S
cia peuce dy Wood	Large pyramidal shrub or medium tree, dense blue-grey needle foliage, yellow flowers in autumn, large decorative flat seed pods. Excellent bird habitat.	5–10m	4–5m	Arid S. ar	•		•		•			H	S
cia pilosa	Small shrub or spreading groundcover, short hairy leaves; profuse creamy yellow ball flowers mainly in spring, also sporadic.	30cm–1m	1–3m	Temp	•		•		•	•	2		S
cia plicata	Small to medium mounding shrub, soft hairy pinnate foliage, rounded yellow flowers winter–spring. Very decorative.	1.5–2.5m	1–2.5m	Temp	•				•	•			S
cia podalyriifolia nt Morgan attle	Tall shrub or small tree, rounded silvery leaves (the outstanding feature), golden racemes of flowers winter–spring.	4–5m	3–4m	Temp S. tr S. ar	•		•		•	•	2		S
cia pravissima ns Wattle	Small to medium pendulous shrub or small tree, triangular leaves, massed yellow flowers in spring. Fast growing and adaptable; a useful screen.	1.5–8m	1–8m	Temp S. tr	•		•		•	•	2	H	S
cia pravissima den Carpet'	Cascading form of the above. Useful for banks, walls and tall pipe sections.	50cm	3–5m	Temp S. tr	•		•		•	•	2	H	S
cia prominens den Rain Wattle	Tall shrub or medium tree, crowded grey foliage, yellow flowers in spring. Extremely attractive as a screen.	4–15m	2–12m	Temp S. tr	•				•	•	2	L	S
cia pruinosa ty Wattle	Medium shrub or small tree, branches with frosted appearance, feathery foliage, bright yellow racemes of flowers winter–spring.	3–8m	3–5m	W. te S. tr S. ar	•		•		•			H	S
cia pubescens	Medium to large shrub, hairy feathery foliage, dense yellow racemes of perfumed flowers in spring. May form clumps by suckering.	1.5–5m	1–3m	Temp S. tr	•				•	•	2	L	S
cia pulchella tern Prickly ses	Small to medium open shrub, slightly prickly stems, feathery foliage, golden flowers at various times, mainly late winter–spring.	50cm–1.5m	1–1.5m	Temp S. tr	•				•	•			S

			Height	Width	Climatic zones	Soil types							
						moist, well drained	wet	dry	dry limy	full sun	filtered sun	coastal regions	frosty regions
Acacia pycnantha Golden Wattle	Large shrub or small tree, large drooping leaves, massed golden racemes of flowers winter–spring. Attractive as a copse. Australia's national emblem.		3–10m	1–6m	Temp S. tr S. ar	•		•		•	•	2	H
Acacia pyrifolia	Medium to large shrub, silver-grey foliage, bright yellow flowers autumn–winter–spring. Ornamental shrub for dry regions.		3–5m	1.5–3m	W. te Trop Arid	•		•		•			
Acacia retinodes Wirilda	Spreading large shrub or small tree, long slender pendulous leaves, lemon yellow flowers most of the year. Fast growing, hardy and adaptable.		4–7m	3–4m	Temp S. tr	•		•		•	•	2	H
Acacia riceana	Medium to tall shrub, crowded short needle leaves, abundant lemon yellow flowers in spring. Excellent as bird habitat, and in wet areas.		4–5m	3–5m	Temp S. tr	•	•			•	•		H
Acacia rigens	Medium to large compact rigid shrub, spiny grey leaves, rounded golden flowers winter–spring–early summer. Good screen or windbreak for dry areas.		2–4m	3–4m	W. te S. ar	•		•		•	•		H
Acacia rossei	Medium to large dense shrub, sticky narrow flat leaves, rounded yellow flowers winter–spring–summer. Drought resistant and ornamental.		2–5m	2–3.5m	W. te S. ar	•		•		•	•	2	H
Acacia rostellifera	Medium to large shrub, long flexible leaves with hooked point, golden yellow flowers in early summer. Coastal and inland forms occur.		3–5m	3–5m	W. te S. ar	•		•	•	•	•	1	L
Acacia rotundifolia	Small to medium compact shrub, rounded hairy leaves, massed bright yellow flowers late winter–spring–early summer. Very decorative.		1–2.5m	1.5–3m	Temp S. ar	•		•		•	•		H
Acacia rubida	Large shrub or medium tree, long narrow foliage, showy yellow flowers winter–spring–early summer. Useful for shade and windbreak.		4–12m	3–7m	Temp S. tr	•		•		•	•		H
Acacia rupicola	Small to medium shrub, prickly rigid foliage, rounded cream to yellow flowers spring–summer. Hardy and adaptable; grows well in shade.		1–2m	1–1.5m	Temp	•		•		•	•		H
Acacia salicina Coobah	Small to medium willow-like tree, long slightly wavy foliage, yellow ball flowers winter–late spring. Attractive screen or windbreak for inland gardens.		5–10m	3–5m	Temp S. tr	•				•	•	2	H
Acacia saligna Golden Wreath Wattle	Large spreading shrub or medium tree, long curved leaves, bright golden globular flowers in spring. Decorative and fast growing; useful shade and shelter tree.		3–10m	4–7m	Temp S. tr S. ar	•				•	•	2	H

Temp — temperate
W. te — warm temperate
Trop — tropical
S. tr — sub-tropical
S. ar — semi-arid

L — light
H — heavy
N — nectar-feeding
S — seed-eating
F — fruit-eating

mp — temperate   L — light
te — warm temperate   H — heavy
op — tropical   N — nectar-feeding
tr — sub-tropical   S — seed-eating
ar — semi-arid   F — fruit-eating

		Height	Width	Climatic zones	Soil types				full sun	filtered sun	coastal regions	frosty regions	bird attraction
					moist, well drained	wet	dry	dry limy					
acia schinoides	Small to medium tree, branches covered with a white waxy bloom, pinnate leaves, pale yellow flowers in long racemes in summer.	4–13m	3–7m	Temp S. tr S. ar	•				•	•		L	S
acia sclerophylla	Small to medium shrub, narrow rigid leaves, almost covered in golden yellow ball flowers in spring.	1–2m	2–4m	Temp S. ar	•		•	•	•	•		H	S
acia sedifolia	Low spreading shrub, small hooked foliage, profuse yellow ball flowers in spring.	1–2m	1–2m	Temp S. ar	•		•		•			L	S
acia sophorae	Small to large broad spreading shrub, broad long leaves, golden rod flowers winter–spring. Quick growing; used for sand stabilising.	1–8m	4–10m	Temp S. tr S. ar	•		•	•	•		1	H	S
acia spathulifolia	Small to medium bushy shrub, fleshy oblong leaves, masses of yellow ball flowers in spring. Ornamental.	1–2m	2–3m	Temp S. ar			•	•		•	1	L	S
acia spectabilis Mudgee Wattle	Medium to large shrub, feathery silver-grey foliage, golden racemes of flowers winter–spring. Spectacular.	3–4m	2–4m	Temp S. tr S. ar	•		•		•	•		H	S
acia stricta	Medium to large upright shrub, grey-green foliage, yellow ball flowers winter–spring.	2–5m	1–4m	Temp S. tr	•		•		•	•		H	S
acia suaveolens	Small to medium spreading shrub, smooth grey leaves, creamy perfumed flowers autumn–winter–spring. Decorative coastal plant.	1–3m	2–5m	Temp S. tr	•		•	•	•	•	1		S
acia subulata	Medium to large shrub, fine foliage, racemes of yellow ball flowers spring–summer. Showy and graceful.	1.5–4m	1–2.5m	Temp S. tr	•		•		•	•		L	S
acia tayloriana	Small ground-covering plant, hairy fern-like foliage, cream ball flowers in summer.	prostrate	70cm–1m	Temp S. tr	•		•		•	•			S
acia terminalis Sunshine Wattle	Small to medium shrub; multi-coloured red, bronze and gold pinnate foliage; pale to bright yellow flowers autumn–winter–spring. Low form available.	30cm–3m	1–2m	Temp S. tr	•		•		•	•		1	S
acia tragonophylla	Large rigid, much branched shrub; prickly foliage, yellow ball flowers winter–spring. Hardy ornamental shrub for dry sites.	3–5m	4–6m	W. te S. ar	•		•	•	•	•		H	S

				Height	Width	Climatic zones	Soil types							
							moist, well drained	wet	dry	dry limy	full sun	filtered sun	coastal regions	frosty regions
Acacia trigonophylla	Small to medium rigid shrub, narrow pointed foliage, golden ball flowers in spring. Ornamental and suited to a range of soils.			1–2.5m	1–2m	Temp S. ar	•		•		•	•		H
Acacia triptera	Small to medium shrub, winged rigid foliage, bright yellow rod flowers in spring. Hardy in dry conditions.			1–2.5m	1–4m	Temp S. tr S. ar	•		•		•	•		H
Acacia truncata	Small to medium spreading shrub, wedge-shaped foliage, rounded yellow flowers winter–spring. Common on W.A. coastal limestones.			1–2.5m	2–4.5m	Temp S. tr S. ar	•		•	•	•		1	
Acacia ulicifolia	Small open rigid shrub, narrow prickly leaves, cream to yellow ball flowers autumn–winter.			1–2m	1–2m	Temp S. tr	•				•			H
Acacia ulicifolia var. brownei	Small compact shrub, fine pointed foliage, bright golden ball flowers winter–spring. Very showy and hardy.			60cm–1m	60cm–1m	Temp S. tr	•		•		•	•		H
Acacia uncinata	Medium to large open shrub, orbicular stem-clasping leaves, bright yellow ball flowers most of the year. Extremely hardy.			2–4m	1.5–3m	Temp S. ar	•		•		•			H
Acacia urophylla	Medium to large shrub, wavy foliage, plentiful yellow flowers winter–spring.			3–4m	2–4m	Temp S. tr	•		•		•			L
Acacia varia	Small shrub with many forms, ferny foliage, short bright yellow rod flowers in spring. Very showy and decorative.			30–45cm	50cm–1m	Temp	•		•		•	•		
Acacia venulosa	Small to large arching shrub, stiff leaves, clusters of bright yellow ball flowers winter–spring.			60cm–4m	90cm–2m	Temp S. ar	•		•		•	•		H
Acacia verniciflua	Variable medium to large shrub, sticky foliage, many bright yellow ball flowers winter–spring–summer. Ornamental and hardy.			3–5m	3–5m	Temp S. tr	•		•		•	•		H
Acacia verticillata	Medium to large shrub, fine prickly foliage clustered around the stems, lemon yellow rod flowers winter–spring–summer.			2–5m	1.5–4m	Temp S. tr	•					•	•	
Acacia vestita	Large pendulous shrub, soft grey hairy foliage, open racemes of golden yellow flowers in spring. Popular and attractive.			3–6m	3–5m	Temp S. tr	•				•	•		H

Temp — temperate
W. te — warm temperate
Trop — tropical
S. tr — sub-tropical
S. ar — semi-arid

L — light
H — heavy
N — nectar-feeding
S — seed-eating
F — fruit-eating

						mp — temperate							

Legend:
- mp — temperate
- te — warm temperate
- ɔp — tropical
- ɾ — sub-tropical
- ar — semi-arid
- L — light
- H — heavy
- N — nectar-feeding
- S — seed-eating
- F — fruit-eating

		Height	Width	Climatic zones	moist, well drained	wet	dry	dry limy	full sun	filtered sun	coastal regions	frosty regions	bird attraction
acia victoriae	Large shrub or small tree, glaucous foliage, creamy yellow ball flowers spring–summer. Useful hedge or low windbreak.	4–10m	4–7m	W. te S. ar	•		•		•	•		H	S
mena australis d Apple	Small to large dense spreading tree; cream flowers in spring, followed by globular red fruit autumn–winter.	6–20m	4–12m	Temp Trop S. tr	•	•				•			F N
mena smithii ɛek Lilly Pilly	Small to large tree, shiny foliage; small greenish flowers in spring, followed by globular pink-purple fruit in winter. Attractive and easy to grow.	8–20m	4–15m	Temp Trop S. tr	•	•				•			F N
tinodium nninghamii	Fine-stemmed herb, pink-and-white daisy flowers in spring. Rockery or container plant.	30–90cm	30–60cm	Temp	•				•	•	2		
tinodium sp. nova	Similar habit and growth to the above, but with smaller flowers.	30cm	30cm	Temp	•				•	•	2		
tinostrobus ɹminatus ɹarf Cypress	An often prostrate suckering conifer, small crowded leaves, decorative seed cones. Useful for soil binding, though slow growing.	50cm–3m	1–5m	W. te S. ar	•		•	•	•	•		L	S
tinostrobus ramidalis ɹamp Cypress	Large shrub or small dense tree, small crowded leaves, conical seed cones. Very effective windbreak for rural sites.	3–8m	2–5m	Temp S. tr S. ar	•		•	•	•	•	2	L	S
tinotus helianthi nnel Flower	Small shrub, deeply divided woolly foliage, white velvety flowers spring–late summer. Beautiful container or rockery plant.	30cm–1m	60cm–1m	Temp	•				•	•	2		
enanthos ɾbigera	Small upright shrub, erect foliage, tubular red flowers winter–spring.	50cm–1m	70cm–1m	Temp	•		•		•	•		H	N
enanthos cuneata	Small to medium shrub, grey foliage, tubular pink to purple flowers spring–summer.	50cm–3m	1–3m	Temp	•		•		•	•		H	N
enanthos ɛisneri	Small, usually spreading shrub; divided foliage, tubular red to purple flowers mostly in summer.	1–2m	1–2m	Temp	•		•		•	•	2	H	N
enanthos ovata	Small spreading shrub, spathulate leaves, tubular scarlet flowers most of the year.	1–1.5m	75cm–1m	Temp	•		•		•	•			N

		Height	Width	Climatic zones	Soil types							
Temp — temperate L — light W. te — warm temperate H — heavy Trop — tropical N — nectar-feeding S. tr — sub-tropical S — seed-eating S. ar — semi-arid F — fruit-eating					moist, well drained	wet	dry	dry limy	full sun	filtered sun	coastal regions	frosty regions
Adenanthos sericea	Small to large shrub, finely divided silvery foliage, small tubular orange or red flowers most of the year.	1.5–6m	2.5–5m	Temp S. ar	•		•	•	•	•	1	L
Agapetes meiniana	Rainforest climber, large shiny leaves, red-pink tubular flowers most of the year. Ideal for baskets. Adapts to cold climates.	climber	light	Temp Trop S. tr	•					•		
Agathis robusta Kauri Pine	Tall symmetrical pine, dark glossy foliage, large seed cones. Attractive indoor or patio tub plant, or beautiful in large gardens.	20–50m	10–25m	Temp Trop S. tr	•				•	•		
Agonis flexuosa Willow Peppermint	Spreading large shrub or large tree, fine weeping foliage, small white flowers spring–summer. Excellent shade and shelter tree, especially in coastal areas.	8–15m	5–10m	Temp S. tr	•		•		•	•	2	
Agonis flexuosa *nana*	Small compact shrub, fine foliage, small white flowers spring–summer. Attractive low hedge.	1–1.5m	1–1.5m	Temp S. tr	•		•		•	•	2	
Agonis flexuosa variegated forms	Several variegated forms are available, but are much slower growing and smaller than the traditional form.	3–4m	2–3m	Temp S. tr	•		•		•	•	2	
Agonis juniperina	Tall slender shrub or medium tree, fine foliage, small white flowers spring–summer. Attractive cut flower.	4–12m	2–5m	Temp S. tr	•				•	•		
Agonis linearifolia	Medium to large shrub, fine foliage, small white flowers spring–summer. Attractive cut flower.	2–5m	2–3m	Temp S. tr	•				•	•		
Agonis parviceps	Small to medium dense shrub, fine foliage; small white flowers winter-spring, excellent for cutting.	1–3m	1–3m	Temp S. tr	•				•	•		
Agrostocrinum *scabrum* Blue Grass Lily	Dwarf tufting lily, fine foliage, 6-petalled blue flowers spring–summer.	60cm	45cm	W. te	•				•	•		L
Albizia lophantha Cape Wattle	Large shrub or medium tree, fern-like foliage, yellow brush flowers most of the year. Fast growing.	3–10m	2–8m	Temp S. tr	•		•	•	•	•	1	L
Alectryon coriaceus Beach Alectryon	Small to large shrub, leathery elliptical leaves, shiny coppery bronze new growth, insignificant flowers in spring, attractive edible red and black seeds.	2–6m	2–5m	W. te Trop S. tr	•		•		•	•	1	L

mp — temperate te — warm temperate op — tropical tr — sub-tropical ar — semi-arid	L — light H — heavy N — nectar-feeding S — seed-eating F — fruit-eating		**Height**	**Width**	Climatic zones	**Soil types**						
						moist, well drained	wet	dry	dry limy	full sun	filtered sun	coastal regions	frosty regions	bird attraction

Name	Description	Height	Width	Climatic zones	moist, well drained	wet	dry	dry limy	full sun	filtered sun	coastal regions	frosty regions	bird attraction
ocasia acrorrhiza njevoi	Fleshy-stemmed plant arising from rhizome, large flat leaves, hooded pale green perfumed flowers in summer. Rainforest plant, attractive with ferns.	1.5–2m	1–1.5m	Temp Trop S.tr	•					•			
ohitonia excelsa	Medium to large tree, shiny foliage, showy bunches of white flowers summer–autumn. Attractive container plant.	7–25m	5–10m	W. te Trop S.tr	•					•		L	S
ohitonia petriei nk Ash	Medium to large tree, ovate silver-backed leaves, clusters of cream flowers in spring. Fast growing; useful for regeneration in moist shaded areas.	10–25m	6–9m	W. te Trop S.tr	•					•		L	
pinia caerulea tive Ginger	Multi-stemmed rainforest plant, lush glossy leaves with red undersides; perfumed white flowers spring–summer, blue berries. Attractive tub plant.	1–2.2m	1–1.5m	Temp Trop S.tr	•					•		L	S
yogyne hakeifolia biscus	Small to medium shrub, finely divided foliage, large pink flowers with darker centres in summer.	1–3.5m	75cm–3m	Temp S.tr S.ar	•		•		•			L	
yogyne huegelii biscus	Small to medium shrub, broadly palmate foliage; white, yellow, mauve-blue or purple flowers spring–summer–autumn.	1.5–3m	1.5–2.5m	Temp S.tr S.ar	•		•		•			L	
norphospermum hitei sty Plum	Medium to large rainforest shrub or small tree, bright rust-coloured new growth, small creamy flowers autumn–winter, large blue-black edible fruit spring–summer.	3–9m	3–6m	W. te Trop S.tr	•					•		L	F
ngophora costata	Medium to large tree; smooth pink, cream or orange trunk; long smooth leaves, massed white flowers in summer. Stately sensuous parkland or garden tree.	8–18m	6–10m	Temp Trop S.tr	•		•		•	•	1	L	N
ngophora ribunda	Medium to large tree, open spreading canopy, masses of nectar-rich cream blossoms in spring. Excellent shade tree.	10–25m	6–15m	Temp S.tr	•		•		•	•	1	L	N
ngophora hispida	Large angular spreading shrub or small tree, large grey leaves, red buds and large bunches of cream flowers spring–summer. Unusual form, attractive in the landscape.	3–6m	3–5m	Temp S.tr	•				•	•	2	L	N
nigozanthos color	Dwarf plant, fine grey strap leaves, red-and-green kangaroo paw flowers spring–summer–autumn.	30–60cm	30–80cm	Temp S.ar	•		•		•	•		L	N
nigozanthos ig Red'	Small vigorous plant, strap leaves; tall stems of bright scarlet kangaroo paw flowers in spring, excellent for cutting.	1–1.5m	1–1.5m	Temp S.tr S.ar	•				•	•	2	L	N

		Height	Width	Climatic zones	Soil types				full sun	filtered sun	coastal regions	frosty regions
Temp — temperate L — light W. te — warm temperate H — heavy Trop — tropical N — nectar-feeding S. tr — sub-tropical S — seed-eating S. ar — semi-arid F — fruit-eating					moist, well drained	wet	dry	dry limy				
Anigozanthos 'Bush Baby'	Compact dwarf plant, many-flowered stems of pinky gold kangaroo paws most of the year. Excellent for rockery or container.	20–40cm	30–60cm	Temp S. tr S. ar	•				•	•		L
Anigozanthos 'Bush Dawn'	Small vigorous plant, bright green foliage, beautiful yellow kangaroo paw flowers on tall stems spring–summer–autumn.	60cm–1m	80cm–1m	Temp S. tr S. ar	•				•	•		L
Anigozanthos 'Bush Emerald'	Small plant, grey-green strap foliage, green stems bearing red-and-green kangaroo paw flowers spring–summer.	60cm–1m	80cm–1m	Temp S. tr S. ar	•				•	•		L
Anigozanthos 'Bush Flame'	Small plant, grey-green strap foliage, green to red stems bearing vivid orange-red kangaroo paw flowers spring–summer. Particularly colourful.	50–70cm	50–80cm	Temp S. tr S. ar	•				•	•		L
Anigozanthos 'Bush Glow'	Small plant, lush strap foliage, spectacular glowing orange-yellow kangaroo paw flowers throughout the warm months.	50–70cm	50–80cm	Temp S. tr S. ar	•				•	•		L
Anigozanthos 'Bush Ranger'	Dwarf plant, dark foliage, beautiful deep red kangaroo paw flowers spring–summer–autumn. Particularly striking.	30–50cm	30–50cm	Temp S. tr S. ar	•				•	•	2	L
Anigozanthos 'Dwarf Delight'	Dwarf plant, bright green foliage, many-flowered heads of vivid orange-red kangaroo paws spring–summer.	60cm	60cm	Temp S. tr S. ar	•				•	•	2	L
Anigozanthos 'Early Spring'	Dwarf plant, narrow leaves, bright red kangaroo paw flowers in early spring. A delightful 'fill-in' plant.	30–60cm	30–50cm	Temp Trop S. tr S. ar	•				•	•		L
Anigozanthos 'Emerald Glow'	Dwarf plant, pink stems bearing glowing emerald kangaroo paw flowers spring–summer. Excellent for container.	40–60cm	40–60cm	Temp Trop S. tr S. ar	•				•	•		L
Anigozanthos flavidus	The tallest kangaroo paw; long strap leaves; tall stems of flowers with colours varying from yellow-green to pink, orange or red spring–summer–autumn.	2m	1.5m	Temp Trop S. tr S. ar	•	•	•		•	•	2	L
Anigozanthos 'Harmony'	Small plant, bright green foliage, tall multi-branched bright red stems bearing vivid yellow kangaroo paw flowers spring–summer–autumn.	80cm–1.2m	60cm–1.2m	Temp Trop S. tr S. ar	•				•	•		L
Anigozanthos humilis Cat's Paw	Dwarf plant, curved grey leaves, gold suffused with red kangaroo paw flowers spring–summer–autumn. Charming in container or raised bed.	10–30cm	30–80cm	Temp S. tr S. ar	•				•	•		L

					Soil types								
		Height	Width	Climatic zones	moist, well drained	wet	dry	dry limy	full sun	filtered sun	coastal regions	frosty regions	bird attraction
igozanthos *nglesii*	Small plant, grey-green strap leaves, furry red-and-green kangaroo paw flowers mainly in spring but often throughout the year.	60cm–1m	30cm	Temp S. ar	•		•		•	•		L	N
igozanthos *cherrimus*	Small plant, grey-green strap leaves, tall stems bearing vivid yellow kangaroo paw flowers mainly in spring. Best grown in deep sand.	60cm–1m	30cm	Temp S. ar	•		•		•	•		L	N
igozanthos *d Cross'*	Small vigorous plant, strap leaves, tall multi-branched stems, many showy burgundy kangaroo paw flowers spring–summer– autumn. Excellent cut flower.	80cm–1m	80cm–1m	Temp Trop S. tr S. ar	•				•	•		L	N
igozanthos rufus	Small plant, grey strap leaves, grey stems bearing rich blood red kangaroo paw flowers late winter–spring. Best grown in deep sand.	50–90cm	50–90cm	Temp S. ar	•		•		•	•	2	L	N
igozanthos viridis	Dwarf plant, fine grey-green leaves, green stems bearing vivid green kangaroo paw flowers often throughout the year. Particularly good for moist sandy areas.	60cm	30cm	Temp S. tr S. ar	•	•			•			L	N
opterus *cleayanus* *cleay Laurel*	Medium to large shrub, umbrella of large bronze and green leaves, white flowers in clusters late spring–summer. Moist shaded site or indoors.	1.5–3.5m	1–2.5m	Temp Trop S. tr	•					•		L	
tus ericoides *strate*	Prostrate compact groundcover, crowded linear leaves, yellow-and- orange pea flowers spring– summer. Excellent coastal rockery, container or basket plant.	prostrate	1–2m	Temp S. tr	•		•	•	•	•	1	L	
aucaria bidwillii *nya Pine*	Large symmetrical tree, radiating branches, prickly lanceolate leaves, large seed cones. Slow growing, but makes a beautiful containerised Christmas tree.	20–30m	10–20m	Temp Trop S. tr	•				•	•			S
aucaria *nninghamii* *op Pine*	Medium to large tree, straight trunk with circular hoops, crowded linear leaves, large seed cones. Beautiful shapely container plant; also grown for timber.	10–30m	6–20m	Temp Trop S. tr	•				•	•			S
aucaria *erophylla* *rfolk Island Pine*	Medium to large tree, symmetrical branches, crowded foliage. Attractive container plant; often used in foreshore plantations.	10–25m	6–20m	Temp Trop S. tr	•		•	•	•		1		S
chidendron *ndiflorum* *ce-flower Tree*	Large shrub, pinnate foliage, beautiful lightly perfumed crimson-and-white fluffy flowers in summer, orange capsules with shiny black seeds.	3–8m	2–5m	W. te Trop S. tr	•					•		L	S
chirhodomyrtus *ckleri* *se Myrtle*	Medium to large weeping shrub, glossy lanceolate leaves, delicate pink-and-white flowers in spring, orange berries. Attractive; for open or shaded sites.	3–5m	1.5–3m	Temp Trop S. tr	•				•	•		L	F

mp — temperate	L — light
te — warm temperate	H — heavy
op — tropical	N — nectar-feeding
r — sub-tropical	S — seed-eating
ar — semi-arid	F — fruit-eating

		Height	Width	Climatic zones	moist, well drained	wet	dry	dry limy	full sun	filtered sun	coastal regions	frosty regions
Archontophoenix alexandrae Alexandra Palm	Large palm with spreading fronds. Attractive and useful for tropical gardens, especially when grown in groups.	12–25m	3–7m	Trop S.tr	•	•			•	•		
Archontophoenix cunninghamiana Bangalow Palm	Tall slender palm with spreading fronds. Used widely in tropical gardens; very handsome grown in groups.	15–25m	4–7m	Trop S.tr	•	•			•	•		
Argyrodendron actinophyllum Black Booyong	Large tree in natural habitat, distinctive shiny palmate leaves, white flowers in late summer, winged seeds. Suitable for large gardens; handsome tub plant.	20–30m	10–15m	W.te Trop S.tr	•					•		
Astartea fascicularis	Small shrub, fine foliage, massed white or pink flowers winter–spring–summer. Responds to pruning.	1–2m	1–2m	Temp S.tr	•				•	•		L
Astartea heteranthera	Small shrub, fine foliage, white flowers winter–spring. Responds to pruning.	80cm–1m	70cm–1.2m	Temp S.tr	•				•	•		L
Astartea 'Winter Pink'	Small compact shrub, fine foliage, deep pink flowers most of the year. Responds to pruning. Excellent cut flower and container plant.	60cm–1m	80cm–1.2m	Temp S.tr	•				•	•		L
Asterolasia asteriscophora	Small open shrub, hairy foliage, bright yellow star flowers in spring. A long-lasting cut flower. Tip prune after flowering.	1–1.5m	1–1.2m	Temp S.tr	•				•	•		L
Astroloma ciliatum	Dwarf conifer-like shrub, dense needle foliage, multi-coloured (red, black and green) tubular flowers winter–late spring. Rockery or container plant.	30–60cm	60cm	Temp S.tr	•		•		•	•		L
Astroloma conostephioides Flame Heath	Compact dwarf shrub, pointed grey foliage, pendent scarlet tubular flowers winter–spring–summer. Eye-catching container plant and cut flower.	30–60cm	60cm	Temp S.tr S.ar	•		•		•	•		H
Astroloma epacridis	Small compact shrub, crowded foliage, orange-red tubular flowers most of the year. Tip pruning beneficial. Rockery plant.	30–80cm	50cm–1.2m	Temp S.tr S.ar	•		•		•	•		L
Astroloma humifusum Cranberry Heath	Prostrate or upright dwarf shrub, small foliage, bright red tubular flowers winter–spring. Very attractive container plant.	prostrate–30cm	60cm–1m	Temp S.tr	•		•		•	•	2	H
Astroloma pinifolium	Small ascending shrub, pine-like foliage, bright yellow tubular flowers spring–summer–autumn. Easily grown in a container.	30cm–1m	50cm–1.5m	Temp S.tr S.ar	•		•		•			H

Legend:
Temp — temperate
W. te — warm temperate
Trop — tropical
S. tr — sub-tropical
S. ar — semi-arid
L — light
H — heavy
N — nectar-feeding
S — seed-eating
F — fruit-eating

Legend:

- p — temperate
- e — warm temperate
- o — tropical
- — sub-tropical
- — semi-arid

- L — light
- H — heavy
- N — nectar-feeding
- S — seed-eating
- F — fruit-eating

	Description	Height	Width	Climatic zones	Soil types moist, well drained	wet	dry	dry limy	full sun	filtered sun	coastal regions	frosty regions	bird attraction
ertonia rsifolia te Oak	Mostly a large shrub or small tree; variable, frequently lobed foliage; brown flowers in autumn, edible decorative blue fruit.	8–15m	4–8m	W.te Trop S.tr	•				•	•			F N
olex cinerea st Saltbush	Small to medium spreading shrub, silver-grey foliage, purplish cream flowers spring–summer. Excellent coastal and sand-binding plant.	1–2m	2–3m	Temp S.tr Arid S.ar	•		•	•	•		1	L	S
olex nummularia	Small to medium spreading shrub, furry silvery white leaves, yellow-brown flowers most of the year. Useful fodder plant for dry soils, and roadside planting.	1–3m	2–4m	Temp S.tr Arid S.ar	•		•	•	•		1	H	S
olex godioides	Low to medium spreading shrub, grey foliage which can be grazed, flowers insignificant. Hardy and adaptable.	50cm–2m	1–2m	Temp S.tr Arid S.ar	•		•	•	•		1	H	S
tromyrtus dulcis	Mounding ground-covering plant, bronze foliage; masses of fluffy white flowers autumn–winter, followed by edible fruit. Regular pruning beneficial.	30–60cm	1–2m	Temp Trop S.tr S.ar	•				•	•	2	L	F N
tromyrtus oclada vety Myrtle	Small to medium rainforest shrub; glossy foliage, soft new growth; pink-and-white flowers in summer, black olive-like fruit attractive to birds. Adaptable.	1–4m	1–2.5m	W.te Trop S.tr	•				•	•		L	F
tromyrtus uifolia	Small to medium shrub, linear foliage; white flowers in summer, followed by edible fruit. Prefers some shade.	1–3m	1–2m	Temp Trop S.tr	•					•		L	F N
khousia odora non-scented yrtle	Small to medium shapely tree; pale green, strongly lemon-scented leaves; fluffy cream flowers summer–autumn.	8–20m	6–10m	Trop S.tr	•				•	•		L	
khousia rtifolia y Myrtle	Medium to large dense shrub; pointed lanceolate leaves, copper new growth; masses of fluffy cream flowers winter–spring–summer. Hardy and adaptable.	2–7m	1.5–3m	Temp Trop S.tr	•				•	•		L	
ckea astarteoides	Small dainty shrub, fine aromatic foliage, masses of tiny pink flowers summer–autumn. Responds to pruning.	80cm–1.5m	70cm–1.5m	Temp S.tr	•				•	•		L	
ckea nphorosmae	Small arching shrub, crowded fine aromatic foliage, massed shell-pink-and-white flowers along stems in spring. Grows well in container.	30–90cm	40cm–1m	Temp S.ar	•		•		•	•		L	
ckea crenatifolia	Small to medium erect slender shrub, dainty crowded aromatic foliage, massed white flowers in summer. Excellent for narrow areas.	1–3m	90cm–2m	Temp S.tr	•					•		H	

		Height	Width	Climatic zones	moist, well drained	wet	dry	dry limy	full sun	filtered sun	coastal regions	frosty regions

Legend:
Temp — temperate
W. te — warm temperate
Trop — tropical
S. tr — sub-tropical
S. ar — semi-arid
L — light
H — heavy
N — nectar-feeding
S — seed-eating
F — fruit-eating

Soil types

		Height	Width	Climatic zones	moist, well drained	wet	dry	dry limy	full sun	filtered sun	coastal regions	frosty regions
Baeckea densifolia	Small arching shrub, fine stems, dense narrow aromatic foliage, dainty white flowers along stems in summer. Prune lightly after flowering.	50cm–1.2m	50–70cm	Temp Trop	●				●	●		L
Baeckea grandiflora	Small shrub, tiny aromatic leaves; large showy white to shell pink flowers in spring, also sporadic. Grows well in container. Prune lightly after flowering.	45–90cm	45–80cm	W. te S. ar	●		●		●			L
Baeckea imbricata	Small shrub, attractive small aromatic leaves, white flowers spring–summer. Prune lightly after flowering.	50cm–1.2m	60cm–1.2m	Temp S. tr	●				●	●		H
Baeckea linifolia	Small to medium softly arching open shrub, slender fine aromatic leaves, small white flowers in summer. Attractive light screen; graceful beside pools.	1–2.5m	75cm–1.5m	Temp S. tr	●	●			●	●		L
Baeckea ramosissima	Small dainty plant of variable habit, tiny crowded aromatic leaves, striking masses of white to deep pink flowers winter–spring–summer. Showy container plant.	prostrate–1m	30cm–1m	Temp	●		●		●	●		L
Baeckea utilis	Small to medium upright dense shrub, crowded aromatic foliage, massed creamy white flowers in summer. Attractive screening plant. Prune after flowering.	1–2.2m	1–2m	Temp S. tr	●	●			●	●		H
Baeckea virgata	Small to medium lightly arching shrub, fine aromatic foliage, white flowers spring–summer. Several prostrate cultivar forms are available. Prune all forms.	1–2.5m	1–2m	Temp S. tr	●				●	●		H
Banksia aemula	Similar to *B. serrata*. Large shrub or small tree, occasionally dwarfed; shiny serrated leaves, conspicuous pale yellow flowers in winter, followed by large fruit.	1–7m	2–7m	Temp Trop S. tr	●	●			●	●	2	L
Banksia ashbyi	Medium to large dense shrub, stiff foliage; showy orange flowers mainly in winter, excellent for cutting.	3–6m	2–5m	W. te S. ar	●		●	●	●			L
Banksia attenuata	Tall shrub or tree, narrow toothed foliage, bright yellow flowers prominently displayed spring–summer.	4–15m	2–7m	W. te S. ar	●		●		●	●	2	L
Banksia audax	Small to medium shrub, rigid toothed leaves, bright orange-gold flowers spring–summer.	1–2m	1.5–2.5m	W. te S. ar	●		●		●	●		H
Banksia baueri	Compact dense medium shrub, soft new growth; large woolly yellow-grey flowers, occasionally rusty orange, autumn–winter.	2–3m	2–3m	W. te S. ar	●		●		●	●	2	H

LEFT:
When considering the planting of containers, compatibility of pot and plant size, shape of plant and texture should all be considered. This plain ball pot with a slight pink tinge is a perfect receptacle for *Actinodium cunninghamii.*

BELOW:
These two pictures of fixed and mobile gardens around an office illustrate that both permanent and seasonal beauty can complement even an ordinary building. Great effect in a confined area is achieved with imaginative use of various materials.

RIGHT:
Crowea exalata
'Australflora Harlequin'

Beautiful and tough are two descriptions for this low-growing shrub, flowering in autumn and winter, and making a lovely sight as it cascades across the ground or down banks. Not only does it thrive in temperate conditions, experience has shown it to be extremely drought resistant.

LEFT:
Possibly the smallest member of the patersonias, *Patersonia longifolia* is one of a number of mostly purple, blue, or occasionally white or yellow flag flowers related to the iris. They have simple strap-like foliage and make an attractive group or border planting.

RIGHT:
Isopogon anemonifolius
'Woorikee 2000'

Even when not in flower this dwarf shrub, with its much divided foliage, is very attractive. As a container plant, or in a rockery or cottage garden, it offers year-round appeal, especially when covered with its unusual flowers from spring to early summer.

np — temperate	L — light
te — warm temperate	H — heavy
p — tropical	N — nectar-feeding
r — sub-tropical	S — seed-eating
r — semi-arid	F — fruit-eating

Name	Description	Height	Width	Climatic zones	moist, well drained	wet	dry	dry limy	full sun	filtered sun	coastal regions	frosty regions	bird attraction
...ksia baxteri	Medium to large open shrub, long triangular-lobed foliage, showy lemon-and-white flowers spring–summer–autumn. Attractive cut flower.	3–3.5m	2–2.5m	W. te S. ar	•		•		•	•	2	H	N S
...ksia blechnifolia	Prostrate creeping plant, deeply lobed foliage, beautiful pinky bronze flowers in spring.	prostrate	2–3.5m	Temp S. ar	•		•		•	•		L	N S
...ksia brownii	Medium to large upright shrub, beautiful ferny foliage, conspicuous bright red-gold flowers in winter. Attractive.	2–5.5m	1–4m	W. te	•				•	•	2	L	N S
...ksia burdettii	Large bushy shrub or small tree, attractive lobed foliage, showy orange-and-white flowers summer–autumn.	3–6m	3–6m	W. te S. ar	•		•	•	•	•		H	N S
...ksia caleyi	Medium to large bushy shrub, stiff grey foliage, pendent flowers of creamy pink to deep pink in spring.	2–3.5m	2–4m	Temp S. ar	•		•		•	•		H	N S
...ksia candolleana	Small many-stemmed shrub, stiff toothed foliage, bright yellow flowers autumn–winter, attractive fruit.	90cm–1.5m	1.5–3m	W. te S. ar	•		•		•	•		H	N S
...ksia canei	Small to medium shrub, short dark leaves, lemon flowers tinged with mauve summer–autumn–late winter.	1–2m	1–2.5m	Temp S. ar	•		•		•	•		H	N S
...ksia coccinea	Medium to large narrow or spreading shrub, rounded grey leaves, large scarlet-and-grey flowers winter–spring–summer.	3–4m	2–2.5m	Temp S. ar	•		•		•	•	1	H	N S
...ksia conferta	Medium to large shrub, slightly toothed stiff foliage, erect lemon brushes summer–autumn–winter.	2–4m	2–3m	Temp S. tr	•				•	•		L	N S
...ksia androides	Low compact spreading shrub, crowded toothed leaves, small but plentiful golden brown flowers spring–summer.	20cm–1.5m	60cm–2m	Temp S. ar	•		•		•	•	1	L	N S
...ksia ericifolia	Small to large dense shrub, short narrow leaves, many showy orange to deep burgundy flowers autumn–winter–spring.	1.2–7m	1.5–2.5m	Temp S. tr	•				•	•	2	L	N S
...ksia ericifolia arf	Small compact shrub, short narrow leaves, spectacular deep red-gold flowers autumn–winter–spring.	1.2–1.6m	1.5–2m	Temp S. tr	•				•	•	2	L	N S

		Height	Width	Climatic zones	Soil types							
					moist, well drained	wet	dry	dry limy	full sun	filtered sun	coastal regions	frosty regions
Banksia gardneri	Prostrate creeping plant, upright grey wavy-edged foliage, rusty brown flowers along the stems in spring.	prostrate–30cm	1–2.5m	Temp S. ar	•		•		•	•		L
Banksia 'Giant Candles'	Medium to large shrub, fine dark foliage, exceptionally tall golden orange flower spikes autumn–winter–spring.	3–5m	2–4m	Temp Trop S. tr	•				•	•		L
Banksia grandis	Large shrub or medium tree, handsome lobed foliage; spectacular flowers, blue-green in bud, changing to gold then bronze, mainly spring–summer.	5–10m	3–8m	Temp S. ar	•		•		•	•		L
Banksia hookeriana	Medium to large bushy shrub, crowded fine-toothed foliage, showy orange-and-white flowers winter–spring.	1.5–3.5m	2–5m	W. te S. ar	•		•		•			H
Banksia integrifolia	Small shrub to erect tall tree, dark green silver-backed leaves, masses of bright lemon flowers summer–autumn–mid-winter.	2.5–20m	2–10m	Temp Trop S. tr	•		•		•	•	1	L
Banksia integrifolia 'Australflora Roller Coaster'	Ground-covering form of the above.	prostrate–20cm	2.5m	Temp Trop S. tr	•		•		•	•	1	L
Banksia laevigata ssp. *laevigata*	Open medium shrub, grey-green leaves with bronze new growth, conspicuous lemon 'cricket ball' flowers late spring–summer.	2–3m	1.5–2.5m	W. te S. ar	•		•		•	•		H
Banksia laricina	Small bushy shrub, fine narrow leaves; pale yellow flowers autumn–winter, followed by rose-shaped fruit.	1–1.5m	1.2–2m	W. te S. ar	•		•		•	•	2	
Banksia lemanniana	Medium to large dense shrub, stiff leaves, conspicuous pendent waxy lemon flowers spring–summer.	2–3m	2–3.5m	W. te S. ar	•		•		•	•	2	H
Banksia lindleyana	Medium to large shrub, pale green foliage, clear yellow flowers summer–early autumn.	2–4m	2–4.5m	W. te S. ar	•		•		•	•		H
Banksia littoralis	Small to medium tree, bushy crown of fine dense foliage, brilliant yellow flowers autumn–winter.	5–12m	3–9m	Temp S. tr	•				•	•	2	L
Banksia marginata	Low compact shrub to dense medium tree, crowded short leaves, profuse bright lemon flowers late summer–autumn–winter.	50cm–10m	1–5m	Temp S. tr	•		•		•	•	2	H

Temp — temperate
W. te — warm temperate
Trop — tropical
S. tr — sub-tropical
S. ar — semi-arid

L — light
H — heavy
N — nectar-feeding
S — seed-eating
F — fruit-eating

p — temperate   L — light
e — warm temperate   H — heavy
o — tropical   N — nectar-feeding
 — sub-tropical   S — seed-eating
 — semi-arid   F — fruit-eating

		Height	Width	Climatic zones	Soil types				full sun	filtered sun	coastal regions	frosty regions	bird attraction
					moist, well drained	wet	dry	dry limy					
ksia media	Small to large bushy shrub, shiny toothed leaves, bright lemon yellow brushes in winter.	1.5–5m	2–5m	W. te	•		•		•	•	1	H	N S
ksia meisneri	Small multi-branched shrub, crowded small bright green leaves, many small honey-gold flowers in winter, attractive small fruit.	70cm–1.5m	1–2m	W. te S. ar	•		•		•	•		L	N S
ksia menziesii	Large compact shrub or medium tree, grey-green stiff leaves, beautiful pink-and-silver flowers autumn–winter–summer, attractive fruit.	5–15m	5–10m	W. te S. ar	•		•		•	•	2	L	N S
ksia nutans	Small to medium bushy shrub, dense blue-green linear leaves, pendent bronze-purple flowers in summer, attractive fruit.	1–2m	1–2.5m	W. te S. ar	•		•		•	•	2	L	N S
ksia oblongifolia (. B. aspleniifolia)	Small to medium shrub, stiff dark oblong slightly toothed leaves, rust coloured woolly new growth; pale yellow flowers, blue-grey in bud, autumn–winter.	60cm–3m	1.5–3m	Temp Trop S. tr	•				•	•	2	L	N S
ksia occidentalis	Small to large dense shrub, fine linear leaves, conspicuous red-and-gold flowers late spring–summer.	50cm–6m	1.5–4.5m	Temp S. ar	•	•			•	•	2	L	N S
ksia oreophila	Medium shrub, bluish green smooth leaves; flowers creamy in bud, opening to silvery mauve in winter.	1.5–3m	1.5–2.5m	W. te S. ar	•		•		•	•		H	N S
ksia ornata	Small to medium spreading bushy shrub, grey-green serrated leaves; creamy yellow flowers, occasionally orange, mainly in winter.	60cm–2.5m	1–2.5m	W. te S. ar	•		•	•	•	•	2	H	N S
ksia paludosa	Small to medium open shrub, bright green leaves on yellow stems; flower buds bronze-gold, opening to yellow, mainly in winter.	50cm–1.5m	80cm–1.2m	Temp S. tr	•		•		•	•	2	L	N S
ksia petiolaris	Prostrate creeping plant; broad wavy toothed grey foliage, a beautiful bronze when new; pink to red-gold flowers spring–summer–autumn.	prostrate	2–3.5m	Temp S. ar	•		•		•	•		H	N S
ksia pilostylis	Small to large bushy shrub, narrow toothed leaves, creamy yellow flowers spring–summer.	30cm–4m	2.5–4m	W. te S. ar	•		•	•	•	•	2	H	N S
ksia praemorsa	Small to large shrub, dense stiff foliage, rich bronze-gold flowers tinged with maroon and pale green in spring.	1–4m	1–3m	Temp S. ar	•		•	•	•	•	1	L	N S

Temp — temperate
W. te — warm temperate
Trop — tropical
S. tr — sub-tropical
S. ar — semi-arid

L — light
H — heavy
N — nectar-feeding
S — seed-eating
F — fruit-eating

		Height	Width	Climatic zones	moist, well drained	wet	dry	dry limy	full sun	filtered sun	coastal regions	frosty regions
Banksia prionotes	Large shrub or medium tree, long wavy toothed grey leaves, showy orange-and-cream flowers most of the year.	4–12m	4–7m	W. te S. ar	•		•	•	•		2	L
Banksia pulchella	Small shrub, short linear leaves, dainty honey-gold flowers most of the year, small rounded fruit.	60cm–1.5m	1–1.8m	W. te S. ar	•		•		•	•	2	L
Banksia quercifolia	Medium to large upright shrub, smooth serrated wavy leaves, attractive red-and-green buds open to yellow or bronze flowers autumn–winter.	2–4m	1.3–2.5m	W. te S. ar	•		•		•	•	2	L
Banksia repens	Creeping plant with underground stems; beautiful lobed foliage, bronze-gold when new; pink-and-cream flowers in spring.	prostrate	2–4m	Temp S. ar	•		•		•	•	2	H
Banksia robur	Small to medium open shrub; broad robust leaves, bronze new growth; bronze-green buds; golden brown flowers most of the year. Handsome.	50cm–2m	50cm–2m	Temp Trop S. tr	•	•			•	•	2	H
Banksia sceptrum	Medium to large shrub, blunt grey-green leaves, plentiful showy rich gold flowers in summer.	2–6m	2–4.5m	W. te S. ar	•		•	•	•	•		L
Banksia serrata	Small to large tree, stiff serrated leaves; silver-grey-and-yellow flowers summer–autumn–late winter, followed by 'Bad Banksia Men' seed cones.	6–20m	4–12m	Temp Trop S. tr	•		•		•	•	1	
Banksia serrata 'Austraflora Pygmy Possum'	Low spreading shrub, stiff serrated leaves, silver-grey-and-yellow flowers conspicuously displayed above foliage spring–summer. Handsome groundcover.	prostrate–30cm	2–3m	Temp Trop S. tr	•		•		•	•	1	
Banksia solandri	Variable shrub, robust oak-like leaves, rich purplish brown perfumed woolly flowers in spring. Handsome.	2–6m	1.5–4m	Temp	•		•		•	•	2	
Banksia speciosa	Spreading large shrub or small tree, long triangular-lobed leaves, showy cream-and-lemon flowers throughout the year.	5–7m	7–8m	W. te S. ar	•		•		•	•	2	L
Banksia sphaerocarpa	Medium shrub, fine blue-green linear foliage, purplish gold globular flowers summer–autumn–late winter.	1.5–2.5m	2–3.5m	W. te S. ar	•		•		•	•		L
Banksia spinulosa	Small to medium shrub, crowded fine linear foliage, honey-gold flowers with black or dark red styles in profusion late autumn–summer–early spring.	1–3.5m	1.2–4m	Temp Trop S. tr	•		•		•	•		H

			Height	Width		**Soil types**							
					Climatic zones	moist, well drained	wet	dry	dry limy	full sun	filtered sun	coastal regions	frosty regions	bird attraction

Legend:
- np — temperate · L — light
- e — warm temperate · H — heavy
- o — tropical · N — nectar-feeding
- — sub-tropical · S — seed-eating
- r — semi-arid · F — fruit-eating

Name	Description	Height	Width	Climatic zones	moist, well drained	wet	dry	dry limy	full sun	filtered sun	coastal regions	frosty regions	bird attraction
ksia spinulosa 'nday Candles'	Compact dwarf shrub, fine crowded foliage, large quantities of gold flowers with dark red styles early autumn–winter–spring.	15–45cm	50cm–1m	Temp Trop S.tr	●		●		●	●	1	L	N S
ksia spinulosa 'narvon Gold'	Compact shapely medium shrub, bright green linear foliage, pure gold flowers winter–spring. Responds to pruning.	1.5–2.5m	1.5–2m	Temp S.tr S.ar	●		●		●	●		L	N S
ksia verticillata	Large dense shrub, blunt leaves, golden flowers summer–autumn. Handsome coastal screening plant.	1.5–6m	3–5m	Temp	●		●		●	●	1	L	N S
ksia victoriae	Large spreading shrub, stiff triangular-lobed foliage, beautiful cream-and-pinky-orange flowers in summer.	3–4.5m	3.5–5m	W.te S.ar	●		●		●			L	N S
ksia violacea	Small shrub, fine linear foliage, globular flowers of violet tinged with greenish gold late spring–summer.	50cm–1.2m	90cm–2m	W.te S.ar	●		●		●		2	L	N S
klya syringifolia wn of Gold	Large shrub or small tree, attractive shiny heart-shaped leaves, masses of gold flowers in summer. Prefers warm climates.	5–8m	3–5m	W.te Trop S.tr	●					●		L	
era rubioides	Small to medium dense shrub, crowded bronze-green foliage, pink or white open-petalled flowers most of the year. Prostrate forms available. Prune regularly.	1–2m	1.2–2.2m	Temp Trop S.tr	●	●			●	●	1	L	
era sessiliflora	Dense medium shrub, crowded dark foliage, vivid purple (occasionally white) flowers massed along stems in spring. Prune regularly.	1.5–2.2m	2–2.5m	Temp Trop S.tr	●	●			●	●		L	
ufortia ussata	Small to medium upright shrub, neatly arranged foliage, large deep red flower spikes summer–early autumn. Tip pruning recommended.	1–1.5m	80cm–1m	Temp S.tr	●				●	●		L	N
ufortia elegans	Small to medium upright shrub, short curved foliage, beautiful pink to purple flowerheads spring–summer. Tip pruning recommended.	1.2–1.8m	80cm–1.2m	Temp S.tr	●				●	●	2	L	N
ufortia cephala	Small dense shrub, pale green foliage, vivid red globular flowerheads in spring. Tip pruning recommended.	40–70cm	50cm–1m	Temp S.tr	●				●	●		L	N
ufortia rophylla	Small spreading shrub, arching branches; narrow, often hairy, grey foliage; bright scarlet to purple-red open flowerheads in spring. Tip prune regularly.	40cm–1.2m	90cm–1.2m	Temp	●				●	●		L	N

		Height	Width	Climatic zones	Soil types				full sun	filtered sun	coastal regions	frosty regions
					moist, well drained	wet	dry	dry limy				
Temp — temperate L — light												
W. te — warm temperate H — heavy												
Trop — tropical N — nectar-feeding												
S. tr — sub-tropical S — seed-eating												
S. ar — semi-arid F — fruit-eating												
Beaufortia orbifolia	Small to medium open upright shrub, neat compact foliage; pale green-and-red bottlebrush flowerheads, aging to bright red, summer–autumn. Tip prune.	1.2–1.5m	80cm–1.2m	Temp	•		•		•	•		H
Beaufortia purpurea	Dwarf to small shrub, tiny narrow leaves, pompom flowerheads of irridescent purple-red spring–summer–autumn. Container plant. Tip prune regularly.	30–60cm	60–90cm	Temp S. tr	•				•	•		L
Beaufortia schaueri	Dwarf to small shrub, tiny leaves; mauve or pink pompom flowerheads spring–summer, also sporadic. Container or rockery plant. Tip pruning recommended.	40–80cm	40–90cm	Temp S. ar	•		•		•	•	2	L
Beaufortia sparsa	Upright medium shrub, long stems covered in neat bright green foliage, showy flame-orange brushes late summer–autumn. Tip pruning recommended.	1.5–1.8m	1.2–1.5m	Temp S. tr	•				•	•		L
Beaufortia squarrosa	Small to medium compact shrub, dense bright green foliage; massed scarlet, honey-gold or lemon open flowerheads spring–summer–autumn. Tip prune.	1.2–3m	1–2.2m	Temp S. ar	•		•		•	•	2	L
Billardiera bicolor	Trailing climber, smooth grey-green foliage, delicate open-petalled flowers of creamy white striped with purple most of the year.	climber	light	Temp Trop S. tr	•		•		•	•		L
Billardiera bignoniacea	Dainty fine-stemmed twining plant, scattered woolly leaves, pale lemon-and-orange bells spring–summer which are vivid in a shaded spot.	climber	light	Temp S. tr	•				•	•		L
Billardiera cymosa	Twining climber, short slender leaves; clusters of pale blue to mauve or pink open bells, occasionally white, spring–summer.	climber	light	Temp Trop S. tr S. ar	•		•	•	•	•		H
Billardiera drummondiana var. *collina*	Dainty twining climber, small toothed foliage, intense china blue open bells spring–summer.	climber	light	Temp S. tr	•		•		•	•		L
Billardiera erubescens	Twining climber, broad glossy leaves, rich crimson-orange bells in clusters spring–summer.	climber	light	Temp S. tr	•		•		•	•		L
Billardiera longiflora	Slender twining climber, narrow leaves; vivid lime green bells often tinged with purple in spring, followed by purple-blue berries.	climber	light	Temp Trop S. tr	•				•	•		L
Billardiera ringens	Slender climber, smooth glossy leaves; large clusters of spectacular vivid orange-red bells spring–summer, also sporadic.	climber	light	Temp S. tr S. ar	•		•	•	•	•	2	L

mp — temperate	L — light			
te — warm temperate	H — heavy			
ap — tropical	N — nectar-feeding			
r — sub-tropical	S — seed-eating			
ar — semi-arid	F — fruit-feeding			

Name	Description	Height	Width	Climatic zones	moist, well drained	wet	dry	dry limy	full sun	filtered sun	coastal regions	frosty regions	bird attraction
llardiera scandens	Tiny climber or twining plant, pale green woolly foliage; yellow-green bells most of the year, followed by green berries.	climber	light	Temp S.tr	•				•	•		L	S
llardiera variifolia	Slender climber, dark green hairy leaves, clusters of rich purple-blue bell flowers summer–autumn.	climber	light	Temp S.tr	•		•		•	•		L	S
ndfordia ndiflora ristmas Bells	Sparse narrow-leaved reedy tuft; tall stems bearing crown of large waxy scarlet-and-gold bells, occasionally pure gold, late spring–summer. Container plant.	30–90cm	30–60cm	Temp Trop S.tr	•	•			•	•		L	N
ndfordia nobilis ristmas Bells	Small reedy clump, clusters of dainty scarlet-and-gold waxy bells on slender stems late spring–summer. Best as container plant.	30–50cm	30cm	Temp Trop S.tr	•	•			•	•		L	N
ea hygroscopica ck Violet	Similar to an African violet; rosette of soft woolly leaves, many stems of pale to deep mauve flowers in clusters summer–autumn. Container plant.	10–15cm	10–20cm	Temp Trop S.tr	•					•			
ronia emonifolia	Small dainty shrub, trifoliolate aromatic toothed leaves, pale pink or pink-and-white flowers in spring. Container plant. Tip pruning recommended.	30–90cm	40–90cm	Temp S.ar	•		•		•	•		L	
ronia citriodora	Rounded dwarf shrub; strongly lemon-scented, dark pinnate leaves; palest pink to white flowers spring–summer. Container plant. Tip prune.	30–60cm	50cm–1m	Temp	•				•	•		L	
ronia clavata	Small to medium bushy shrub, fine aromatic foliage, pale green lightly perfumed bell flowers spring–summer. Tip pruning recommended.	1–1.8m	1–1.5m	Temp	•				•	•	2	L	
ronia crenulata	Small shrub, aromatic foliage, showy pink open-petalled flowers late winter–spring–early summer. Tip pruning recommended.	60–90cm	60cm–1.2m	Temp	•				•	•		L	
ronia deanei	Small upright shrub, narrow aromatic leaves, dainty open-petalled flowers of white to deep pink in spring. Tip pruning recommended.	60cm–1m	40–80cm	Temp S.tr	•	•			•	•		L	
ronia denticulata	Small upright shrub; slightly toothed, aromatic grey-green leaves; massed mauve-pink flowers (occasionally white) in spring. Tip prune.	60cm–1.2m	80cm–1m	Temp S.tr	•				•	•		H	
ronia filifolia	Dainty dwarf shrub, fine linear reddish bronze aromatic foliage, tiny pink flowers scattered over foliage all year. Container plant. Tip pruning recommended.	30–60cm	50cm–1m	Temp S.ar	•		•		•	•		L	

				Height	Width	Climatic zones	Soil types							
Temp — temperate	L — light						moist, well drained	wet	dry	dry limy	full sun	filtered sun	coastal regions	frosty regions
W. te — warm temperate	H — heavy													
Trop — tropical	N — nectar-feeding													
S. tr — sub-tropical	S — seed-eating													
S. ar — semi-arid	F — fruit-eating													

		Height	Width	Climatic zones	moist, well drained	wet	dry	dry limy	full sun	filtered sun	coastal regions	frosty regions
Boronia floribunda	Small shrub, dense pinnate aromatic foliage, clusters of showy fragrant pale to deep pink flowers in spring. Tip pruning recommended.	90cm–1.5m	60cm–1.2m	Temp S. tr	•				•	•		L
Boronia fraseri	Small shrub, smooth bronze-green pinnate aromatic foliage, large open musk pink flowers in clusters in spring. Tip pruning recommended.	60cm–1m	80cm–1.2m	Temp S. tr	•		•		•	•		L
Boronia heterophylla	Medium shrub, dense pinnate aromatic foliage, masses of lightly fragrant deep pink bell flowers in spring. Popular cut flower. Tip pruning recommended.	1–2m	60cm–1.2m	Temp S. tr	•				•	•		L
Boronia inornata	Dainty rounded dwarf shrub; fine aromatic foliage, covered in pink flowers winter–spring–summer. Beautiful container plant. Tip pruning recommended.	30–60cm	60–90cm	Temp S. ar	•		•		•	•		H
Boronia megastigma Brown Boronia	Small shrub, fine compact aromatic foliage, masses of highly fragrant brown bells in spring. Several forms in cultivation. Container plant. Tip prune.	30cm–1.2m	40cm–1m	Temp S. tr	•				•	•		L
Boronia microphylla	Small rounded shrub, pinnate aromatic foliage, clusters of deep pink flowers spring–early summer. Container plant. Tip pruning recommended.	60cm–1m	60cm–1m	Temp S. tr	•				•	•		L
Boronia mollis	Medium shrub, soft pinnate aromatic foliage, massed pink open-petalled flowers in spring. Cultivar 'Lorne Pride' particularly attractive. Prune regularly.	1–2m	1–1.5m	Temp S. tr	•				•	•		H
Boronia muelleri 'Sunset Serenade'	Compact dwarf shrub, pinnate aromatic foliage; masses of showy pink-and-white flowers throughout the year, especially spring. Container plant. Tip prune.	60–90cm	60cm–1m	Temp S. tr	•				•	•		L
Boronia pilosa	Small shrub, grey soft pinnate aromatic foliage, profuse clusters of deep pink flowers spring–summer. Double-flowered form ('Rose Blossom') available.	30cm–1m	45–80cm	Temp	•				•	•		L
Boronia pinnata	Medium shrub, aromatic pinnate foliage, festoons of deep and pale pink fragrant flowers in spring. Popular and easily grown. Tip prune regularly.	1–2m	1–1.5m	Temp S. tr	•				•	•		L
Boronia serrulata Sydney Rock Rose	Small dainty shrub, silky stem-clasping aromatic foliage, dense clusters of vivid pink bells in spring. Long-flowering container plant. Tip pruning recommended.	60cm–1m	70cm–1m	Temp S. tr	•				•	•		L
Bossiaea cordigera	Low spreading shrub, tangled wiry stems, tiny heart-shaped leaves, delicate red-and-yellow pea flowers spring–summer.	20–50cm	1–2.5m	Temp	•		•		•	•		L

		Height	Width	Climatic zones	Soil types				full sun	filtered sun	coastal regions	frosty regions	bird attraction
					moist, well drained	wet	dry	dry limy					

Legend:

ıp — temperate	L — light
e — warm temperate	H — heavy
p — tropical	N — nectar-feeding
— sub-tropical	S — seed-eating
r — semi-arid	F — fruit-eating

Name	Description	Height	Width	Climatic zones	moist, well drained	wet	dry	dry limy	full sun	filtered sun	coastal regions	frosty regions	bird attraction
siaea dentata	Open medium shrub, triangular foliage, pendent pea flowers of orange-red tinged with green or deep red autumn–winter–spring. Graceful.	1–2.5m	1–2m	Temp S.tr	•		•		•	•		L	
siaea linophylla	Weeping medium shrub, linear bronze-green foliage, showy golden pea flowers winter–spring. Graceful.	1–1.8m	1–1.8m	Temp S.tr	•		•		•	•		L	
chychiton rifolius ne Tree	Medium to large spreading tree, shiny leaves variable in shape, large panicles of scarlet bells in warm months. Very ornamental; slow growing in the south.	6–15m	6–12m	Temp Trop S.tr	•				•	•		L	N S
chychiton color ebark	Medium tree, broad hairy leaves, large pink or red bells in warm months, decorative fruiting follicles. Handsome parkland tree; partly or wholly deciduous.	8–10m	6–8m	Temp Trop S.tr	•				•	•		L	N S
chychiton gorii ert Kurrajong	Small tree, bright green foliage, creamy yellow to brown bells after rains, decorative fruiting follicles. Shade tree for arid regions; drought resistant.	4–8m	4–6m	W.te Arid S.ar	•		•		•			H	N S
chychiton ulneus rajong	Small to large tree, bright shiny foliage, cream or pink bells blotched inside with red spring–summer, decorative boat-shaped fruiting follicles.	8–16m	5–12m	Temp S.ar	•		•	•	•	•	1	H	N S
chychiton estris tle Tree	Medium to large tree, swollen trunk, deeply divided or entire foliage, creamy bells in spring. Grown in parklands for its unusual trunk; partly deciduous.	5–10m	5–6m	Arid S.ar	•		•	•	•			L	N S
chycome ustifolia	Carpeting plant, small grey leaves, masses of dainty pink or mauve daisies on slender stems all year. Groundcover or border plant. Prune regularly.	15cm	1–1.5m	Temp S.tr	•		•		•	•		L	
chycome ersifolia	Dwarf creeping clump of daintily lobed foliage, pretty white daisies on long stems all year. A 'cottage garden' plant. Light pruning recommended.	10–30cm	15–50cm	Temp	•	•			•	•	2	L	
chycome ridifolia	Self-seeding annual herb, naturally carpeting among other plants; small soft leaves; dainty white, pink, blue or mauve daisies cover plant most of the year.	10–25cm	60cm–1m	Temp S.ar	•		•	•	•	•	1		
chycome ltifida	Spreading mound of fine divided foliage; masses of white, pale pink, mauve or deep purple daisies all year. Constant pruning maintains shape and flowering.	10–20cm	60cm–1m	Temp Trop S.tr	•		•		•	•		L	
chycome ltifida var. atata	Tiny mound of crowded foliage, mauve daisies at foliage level all year if regularly pruned. Charming in container or rockery.	prostrate	60cm	Temp Trop S.tr	•		•		•	•		L	

		Height	Width	Climatic zones	Soil types								
					moist, well drained	wet	dry	dry limy	full sun	filtered sun	coastal regions	frosty regions	

Temp — temperate
W. te — warm temperate
Trop — tropical
S. tr — sub-tropical
S. ar — semi-arid

L — light
H — heavy
N — nectar-feeding
S — seed-eating
F — fruit-eating

		Height	Width	Climatic zones	moist, well drained	wet	dry	dry limy	full sun	filtered sun	coastal regions	frosty regions	
Brachycome sp. Pilliga	Prostrate suckering tufting clump, pansy-like leaves, vivid pink daisies (which last well as a picked posy) all year.	5cm	1–2m	Temp S. ar	•		•		•	•			L
Brachysema lanceolatum Swan River Pea	Small to medium spreading shrub which can also climb; broad silvery leaves, scarlet pea flowers winter–spring. Hardy and reliable. Regular pruning recommended.	1–2m	1–2m	Temp S. tr S. ar	•		•	•	•	•	1		L
Brachysema latifolium	Dense matting creeper; oval leaves, dark grey-green above, silky white below; orange-red pea flowers winter–spring.	prostrate	1–1.5m	Temp S. tr	•		•		•	•			L
Brachysema praemorsum	Matting creeper, shield-shaped light green foliage; flowers in pairs, opening cream but aging to red, spring–summer.	prostrate–30cm	1–1.5m	Temp S. tr	•				•	•			L
Brachysema sericeum black-red	Small rounded compact shrub, firm grey-green leaves, blackish red pea flowers hidden among foliage mostly winter–spring–summer. Hardy landscape plant.	prostrate–60cm	1.5–2.5m	Temp S. tr	•		•		•	•			L
Brachysema sericeum cream	Low spreading mound, soft grey foliage, pale cream flowers winter–spring–summer. Excellent landscape plant.	prostrate–45cm	1.5–3m	Temp S. tr	•		•		•	•			L
Brachysema species	Similar to *B. latifolium* but more commonly grown. Creeping matting habit, smooth glossy oval leaves, blunt orange-red pea flowers winter–spring.	prostrate	60cm–1m	Temp S. ar	•		•		•	•			L
Buckinghamia celsissima Ivory Curl Flower	Tall rainforest shrub or medium tree; variable foliage, entire or lobed; spectacular long racemes of fragrant creamy flowers summer–autumn.	4–12m	1.5–10m	Temp Trop S. tr	•				•	•			L
Bulbine bulbosa Bulbine Lily	Dwarf grassy lily, long onion-like leaves, tall fleshy stems topped with bright yellow flowers in spring.	45cm	30cm	Temp Trop S. tr	•				•	•			H
Bulbine semibarbata Leek Lily	Similar to previous species, but smaller in stem and flower. Both give an ephemeral 'wildflower' quality to gardens, self-seeding easily.	20–30cm	20–30cm	Temp S. tr	•		•		•	•			H
Bursaria spinosa Sweet Bursaria	Medium to large spreading shrub, small blunt leaves; massed panicles of creamy white perfumed flowers in summer, highly attractive to butterflies.	2–5m	1–2.5m	Temp Trop S. tr	•		•	•	•	•	2		H
Caldcluvia paniculosa	Large shrub, pinnate leaves with pink new growth, panicles of white flowers in spring. Very beautiful; for indoors or protected sites.	3–8m	2–4m	W. te Trop S. tr	•					•			

	L — light
np — temperate	H — heavy
te — warm temperate	N — nectar-feeding
p — tropical	S — seed-eating
' — sub-tropical	F — fruit-eating
r — semi-arid	

Name	Description	Height	Width	Climatic zones	moist, well drained	wet	dry	dry limy	full sun	filtered sun	coastal regions	frosty regions	bird attraction
ectasia cyanea sel Lily	Dwarf many-stemmed lily, stem-clasping foliage, metallic blue flowers with yellow-orange centres spring–summer.	10–30cm	60cm–1.2m	Temp S. ar	•		•		•	•		H	
licoma ratifolia	Medium to large shrub, soft toothed foliage, fluffy yellow wattle-like flowers spring–summer. Ornamental, especially in shaded sites.	2–3.5m	1.5–2.5m	Temp S. tr	•				•	•		L	
listemon chyandrus	Small to medium shrub, short prickly foliage, small orange bottlebrush flowers in summer and occasionally at other times. Prune after flowering.	1–4m	60cm–2.2m	Temp S. tr	•	•			•	•		H	N
listemon rgundy'	Medium shrub, dense foliage, burgundy bottlebrush flowers spring–summer. Retain shape and promote further flowering by pruning.	2–3m	1.5–2.5m	Temp Trop S. tr	•	•			•	•		H	N
listemon citrinus straflora ebrand'	Low spreading shrub, short stiff leaves, large bright red brushes spring–summer–autumn. Promote further blooms by pruning after each flowering.	50–80cm	2–3m	Temp Trop S. tr	•	•			•	•		L	N
listemon citrinus lendens'	Also known as C. 'Endeavour'. Large shapely semi-weeping shrub, crowded foliage; bright red brushes spring–summer, also other times if regularly pruned.	2–4m	2–3m	Temp Trop S. tr	•	•			•	•	•	L	N
listemon citrinus nite Ice'	Low spreading shrub, short stiff leaves, large white brushes late spring–summer. Prune after flowering.	60cm–1m	2–3m	Temp Trop S. tr	•	•			•	•		L	N
listemon mboynensis	Low spreading to large shrub, large leaves; pink, red or crimson brushes most of the year. Pruning improves shape and flowering.	60cm–3m	2–2.5m	Temp Trop S. tr	•				•	•		L	N
listemon ureka'	Medium to large upright shrub; stiff crowded leaves, pink new growth; vivid pink brushes in spring. Regular pruning improves shape and promotes flowering.	2–4m	1–2.5m	Temp Trop S. tr	•	•			•	•		L	N
listemon rmosus	Large shrub or small tree; narrow rigid foliage, bright new growth; red brushes in spring. Prune to promote compact habit.	3–6m	2–4m	Temp Trop S. tr	•	•			•	•		L	N
listemon enoa River'	Medium upright multi-stemmed shrub, narrow pointed foliage, lustrous cerise-mauve flowers autumn and spring. Prune to promote further flowering.	1.5–2.5m	1–2.2m	Temp Trop S. tr	•		•		•	•		L	N
listemon arkness'	Also known as C. 'Gawler'. Large weeping shrub, pendulous foliage, brilliant scarlet brushes autumn and spring. Prune to promote further flowering.	3–4m	2–3m	Temp Trop S. tr	•	•		•	•	•	2	L	N

			Height	Width	Climatic zones	Soil types							
						moist, well drained	wet	dry	dry limy	full sun	filtered sun	coastal regions	frosty regions
Callistemon 'King's Park Special'	Large upright shrub, grey-green foliage, lustrous bright red brushes massed over shrub spring–summer. Excellent street tree. Prune to promote flowering.		3–4.5m	2–3.5m	Temp Trop S.tr	•	•			•	•	2	L
Callistemon linearis	Weeping medium shrub, fine silvery foliage, red brushes with yellow tips spring–summer. Prune lightly to promote flowering.		1.5–3m	2–3m	Temp Trop S.tr	•	•			•	•		L
Callistemon macropunctatus	Medium to large shrub, small crowded foliage, showy gold-tipped rose pink brushes late spring–summer. Spectacular. Improved with pruning.		2–4m	2–4m	Temp Trop S.tr	•	•			•	•	2	H
Callistemon 'Mauve Mist'	Medium shrub, broad foliage, beautiful mauve brushes late spring–summer. Can flower at other times when pruned regularly.		2–3m	1.5–2.5m	Temp Trop S.tr	•	•			•	•		L
Callistemon montanus	Large shrub, fine foliage, bright red brushes in spring and autumn. Prune to improve habit and promote flowering.		4–5m	2–3m	Temp Trop S.tr	•	•			•	•		
Callistemon pachyphyllus	Rigid medium shrub, thick leaves, large bright red brushes spring and autumn. Prune heavily to promote compact habit.		2–3m	1–2m	Temp Trop S.tr	•	•			•	•		
Callistemon 'Packer's Selection'	Upright medium shrub, fine foliage, narrow deep red brushes spring–summer. Prune after flowering.		2–3m	1–2m	Temp Trop S.tr	•				•	•		L
Callistemon pallidus	Variable small to large shrub; broad, often grey foliage, silky new growth; large lemon brushes spring–summer and occasionally autumn. Prune after flowering.		1.5–4m	2–3m	Temp S.tr	•		•		•	•	2	H
Callistemon pallidus 'Australflora Candle Glow'	Low arching shrub; grey leaves, silver new growth; bright lemon brushes spring–summer–autumn. Hardy and very showy. Prune to promote flowering.		60–90cm	2–3.5m	Temp S.tr	•		•		•	•	2	H
Callistemon paludosus	Variable large shrub or small tree. Most decorative form has fine silvery foliage, fluffy pink brushes autumn–winter. Prune to promote flowering.		3–7m	2–5m	Temp S.tr	•	•			•	•		H
Callistemon phoeniceus	Small to medium spreading, sometimes open shrub; grey foliage, bright red brushes spring–summer. Low form available. Prune after flowering.		60cm–2.5m	2–4m	Temp S.tr	•	•	•		•	•		L
Callistemon pinifolius	Small spreading shrub, fine foliage, soft green or red brushes spring–summer. Prune lightly to improve flowering.		1–3m	1.5–3m	Temp Trop S.tr	•	•			•	•	2	L

Temp — temperate
W. te — warm temperate
Trop — tropical
S. tr — sub-tropical
S. ar — semi-arid

L — light
H — heavy
N — nectar-feeding
S — seed-eating
F — fruit-eating

		Height	Width	Climatic zones	Soil types				full sun	filtered sun	coastal regions	frosty regions	bird attraction
					moist, well drained	wet	dry	dry limy					
...listemon 'Red Clusters'	Medium shrub, stiff foliage; clusters of red brushes in summer and autumn, especially if pruned regularly.	1–2.5m	1–2m	Temp Trop S. tr	•	•			•	•		L	N
...listemon 'Reeves ...k'	Erect medium shrub, stiff foliage; lustrous pink brushes in summer and autumn, especially if pruned regularly.	2–3m	2–3m	Temp Trop S. tr	•	•			•	•		L	N
...listemon rigidus	Medium shrub, stiff foliage, bright red brushes late spring–summer. Prune to improve habit and promote flowering.	1.5–2.5m	2–2.5m	Temp Trop S. tr	•	•			•	•		H	N
...listemon ...gnus	Large shrub or small tree, white papery bark; dense foliage, superb pink-red new growth; pink or white brushes spring–summer. Prune regularly.	4–10m	2–7m	Temp Trop S. tr	•	•			•	•	2	L	N
...listemon shiressii	Medium to large shrub, papery bark, small crowded leaves, cream brushes spring–summer. Prune while young to encourage bushiness.	4–8m	3–6m	Temp Trop S. tr	•	•			•	•		L	N
...listemon sieberi	Small to medium upright shrub, fine needle foliage, massed pale lemon brushes in summer. The only alpine bottlebrush. Prune to retain compact habit.	1.5–2m	80cm–1.2m	Temp S. tr	•	•			•	•		H	N
...listemon sieberi ...straflora Little ...ber'	Dwarf to small compact mounding shrub, fine dense foliage, pale lemon brushes in summer. Light pruning recommended.	50–80cm	60–90cm	Temp S. tr	•	•			•	•		H	N
...listemon ...ciosus	Small to medium, usually upright shrub; blue-grey foliage, spectacular large rich red brushes spring–summer. Prune to promote further flowering.	60cm–1.8m	1–1.5m	Temp Trop S. tr	•	•			•	•	1	L	N
...listemon ...ulatus	Small to medium arching shrub, fine leaves, bright red or mauve brushes mainly spring–summer. Prune to encourage bushiness and flowering.	1–2m	1.5–2.5m	Temp Trop S. tr	•	•			•	•		L	N
...listemon ...tifolius	Small to medium open shrub, long needle leaves, large crimson brushes late spring–summer. Suitable for semi-arid conditions. Pruning improves flowering.	90cm–2.5m	1.5–2.2m	Temp S. tr S. ar	•		•	•	•	•		H	N
...listemon ...inalis	Weeping large shrub or small tree, usually fine foliage; red brushes on the ends of stems spring–summer and occasionally autumn, especially if pruned.	5–10m	3–5m	Temp Trop S. tr	•	•			•	•	2	L	N
...listemon ...inalis ...tain Cook'	Small to medium shrub, crowded foliage, masses of bright red brushes in spring and autumn. Compact habit further improved by pruning.	1.2–2m	80cm–1.2m	Temp Trop S. tr	•	•			•	•		L	N

mp — temperate
te — warm temperate
op — tropical
tr — sub-tropical
ar — semi-arid

L — light
H — heavy
N — nectar-feeding
S — seed-eating
F — fruit-eating

				Height	Width		Soil types							
						Climatic zones	moist, well drained	wet	dry	dry limy	full sun	filtered sun	coastal regions	frosty regions

Temp — temperate
W. te — warm temperate
Trop — tropical
S. tr — sub-tropical
S. ar — semi-arid

L — light
H — heavy
N — nectar-feeding
S — seed-eating
F — fruit-eating

Name	Description	Height	Width	Climatic zones	moist, well drained	wet	dry	dry limy	full sun	filtered sun	coastal regions	frosty regions
Callistemon viminalis 'Dawson River'	Large shrub or small tree, fine weeping foliage, crimson brushes spring–summer and sometimes autumn. Pruning encourages further flowering.	5–10m	3–5m	Temp Trop S. tr	•	•			•	•		L
Callistemon viminalis 'Hannah Ray'	Large shrub, weeping grey woolly foliage; crimson brushes spring–summer, and occasionally autumn, especially if pruned.	3–5m	2–3m	Temp Trop S. tr	•	•			•	•		L
Callistemon viminalis 'Little John'	Small rounded shrub, crowded blue-grey foliage, deep blood red brushes in spring and autumn. Container plant. Prune lightly to promote further flowering.	60–90cm	1–1.5m	Temp Trop S. tr	•	•			•	•		L
Callistemon viminalis 'Rose Opal'	Small to medium shrub, crowded foliage, rose coloured brushes spring–summer and sporadic if lightly pruned after flowering.	1.5–2m	1–1.5m	Temp Trop S. tr	•	•			•	•		L
Callistemon 'Violaceus'	Medium shrub, stiff crowded foliage; violet coloured flowers spring–summer and sometimes autumn, especially if pruned regularly.	2–3m	2–3m	Temp Trop S. tr	•	•			•	•		L
Callistemon viridiflorus	Small to medium upright shrub, small leaves, dense yellow-green brushes late spring–summer. Prune to encourage bushiness and improve flowering.	1–2m	60cm–1.2m	Temp S. tr	•	•			•	•		H
Callistemon 'Western Glory'	Medium shrub, stiff crowded leaves; large purple-red brushes late spring–summer, occasionally at other times if pruned regularly.	2–2.5m	2–2.5m	Temp S. tr	•	•		•	•	•		L
Callitris columellaris	Medium to tall pyramidal 'cypress pine', tiny crowded blue-green leaves, attractive seed capsules. Ornamental, and good windbreak.	7–15m	4–10m	W. te S. ar	•		•		•	•	1	H
Callitris endlicheri	Small to medium tree, glaucous foliage, attractive seed capsules. Tolerates harsh rocky conditions; a good small shelter tree.	6–15m	2–5m	W. te S. tr	•		•		•		2	H
Callitris macleayana	Small to medium compact or spreading tree; soft fine green foliage, bronze in winter; attractive seed capsules. The only *Callitris* found in rainforests.	4–18m	2–8m	Temp Trop S. tr	•	•				•		H
Callitris oblonga	Small to large shrub, glaucous foliage, attractive seed capsules. Useful in narrow confined areas; suited to cool climates.	1.8–8m	1–3m	Temp	•		•		•	•		H
Callitris preissii ssp. *verrucosa*	Large shrub or small tree, grey-green foliage, decorative seed capsules. Tolerates very dry conditions.	3–7m	2–4m	W. te Arid S. ar	•		•		•			H

		Height	Width	Climatic zones	Soil types								bird attraction
					moist, well drained	wet	dry	dry limy	full sun	filtered sun	coastal regions	frosty regions	
itris rhomboidea	Medium to large shrub, glaucous or green foliage, decorative seed capsules. Hardy container plant; easy to grow in well-drained soils.	5–7m	3–4m	Temp S.tr	•		•		•	•	1	H	S
cephalus wnii er Cushion Bush	Small compact mounding shrub, silver foliage, tiny yellow button flowers spring–summer. Striking contrast plant. Regular pruning essential.	50cm–1m	1–2m	Temp S.tr	•		•	•	•	•	1	L	
stemma oureum land Lily	Dwarf plant, fleshy strap leaves, pink or yellow daffodil-like flowers summer–autumn. Decorative in a container or as a border.	30–60cm	10–20cm	Temp S.ar	•		•		•	•		L	
thamnus drifidus Bush	Medium to large dense shrub, soft needle foliage, profuse scarlet brushes spring–summer. Useful for hedges and low windbreak. Prune regularly.	2–4m	2–4m	Temp S.ar	•		•	•	•	•	1	L	N
thamnus drifidus strate	Low spreading dense shrub, fine needle foliage, scarlet bottlebrush flowers spring–summer. Excellent coastal groundcover. Prune regularly.	15–30cm	1–2m	Temp S.ar	•		•	•	•	•	1	L	N
thamnus sus	Small to medium shrub, hairy grey needle foliage, scarlet bottlebrushes spring–summer. Useful for hedges and foliage contrast. Prune regularly.	1–2m	1–2m	Temp S.ar	•		•		•	•	2	L	N
stegia anella	Light creeping or twining plant, attractive kidney-shaped leaves, pink 'morning glory' flowers spring–summer. Very useful for sand binding.	prostrate	1.5–2.5m	Temp Trop S.tr	•		•	•	•	•	1		
trix alpestris	Small compact shrub, fine aromatic foliage, pink buds and delicate white star flowers spring–summer. Prune lightly after flowering.	1–2m	1–1.8m	Temp S.ar	•		•		•	•	2	H	
trix aurea	Small shrub, slightly hairy soft aromatic foliage, vivid yellow perfumed star flowers spring–summer. Beautiful container plant and cut flower. Prune lightly.	50–80cm	50–80cm	Temp S.ar	•		•		•	•		L	
trix depressa	Small shrub, fine aromatic foliage, masses of yellow-and-cream star flowers spring–summer. Charming container plant. Light pruning is beneficial.	60–90cm	30–50cm	Temp S.ar	•		•		•			L	
trix flavescens	Small compact shrub, fine aromatic foliage, numerous gold star flowers in summer. Container plant. Light pruning is beneficial.	50cm–1.2m	30–80cm	Temp S.ar	•		•		•	•		L	
trix fraseri	Small shrub, fine aromatic foliage, shiny pinky purple star flowers spring–summer–autumn. Beautiful container plant. Light pruning required.	60cm–1.5m	1–1.5m	Temp S.ar	•		•		•	•		L	

		Height	Width	Climatic zones	Soil types							
					moist, well drained	wet	dry	dry limy	full sun	filtered sun	coastal regions	frosty regions
Temp — temperate L — light W. te — warm temperate H — heavy Trop — tropical N — nectar-feeding S. tr — sub-tropical S — seed-eating S. ar — semi-arid F — fruit-eating												
Calytrix glutinosa	Small shrub, fine sticky aromatic foliage, numerous pinky purple star flowers late spring–summer. Showy container plant. Light pruning required.	50cm–1.2m	30cm–1m	Temp S. ar	•		•		•			L
Calytrix sullivanii	Small to medium upright shrub, fine heathy aromatic foliage, numerous white star flowers spring–early summer. Prune regularly.	1–1.8m	1–2.2m	Temp S. ar	•		•		•	•		H
Calytrix tetragona	Small to medium shrub, fine heathy aromatic foliage, white or pink star flowers spring–early summer. Adaptable and very showy. Requires light pruning.	1–2m	80cm–2m	Temp S. ar	•		•		•	•		H
Calytrix tetragona prostrate	Compact dwarf shrub, fine grey aromatic foliage, massed pink star flowers in spring. Container or rockery plant. Tip pruning recommended.	prostrate–30cm	60–80cm	Temp S. ar	•		•		•	•		H
Carpobrotus rossii	Carpeting plant, succulent leaves, large purple or pink flowers mainly spring–summer but also at other times. For binding loose soils.	prostrate	2–4m	Temp S. tr S. ar	•		•	•	•	•	1	
Cassia artemisioides	Small to medium shrub, silvery green pinnate foliage, racemes of bright yellow flowers most of the year. Eye-catching, adaptable shrub for dry regions.	1–2m	1–1.5m	W. te Arid S. ar	•		•		•		2	H
Cassia brewsteri	Large shrub or medium tree, bright green pinnate foliage, cream-and-pink flowers late summer–autumn–winter. Showy shrub for warm climates.	5–10m	4–7m	W. te S. tr Trop	•		•		•		2	
Cassia nemophila	Small to medium shrub, linear or pinnate foliage, bright yellow flowers winter–spring. Many forms and hybrids of this species exist.	1.5–2.5m	2–2.5m	W. te Arid S. ar	•		•		•	•	2	H
Cassia odorata	Small to medium shrub, shiny foliage, perfumed orange or yellow flowers spring–summer–autumn. Well known in cultivation.	1–2m	80cm–1.5m	W. te Arid S. ar	•		•		•	•	1	
Castanospermum australe Black Bean	Medium to large spreading tree, handsome pinnate foliage, showy red or red-yellow pea flowers spring–early summer. Attractive indoor container plant.	4–20m	3–15m	W. te Trop S. tr	•				•	•	2	
Casuarina cristata Belah	Small to large suckering tree, fine foliage, brownish red flowers spring–summer, decorative seed cones. Good shade and shelter tree.	4–20m	2–8m	W. te S. ar Arid	•		•	•	•			H
Casuarina cunninghamiana	Medium to large tree, fine dark foliage, brownish red flowers in summer, decorative seed cones. Very handsome, fast growing, useful for shade and shelter.	10–30m	5–15m	Temp Trop S. tr	•	•			•	•		H

LEFT:
Interesting and efficient use of space can often be determined by pathway design and the accompanying planting. As in this scene, distant views should draw you constantly on, experiencing changing textures and structures as you go; the vistas ahead should always contain mysteries to be unravelled.

BELOW:
Blue-flowering stems of *Orthrosanthus multiflorus* partly hide a solid timber seat beside a shallow pool in the Austraflora gardens. The busyness of this small, lightly fenced area contrasts with the broad, softly textured pathway.

T:
anter box sporting an annual lay of *Helipterum* daisies ng other fine shrubs doubles dividing element in a public park.

Callistemon citrinus 'Australflora Firebrand' (crimson) and *Callistemon pallidus* 'Australflora Candle Glow' (lemon) are frequently combined in both private and broad landscapes. Steep banks or slopes, median strips and carparks are enhanced by this pair, each of which tolerates a wide range of soils and climates, thus making them popular choices for difficult situations.

p — temperate	L — light
e — warm temperate	H — heavy
p — tropical	N — nectar-feeding
— sub-tropical	S — seed-eating
— semi-arid	F — fruit-eating

	Height	Width	Climatic zones	Soil types								
				moist, well drained	wet	dry	dry limy	full sun	filtered sun	coastal regions	frosty regions	bird attraction
uarina aisneana	Medium to large tree, fine weeping foliage, flowering sporadic, very large seed cones. Handsome shade and shelter tree for arid zones.	6–15m	3–12m	Arid S. ar	•		•		•			H	S
uarina distyla	Medium shrub, fine grey-green foliage, red-gold flowers, attractive seed cones. Useful for hedges in a range of conditions.	1.5–3m	2–3m	Temp S. tr	•		•		•	•	2		S
uarina isetifolia	Large shrub or tree, fine graceful weeping foliage; reddish flowers autumn–winter, also sporadic; small seed cones. Important for stabilising dunes and for shelter.	6–15m	3–10m	W. te Trop S. tr			•	•	•	•	1		S
uarina glauca	Sturdy small to medium tree, grey-green foliage, reddish brown flowers winter–spring, small cones. Hardy and adaptable; suckers readily; shelter tree.	2–10m	2–10m	Temp S. tr	•	•			•	•	1	H	S
uarina humilis	Small to medium shrub, fine blue-grey foliage; reddish orange flowers in spring, also sporadic; small seed cones. Excellent low windbreak.	60cm–2m	60cm–1.5m	Temp S. tr	•		•	•	•	•	2		S
uarina inophloia	Large shrub or small tree, decorative red peeling bark, fine foliage, bright red flowers in winter. Hardy and adaptable.	4–8m	2.5–5m	W. te S. ar	•		•		•	•	2	H	S
uarina nanniana	Small to medium shrub, fine green or grey foliage, brown flowers winter–spring, attractive seed cones. Adaptable; useful as a windbreak.	1–3.5m	1–2.5m	Temp S. ar	•		•		•	•	2		S
uarina littoralis	Shapely large shrub or small tree, fine foliage, reddish gold flowers in autumn, attractive seed cones. Adaptable; useful and attractive windbreak.	3–9m	1.5–5m	Temp S. tr	•		•		•	•	1	L	S
uarina ellerana	Small to medium shrub, fine grey foliage, rusty red flowers spring–summer–autumn, cylindrical seed cones. Fast growing and adaptable; suited to arid areas.	40cm–3m	1–2m	Temp S. ar	•		•		•	•	2	H	S
uarina nana	Small to medium dense shrub, fine upright foliage, reddish flowers in spring, globular seed cones. Ornamental small screen or low windbreak.	1.5–3.5m	1–2.5m	Temp S. tr	•		•		•	•		H	S
uarina obesa	Medium to large spreading tree, thick grey-green foliage, reddish flowers winter–spring, small seed cones. Shade and shelter tree, wet or saline areas.	6–25m	3–10m	W. te S. ar	•	•	•	•	•	•	1	H	S
uarina paludosa	Small bushy shrub, fine foliage, red-brown flowers autumn–winter–spring, small seed cones. Hardy and adaptable; tolerates heavy though not wet soils.	50cm–1.2m	80cm–1.5m	Temp S. ar	•		•		•	•	2	H	S

Temp — temperate
W. te — warm temperate
Trop — tropical
S. tr — sub-tropical
S. ar — semi-arid

L — light
H — heavy
N — nectar-feeding
S — seed-eating
F — fruit-eating

		Height	Width	Climatic zones	Soil types							
					moist, well drained	wet	dry	dry limy	full sun	filtered sun	coastal regions	frosty regions
Casuarina pinaster	Medium to large pine-like shrub, ornamental conifer-like foliage, red flowers autumn–winter–spring, cylindrical seed cones. Very attractive screen or hedge.	2–4.5m	1.5–2.5m	Temp S. ar	•		•		•	•		H
Casuarina pusilla	Small to medium bushy shrub, fine grey-green foliage, red flowers autumn–winter–spring, small cylindrical seed cones. Excellent as low hedge.	50cm–2.5m	1–2m	Temp S. ar	•		•		•	•	2	L
Casuarina torulosa Rose She Oak	Small to large tree, fine weeping bronze-purple foliage, rusty gold flowers autumn–winter, small seed cones. Very beautiful, especially planted in groves.	6–20m	3–12m	Temp S. tr	•		•		•	•	2	L
Casuarina verticillata Drooping She Oak (syn. *C. stricta*)	Large shrub or small tree, thick drooping foliage, bronze golden flowers in autumn, decorative seed cones. Shade and shelter tree.	3–10m	3–7m	Temp S. tr	•		•		•	•	1	H
Celmisia asteliifolia Snow Daisy	Tufted suckering plant, silver leaves, large white yellow-centred daisies in summer. Flowers well in container or rockery.	15–30cm	20–40cm	Temp	•				•	•		H
Ceratopetalum apetalum Coachwood	Medium to large tree, shiny foliage; white flowers followed by red sepals spring–summer, often flowering when young.	6–15m	3–8m	Temp Trop S. tr	•				•	•		L
Ceratopetalum gummiferum N.S.W. Christmas Bush	Large shrub or medium tree, toothed foliage, masses of white flowers followed by bright red enlarged sepals spring–summer.	6–15m	2–8m	Temp Trop S. tr	•				•	•		L
Chamelaucium ciliatum	Small shrub, fine crowded foliage; pink-and-white teatree-like flowers in spring, aging to red. Tip prune regularly.	30–80cm	20–80cm	Temp S. ar	•		•		•			L
Chamelaucium sp. Walpole	Small to medium conifer-shaped shrub, fine neat foliage, clusters of white teatree-like flowers late spring–summer. Tip prune regularly.	1–1.8m	1–2m	Temp S. ar	•		•		•		1	
Chamelaucium uncinatum Geraldton Wax	Medium to large open shrub, fine foliage; purple, pink, burgundy or white waxy flowers in spring. Popular cut flower. Regular pruning recommended.	2–4.5m	2.5–5m	Temp S. tr S. ar	•		•	•	•			L
Chamelaucium uncinatum x sp. Walpole	Upright to spreading medium shrub, fine foliage, massed clusters of mauve-pink flowers in spring. Excellent cut flower. Regular pruning recommended.	1–2m	60cm–1.5m	Temp S. tr S. ar	•		•		•	•	2	L
Chorilaena quercifolia	Small to medium shrub, hairy oak-like foliage, interesting pendulous cream to red flowers spring–summer. Light pruning recommended.	1.5–3.5m	3–3.5m	Temp	•		•		•	•	1	

np — temperate	L — light
e — warm temperate	H — heavy
p — tropical	N — nectar-feeding
' — sub-tropical	S — seed-eating
r — semi-arid	F — fruit-eating

Name	Description	Height	Width	Climatic zones	moist, well drained	wet	dry	dry limy	full sun	filtered sun	coastal regions	frosty regions	bird attraction
rizema aciculare	Small shrub, needle leaves, numerous bright pink-and-yellow pea flowers winter–spring. Tip pruning recommended.	50cm–1.2m	40–90cm	Temp S. ar	•		•		•	•		L	
rizema datum	Dense small shrub, heart-shaped leaves, multi-coloured (orange, red, yellow and purple) pea flowers winter–spring–summer. Prune after flowering.	50cm–2m	1–2m	Temp S.tr S.ar	•		•		•	•		L	
rizema dicksonii	Small upright shrub, fine curved foliage, multi-coloured (orange, red and yellow) pea flowers spring–summer. Prune after flowering.	60cm–1m	40–80cm	Temp S. ar	•		•		•	•		L	
rizema ersifolium	Lightly climbing plant, fine stems, elliptical foliage, multi-coloured (orange, pink and yellow) pea flowers spring–summer.	climber	light	Temp S.tr S.ar	•		•		•	•			
rizema folium	Small shrub or semi-climber, holly-like leaves; loose bunches of multi-coloured (orange, red and yellow) pea flowers spring–summer.	climber or 1–3m	light or 1–3m	Temp S.tr	•				•	•			
namomum eri ver's Sassafras	Medium to large tree, scented pendulous wavy-edged foliage, creamy tubular flowers in spring. Useful indoors and in warm climates.	8–20m	5–12m	W.te Trop S.tr	•					•			
sus antarctica	Climber, large toothed leaves, insignificant greenish flowers summer–autumn, black inedible fruit. Handsome; for shaded areas, or indoor container.	climber	vigorous	W.te Trop S.tr	•					•			
ytonia tralasica	Small herb which roots at leaf nodes; white or pink flowers spring–summer–autumn. For moist soils, especially bog margins.	prostrate	60cm–1.5m	Temp	•	•			•	•		H	
matis aristata	Twining climber, bronze-green trifoliolate or single leaves; large white shiny star flowers spring–summer, followed by fluffy seed heads.	climber	medium	Temp S.tr	•				•	•		L	
matis rophylla	Light to medium climber or small shrub, divided foliage; greenish cream flowers in spring, followed by fluffy seed heads.	climber or 1m	light–medium or 1–2m	Temp S. ar	•		•	•	•	•	2	L	
matis pubescens	Twining rambling climber, broad trifoliolate leaves, large white star flowers spring–summer, followed by fluffy seed heads.	climber	medium	Temp S.tr	•				•	•		L	
nthus formosus rt's Desert Pea	Low spreading annual, soft grey-green pinnate foliage, scarlet or scarlet-and-black pea flowers summer–autumn. Grown from seed. Spectacular.	prostrate–50cm	1–3.5m	W.te Arid S.ar	•		•	•				L	N S

Temp — temperate
W. te — warm temperate
Trop — tropical
S. tr — sub-tropical
S. ar — semi-arid

L — light
H — heavy
N — nectar-feeding
S — seed-eating
F — fruit-eating

		Height	Width	Climatic zones	Soil types							
					moist, well drained	wet	dry	dry limy	full sun	filtered sun	coastal regions	frosty regions
Commersonia bartramia Brown Kurrajong	Medium to large shrub, straight white trunk, horizontal shallow canopy of large furry leaves, abundant creamy white flowers spring–summer. Hardy.	4–7m	2–4m	Temp Trop S. tr	•				•	•		
Commersonia pulchella	Dwarf shrub, lightly suckering; soft grey-green foliage, dainty shot pink-and-white flowers most of the year. Container plant. Tip prune lightly.	10–40cm	60cm–1.2m	Temp S. ar	•		•		•	•		
Conospermum mitchellii Smokebush	Small to medium erect shrub, narrow stiff foliage, heads of smoky grey or white tubular flowers spring–summer.	1–2.5m	80cm–1.8m	W. te S. ar	•		•		•	•		L
Conospermum patens	Small slender shrub, narrow crowded foliage, smoky grey–blue tubular flowers spring–early summer.	30–90cm	50cm–1.2m	W. te S. ar	•		•		•	•		L
Conospermum stoechadis	Small to medium rounded shrub, narrow rigid foliage; woolly tubular flowers massed over bush in spring, colouring it entirely silver.	80cm–1.8m	1–2m	W. te S. ar	•		•		•			L
Conospermum triplinervium	Medium shrub, upright branches, narrow to broad leaves, densely woolly tubular flowers of silvery white in spring.	1.8–3.5m	2–4m	W. te S. ar	•		•		•	•		L
Conostylis aculeata	Variable mounding clump, long narrow foliage, loose clusters of bright yellow woolly tubular flowers spring–summer. Has proved adaptable in cultivation.	30–50cm	50cm–1.2m	Temp S. ar	•		•		•	•		L
Conostylis bealiana	Tiny tufting plant, crowded narrow leaves, dozens of showy bright golden yellow tubular flowers winter–spring. Rockery or container.	10–20cm	15–30cm	Temp S. ar	•		•		•			L
Conostylis candicans	Dwarf shrub, long narrow silver strap leaves, vivid golden woolly tubular flowers clustered on long stems winter–spring–summer. Showy and adaptable.	30–50m	50–90cm	Temp S. ar	•		•		•			L
Conostylis seorsiflora	Dense matting plant, crowded smooth foliage, open star-like yellow-and-cream flowers spring–summer. Rockery or container.	prostrate	50–90cm	W. te S. ar	•		•		•			L
Conostylis setigera	Dwarf tufting plant, bristly foliage, slender dense clusters of tubular creamy yellow flowers spring–early summer. Rockery or container.	10–30cm	20–50cm	Temp S. ar	•		•		•			L
Conostylis setosa	Compact dwarf plant, twisted bristly foliage, heads of tubular cream or purplish cream woolly flowers spring–early summer. Rockery or container.	20–30cm	10–30cm	Temp	•		•		•	•		L

			L — light
mp — temperate			H — heavy
te — warm temperate			N — nectar-feeding
p — tropical			S — seed-eating
r — sub-tropical			F — fruit-eating
ar — semi-arid			

Name	Description	Height	Width	Climatic zones	Soil types				full sun	filtered sun	coastal regions	frosty regions	bird attraction
					moist, well drained	wet	dry	dry limy					
rdyline petiolaris, broad-leaved Palm Lily	Slender rainforest plant, erect clump-forming stems, broad leaves; pendulous strings of purple flowers spring–summer, shiny bright red berries.	1.5–5m	1–2.2m	Temp Trop S.tr	•					•			S
rdyline stricta, Slender Palm Lily	Slender rainforest plant, erect clump-forming stems, long flat drooping leaves, sprays of blue-purple flowers in summer, dark globular berries. Indoor plant.	1.8–4.5m	1–2m	Temp Trop S.tr	•					•		L	S
rdyline terminalis, Palm Lily	Slender rainforest plant, erect clump-forming stems, large broad leaves, sprays of white to mauve flowers winter–spring, scarlet berries. Hardy.	1.8–6m	1–2.5m	Temp Trop S.tr	•					•		L	S
rea aemula	Small spreading shrub, felty oval leaves; pale purplish green tubular bells in spring, not spectacular but extremely attractive to birds.	30cm–1.8m	60cm–1.5m	Temp S.tr	•		•		•	•		L	N
rea alba	Small to medium dense variable shrub, silver-grey round leaves; waxy open white bells, occasionally soft pink, most of the year. Prune regularly.	20cm–1.8m	1–2.2m	Temp S.tr	•		•	•	•	•	1	L	N
rea khousiana	Small to medium compact shrub, glossy leaves; creamy green to rusty tubular bells winter–spring, luminous in dull weather. Prune regularly.	80cm–1.8m	1–3m	Temp S.tr	•		•	•	•	•	1		N
rea baeuerlenii, f's Cap Correa	Small to medium dense shrub, strongly aromatic glossy leaves, pale green tubular bells with flattened hat-like calyx autumn–winter–spring. Prune regularly.	1–2.2m	1.5–2.5m	Temp S.tr	•					•	2		N
rea calycina	Small to medium compact shrub, pale green felted foliage; pale green tubular bells winter–spring, highly attractive to birds. Regular pruning required.	1–2.5m	1.5–2.5m	Temp	•		•		•	•	2		N
rea decumbens	Low spreading groundcover, dense foliage, dusky pink tubular bells spring–summer. Hardy in many situations; a good 'living mulch'. Light pruning beneficial.	20cm–1.2m	1–1.5m	Temp S.ar	•		•	•	•	•	2	L	N
rea sky Bells' or k Bells'	Well known by both names. Low spreading shrub, dense foliage; salmon pink tubular bells most of the year, especially winter–spring. Prune regularly.	20–60cm	60cm–2m	Temp S.tr	•		•		•	•		L	N
rea glabra	Medium shrub, smooth leaves, pale green to dusky red tubular bells winter–spring. Useful for screening and bird attraction. Regular pruning essential.	1.5–3m	1–2.5m	Temp S.tr S.ar	•		•		•	•	2	L	N
rea lawrenciana	Variable small to large shrub, glossy narrow or broad leaves, tubular bells of bright cream, yellow-green or dusky pink winter–spring. Prune regularly.	2–7m	1.5–5m	Temp S.tr	•	•				•		L	N

	L — light
Temp — temperate	H — heavy
W. te — warm temperate	N — nectar-feeding
Trop — tropical	S — seed-eating
S. tr — sub-tropical	F — fruit-eating
S. ar — semi-arid	

		Height	Width	Climatic zones	Soil types							
					moist, well drained	wet	dry	dry limy	full sun	filtered sun	coastal regions	frosty regions
Correa 'Mannii'	Small to medium shrub, glossy dark foliage, vivid deep pink tubular bells winter–spring. More compact habit under harsh conditions. Prune regularly.	80cm–2m	1.5–2.5m	Temp S.tr S.ar	•		•	•	•	•		L
Correa 'Marian's Marvel'	Small shrub, strong upright stems, glossy foliage, masses of pale pink-and-lemon tubular bells winter–spring. Attractive and adaptable. Prune regularly.	1–1.2m	1–1.5m	Temp S.tr	•			•	•	•		L
Correa pulchella	Variable dwarf shrub or groundcover, short oval leaves, masses of showy salmon to deep vermilion tubular bells autumn–winter–spring. Prune regularly.	prostrate–60cm	1–1.2m	Temp S.tr S.ar	•		•	•	•	•	2	L
Correa reflexa	Numerous forms and habits: prostrate to upright shrubs, variable foliage, green to red-and-yellow tubular bells autumn–winter–spring. Prune regularly.	prostrate–2m	60cm–1.2m	Temp S.tr S.ar	•		•		•	•	2	L
Correa reflexa var. *nummulariifolia*	Compact spreading groundcover, silver-green foliage, pale creamy green tubular bells mostly winter–spring. Excellent for coastal or inland gardens. Prune regularly.	prostrate–10cm	60cm–1.2m	Temp S.tr S.ar	•		•		•	•	1	H
Correa schlechtendalii	Small to medium shrub, grey-green foliage, dusky red bells tipped with green mainly spring–summer–autumn. Prune regularly to encourage bushiness.	50cm–2m	80cm–1.8m	Temp S.tr S.ar	•		•		•	•		L
Cotula coronopifolia	Small creeping plant, bright green foliage, vivid yellow buttons spring–summer. Excellent for bog gardens, beside pools or in moist areas.	10–20cm	1–3m	Temp S.tr	•	•			•	•		L
Cotula filicula	Matting plant, ferny leaves, pale yellow-green buttons spring–summer. For moist shady areas or bog margins.	prostrate	1–2m	Temp S.tr	•	•				•		L
Craspedia glauca	Dwarf clump of broad grey-green foliage, tall stems with globular yellow to orange flowerheads in summer. Container plant.	30–80cm	50cm–1m	Temp S.tr	•				•	•		H
Craspedia globosa	Dwarf tufting plant, silver ribbony foliage, long stems bearing bright golden globular flowerheads spring–summer. Long-lasting cut flower, and dries well.	15–40cm	30–60cm	Temp S.tr	•				•	•		H
Crotalaria cunninghamii Green Bird Flower	Small to medium shrub, soft hairy foliage; long yellow-green bird-like flowers winter–spring, followed by hairy pods.	1–2.5m	50cm–2m	W. te Arid S.tr	•		•		•			
Crowea exalata	Dwarf to small shrub, narrow leaves; pale to deep pink waxy flowers all year, particularly spring–summer. Container or rockery plant. Prune lightly.	40–90cm	50–90cm	Temp S.tr	•		•		•	•	2	L

		Height	Width	Climatic zones	Soil types								
					moist, well drained	wet	dry	dry limy	full sun	filtered sun	coastal regions	frosty regions	bird attraction
p — temperate L — light													
e — warm temperate H — heavy													
o — tropical N — nectar-feeding													
— sub-tropical S — seed-eating													
r — semi-arid F — fruit-eating													
wea exalata straflora Green e'	Dwarf compact shrub, narrow crowded leaves; deep pink waxy flowers most of the year, especially spring–summer. Container plant. Prune lightly.	10–20cm	40–60cm	Temp S.tr	•		•		•	•	2		
wea exalata	Small to medium upright shrub, linear foliage; large showy deep pink flowers most of the year, excellent for cutting. Light pruning beneficial.	80cm–1.2m	1–1.5m	Temp S.tr	•				•	•	2	L	
wea orinda Ecstasy'	Hybrid of C. exalata and C. saligna. Small compact shrub, broad foliage; pale pink waxy flowers most of the year, especially summer–autumn. Tip prune.	60cm–1m	60cm–1.2m	Temp S.tr	•				•	•	2	L	
wea saligna	Variable small shrub, narrow to broad foliage, large waxy pink flowers most of the year. A particularly large-flowered form is available. Light pruning beneficial.	60cm–1m	60cm–1m	Temp S.tr	•				•	•	2		
otandra amara	Dwarf shrub, one form prostrate and compact, one upright. Tiny foliage, masses of white tubular flowers winter–spring. Container plant. Prune lightly.	10–60cm	50–80cm	Temp S.ar	•		•		•	•		L	
ptandra rtechinii	Small compact shrub, crowded foliage, woolly pompom flowerheads of silver-grey winter–spring. Unusual container or rockery plant. Prune lightly.	60cm–1m	50–90cm	Temp S.tr	•				•	•		L	
ptocarya vigata bowiei ssy Laurel	Large rainforest shrub, glossy leaves, cream flowers in spring; red, orange or yellow fruit (a major food source for native pigeons). Tolerates heavy shade.	3–6m	1.5–3m	W.te Trop S.tr	•					•			F S
aniopsis cardioides keroo	Small to medium spreading tree, leathery foliage, fragrant greenish white flowers autumn–winter, leathery orange capsules. Decorative and hardy.	8–15m	5–15m	W.te Trop S.tr	•		•		•	•	1		S
tsia viburnea ive Elderberry	Large shrub, broad toothed leaves; very showy, sweetly scented white star flowers late spring–summer. Regular pruning beneficial.	2–6m	1–2.5m	W.te Trop S.tr	•					•		H	
as media nia Palm	Palm-like plant, thick trunk with arching fronds sprouting from top, large orange fruit. Hardy, generally easily grown but slow.	1–5m	2–5m	Temp Trop S.tr	•					•		L	S
nbopogon biguus nt Grass	Compact glaucous-foliaged grass, curry or citron-smelling stems. Attractive as contrast plant, and around base of rocks. Prune lightly.	30–60cm	10–30cm	Temp S.tr Arid S.ar	•		•		•			L	S
mpiera alata	Low open clump; arching stems, angled and winged; slightly toothed leaves, showy rich blue flowers winter–spring. Prune lightly after flowering.	30–75cm	60cm–1m	Temp S.tr	•		•		•	•		L	

		Height	Width	Climatic zones	Soil types				full sun	filtered sun	coastal regions	frosty regions
					moist, well drained	wet	dry	dry limy				
Dampiera coronata	Low, occasionally suckering herb; basal leaves larger than upper leaves, showy pale to deep blue flowers winter–spring.	30–75cm	1–1.5m	Temp S. tr	•		•		•	•		L
Dampiera diversifolia	Occasionally suckering mat plant; crowded narrow leaves, masses of scented deep blue flowers spring–summer. Container plant. Tip prune.	prostrate	75cm–1.5m	Temp Trop S. tr	•		•		•			L
Dampiera hederacea	Dwarf to small scrambling plant, soft foliage, masses of pale to deep blue flowers winter–spring. Tip pruning beneficial.	30cm–1m	75cm–1.5m	Temp S. tr	•			•	•	•	2	L
Dampiera lanceolata	Dwarf suckering spreading herb, many upright slightly grooved stems, lanceolate leaves; showy deep blue flowers in spring, also sporadic.	30–75cm	75cm–1.5m	Temp S. ar	•		•		•	•	2	L
Dampiera lavandulacea	Dwarf spreading clump, upright or spreading stems, leaves in clusters, many blue to lilac-pink flowers in spring.	20–75cm	1–3m	Temp S. ar	•		•	•	•			L
Dampiera linearis	Extremely variable in habit and leaf, masses of deep purple to sky blue flowers winter–spring. Excellent for rockery or container planting.	30–75cm	50cm–2m	Temp S. tr	•		•		•	•		L
Dampiera purpurea	Small upright shrub, woolly stems, large grey leaves, extremely showy rich purple flowers in large clusters spring–summer. Prune lightly.	75cm–1.2m	50cm–2m	Temp S. tr	•		•		•	•		L
Dampiera rosmarinifolia	Suckering spreading groundcover, upright stems, short blunt leaves, masses of deep blue (occasionally pale pink or white) flowers in spring.	20–60cm	1–3m	Temp S. ar	•		•	•	•	•		H
Dampiera stricta	Dwarf suckering shrub, sparse foliage, bright eye-catching pale to mid-blue flowers winter–spring–summer. Attractive mingled with other small plants.	20–75cm	30cm–2m	Temp S. tr	•		•		•	•		L
Dampiera teres	Dwarf suckering plant, grey stems, silver-grey leaves, silver buds, vivid blue flowers spring–summer. Container plant. Light tip pruning beneficial.	10–50cm	30cm–1m	Temp S. tr S. ar	•		•		•			L
Dampiera trigona	Dwarf to small plant, slender smooth stems, sparse foliage, masses of violet-blue-and-white flowers winter–spring–summer. Container plant. Prune lightly.	20–75cm	40cm–1.2m	Temp S. tr	•		•		•	•	2	L
Darwinia citriodora	Small to medium compact shrub, crowded silvery green lemon-scented foliage, glowing orange-bracted flowers winter–spring–summer. Prune after flowering.	50cm–2m	75cm–1.5m	Temp S. tr S. ar	•		•		•	•	2	L

Temp — temperate
W. te — warm temperate
Trop — tropical
S. tr — sub-tropical
S. ar — semi-arid

L — light
H — heavy
N — nectar-feeding
S — seed-eating
F — fruit-eating

		Height	Width	Climatic zones	moist, well drained	wet	dry	dry limy	full sun	filtered sun	coastal regions	frosty regions	bird attraction
p — temperate L — light warm temperate H — heavy tropical N — nectar-feeding sub-tropical S — seed-eating semi-arid F — fruit-eating													
vinia citriodora traflora spray'	Compact prostrate form, pale silvery green aromatic foliage, many orange-red bracted flowers winter–spring–summer. Container plant. Prune lightly.	prostrate–10cm	50–90cm	Temp S.tr S.ar	•		•		•	•		1	N
vinia collina	Small compact shrub, crowded aromatic foliage, bell-shaped flowerheads with yellow-green bracts autumn–winter–spring. Container plant. Prune lightly.	30cm–1.2m	45cm–1m	Temp S.tr	•				•	•			N
vinia leiostyla	Dwarf to small shrub, fine crowded aromatic leaves, bell-shaped flowerheads with large rose pink bracts in spring. Container plant. Prune lightly.	20cm–1m	45cm–1m	Temp S.tr	•				•	•			N
vinia rostegia	Small compact shrub, crowded aromatic foliage; bell-shaped flowerheads, crimson streaked over cream, winter–spring. Container plant. Prune lightly.	50cm–1.5m	75cm–1.2m	Temp S.tr	•		•		•	•		L	N
vinia meeboldii	Upright medium shrub, crowded aromatic linear leaves; large bell-shaped flowerheads, greenish white with red tips, in spring. Container plant. Prune lightly.	1.5–3m	1.2–1.6m	Temp S.tr	•				•	•		L	N
vinia neildiana	Dwarf to small compact shrub, crowded aromatic linear leaves; squat round flowerheads, green aging to crimson, in spring. Container plant. Prune lightly.	20cm–1m	40cm–1m	Temp S.tr	•		•		•	•			N
vinia oxylepis	Small shrub, crowded aromatic linear leaves, large crimson bell-shaped flowerheads in spring. Container plant. Prune lightly after flowering.	60cm–1m	40–90cm	Temp S.tr	•				•	•			N
winia squarrosa	Small shrub, crowded aromatic bright green leaves, soft pink bell-shaped flowerheads in spring. Container plant. Prune lightly after flowering.	30–90cm	20–75cm	Temp S.tr	•				•	•			N
winia taxifolia macrolaena	Prostrate spreading mat, fine aromatic grey-green foliage, many large deep pink flowerheads mostly in spring. Light tip pruning beneficial.	prostrate	90cm–1.2m	Temp S.tr	•				•	•		L	N
idsonia pruriens	Tall rainforest shrub to medium tree, decorative woolly foliage, large bracts on stems, plum-like edible fruit. Beautiful tub specimen.	3–9m	1.5–5m	Temp Trop S.tr	•					•			F
nella intermedia	Tufting lily, long strap leaves, pale to dark blue flowers on long stems in summer, bright blue berries. Hardy and attractive landscape plant.	30–60cm	60cm–2.5m	Temp Trop S.tr	•		•		•	•	2		F
nella laevis	Tufting lily, long soft strap leaves, clusters of pale blue flowers on long stems spring–summer, dark blue berries. Hardy and attractive landscape plant.	10cm–1m	50cm–1.2m	Temp S.tr S.ar	•		•		•	•		L	F

		Height	Width	Climatic zones	Soil types				full sun	filtered sun	coastal regions	frosty regions
					moist, well drained	wet	dry	dry limy				
Temp — temperate W. te — warm temperate Trop — tropical S. tr — sub-tropical S. ar — semi-arid	L — light H — heavy N — nectar-feeding S — seed-eating F — fruit-eating											
Dianella revoluta	Tufting spreading lily, stiff linear strap leaves, clusters of pale blue flowers on long stems spring–summer, dark blue berries. Hardy and attractive landscape plant.	20cm–1m	50cm–1m	Temp Trop S. tr S. ar	•				•	•	2	H
Dianella tasmanica Flax Lily	Robust spreading lily, thick shiny strap leaves, loose clusters of dark blue flowers on long stems spring–summer, large showy indigo berries. Hardy.	50cm–1.5m	50cm–2m	Temp S. tr	•				•	•		H
Dichanthium sericeum Queensland Blue Grass	Blue-green tufting grass. Very hardy. Attractive habit maintained by pruning.	50–80cm	30–50cm	Temp Trop S. tr	•		•		•			H
Dichondra repens	Creeping mat plant, small kidney-shaped leaves, tiny insignificant cream flowers in spring. Valuable primarily as lawn alternative for moist shaded sites.	prostrate	1–6m	Temp S. tr	•		•		•	•		L
Dichopogon strictus Chocolate Lily	Small tufting lily, soft linear leaves, slender stems bear fragrant violet coloured flowers in spring. Best grown in drifts for wildflower effect.	40cm–1m	40–90cm	Temp S. tr S. ar	•		•		•	•		L
Dillwynia sericea	Small shrub, fine linear foliage, dense clusters of bright orange to pink pea flowers in spring. Prune lightly after flowering.	50cm–1m	30cm–1m	Temp S. tr	•		•		•	•		L
Diplarrena latifolia	Dwarf tufting iris-like plant, strap-like foliage, white flowers with yellow and purple markings in spring. Container or rockery plant.	30–75cm	20–40cm	Temp S. tr	•				•	•		H
Diplarrena moroea	Small tufting clump, strap-like leaves, tall stems bear white iris-like flowers in spring. Provides good foliage contrast among small shrubs.	10–90cm	10cm–1m	Temp Trop S. tr	•		•		•	•		L
Diploglottis campbellii Small-leaved Tamarind	Large rainforest shrub or small tree, spreading pinnate foliage, fragrant creamy brown flowers summer–autumn, decorative red edible fruit. Handsome.	5–15m	2–5m	W. te Trop S. tr	•					•		
Diploglottis cunninghamii Native Tamarind	Large rainforest shrub or small to large tree; handsome pinnate foliage, velvety new growth; yellow-brown flowers in spring, edible orange fruit.	8–20m	2–6m	W. te Trop S. tr	•					•		
Diplolaena angustifolia	Small to medium bushy shrub, grey-green linear foliage, large pendent many-stamened flowerheads of showy crimson to orange winter–spring.	1–2m	75cm–1.5m	Temp S. ar	•		•	•	•		2	
Diplolaena grandiflora	Small to medium shrub, broad furry leaves, very large pendent flowerheads of many pink to red stamens winter–spring.	50cm–2.5m	1m–2.5m	Temp S. ar	•		•	•	•		1	

		Height	Width	Climatic zones	moist, well drained	wet	dry	dry limy	full sun	filtered sun	coastal regions	frosty regions	bird attraction
olaena rocephala	Small to medium compact shrub, blunt woolly leaves; flowerheads with red stamens, smaller than the above but still showy, winter–spring.	50cm–2m	60cm–2m	Temp S.ar	•		•	•	•	•	2		
onaea humifusa	Dense groundcover, crowded obovate leaves; insignificant flowers, followed by light green to pinkish brown hops winter–spring. Tough, hardy and useful.	prostrate	1–2m	Temp S.tr S.af	•	•	•		•	•		H	S
onaea rozyga	Small many-branched shrub, dainty fern-like foliage, insignificant flowers, particularly showy display of brilliant red-gold hops winter–spring.	70cm–1.5m	75cm–1.8m	Temp S.ar	•		•		•	•		H	S
onaea cumbens	Dense ground-covering dwarf shrub, small pointed leaves, tiny green flowers maturing to reddish dark purple hops spring–summer. Hardy and adaptable.	30–60cm	1–2m	Temp S.tr S.ar	•		•		•	•	2	H	S
yanthes excelsa nea Lily	Giant lily, long broad spear-like leaves, robust stems to 5m tall bearing large heads of scarlet flowers spring–summer. Dramatic plant.	1–1.5m	2–3m	Temp Trop S.tr	•				•	•	2		N S
andra calophylla	Prostrate spreading shrub with underground stems, upright leaves with large lobes, mauve to pink flowerheads in spring. Excellent container plant.	prostrate	1–2.5m	W.te S.ar	•		•		•	•		L	N S
andra ferruginea	Dwarf or small shrub, long rigid leaves, large glowing orange protea-like flowerheads late winter–spring.	30cm–1.7m	40cm–2m	W.te S.ar	•		•		•	•		L	N S
andra formosa	Medium to large dense shrub, many crowded, lightly serrated leaves; bright golden flowerheads in spring, excellent for cutting.	3–6m	2–4m	Temp S.ar	•		•		•	•	2	L	N S
andra nivea	Small spreading shrub, long wavy fern-like leaves, multi-coloured flowerheads (bronze, pink and green) winter–spring. Rockery or container plant.	15–85cm	40cm–2m	Temp S.ar	•		•		•	•		L	N S
andra nobilis	Medium shrub, dense triangular-lobed foliage, golden yellow flowerheads winter–spring. Showy plant, excellent for large container.	2–4m	2.5–4m	Temp S.ar	•		•		•			L	N S
andra ycephala	Medium many-branched shrub, prickly foliage, masses of small lemon yellow flowerheads clustered along branchlets winter–spring. Good cut flower.	1.5–3m	1–2m	W.te S.ar	•		•		•	•		L	N S
andra praemorsa	Medium to large shrub; wavy, slightly prickly-toothed foliage; showy yellow or pink-yellow flowerheads winter–spring.	2–3.5m	2–4m	Temp S.ar	•		•		•	•		L	N S

Temp — temperate
W. te — warm temperate
Trop — tropical
S. tr — sub-tropical
S. ar — semi-arid

L — light
H — heavy
N — nectar-feeding
S — seed-eating
F — fruit-eating

		Height	Width	Climatic zones	Soil types							
					moist, well drained	wet	dry	dry limy	full sun	filtered sun	coastal regions	frosty regions
Dryandra proteoides	Small to medium shrub, spreading stiff triangular-lobed narrow leaves; large protea-shaped golden bronze flowerheads winter–spring.	1–2.5m	1–2m	Temp S. ar	•		•		•	•		L
Dryandra quercifolia	Medium to large shrub, wavy pungent-lobed foliage; large showy greenish yellow flowerheads, occasionally pink-toned, autumn–winter–spring.	2–4m	1–3.5m	Temp S. ar	•		•		•	•		L
Dryandra sessilis	Medium to large shrub, stiff grey-green cuneate leaves, profuse creamy yellow flowerheads winter–spring. Showy, and hardy in cultivation.	2–5m	1.5–4m	Temp S. ar	•		•	•	•	•	2	L
Dryandra speciosa	Small shrub, narrow linear leaves, pendent red to soft orange flowerheads partly covered by feathery bracts winter–spring. Container plant.	30cm–1.5m	50cm–1.5m	Temp S. ar	•		•		•	•		L
Dryandra tenuifolia	Variable habit, either prostrate or upright; long narrow leaves, pale yellow to pinkish flowerheads in spring.	15cm–2m	1–3m	Temp S. ar	•		•		•	•		L
Ehretia acuminata Koda	Medium to large rainforest tree, elliptical toothed leaves, perfumed cream flowers in spring, bird-attracting yellow berries. Attractive, fast growing.	10–25m	5–12m	W. te Trop S. tr	•					•		
Elaeocarpus holopetalus	Medium to large tree of cool moist forests, attractive toothed foliage, pink-and-white 'lily of the valley' type flowers spring–early summer, black berries.	10–15m	5–10m	Temp S. tr	•					•		L
Elaeocarpus reticulatus Blueberry Ash	Small to medium tree, glossy foliage, older leaves often autumn-toned, fringed white to deep pink bell flowers spring–early summer, blue berries.	8–12m	3–4m	Temp Trop S. tr	•		•		•	•		L
Elattostachys nervosa Beetroot Tree	Small to medium tree; pinnate foliage, spectacular beetroot red new growth; brownish flowers spring and autumn, black seeds attractive to birds. Hardy.	6–13m	5–8m	Temp Trop S. tr	•					•		L
Endiandra pubens Hairy Walnut	Small to medium or tall rainforest tree; large glossy leaves, hairy red new growth; white flowers autumn and spring, large globular red fruit. Handsome.	10–25m	6–12m	W. te Trop S. tr	•					•		
Epacris breviflora	Small erect shrub; crowded foliage on long stems, topped with large clusters of pure white fragrant flowers spring–summer. Prune after flowering.	60cm–1m	30–60cm	Temp S. tr	•				•	•		L
Epacris impressa Heath	Small wiry shrub, dense foliage; massed tubular flowers of white, pink, scarlet or deep plum autumn–winter–spring. Plant in drifts. Prune after flowering.	60cm–1m	20–60cm	Temp S. tr S. ar	•		•	•	•	•	•	H

p — temperate	L — light
e — warm temperate	H — heavy
a — tropical	N — nectar-feeding
— sub-tropical	S — seed-eating
— semi-arid	F — fruit-eating

	Description	Height	Width	Climatic zones	moist, well drained	wet	dry	dry limy	full sun	filtered sun	coastal regions	frosty regions	bird attraction
cris impressa ing Pink'	Dwarf plant, wiry stems, dense small leaves, masses of shell pink flowers in spring. Container plant. Prune after flowering.	60cm	30–45cm	Temp S. tr S. ar	•		•		•	•		H	N
cris impressa grandiflora	Small slender upright shrub, robust stems, dense small leaves, flowers of similar colour variation to E. impressa.	80cm–1.2m	60–80cm	Temp S. tr	•		•		•	•		L	N
cris impressa grandiflora ble	Small upright shrub, dense small leaves, deep pink rosebud-like flowers winter–spring. Beautiful container plant. Prune after flowering.	60cm–1m	20–60cm	Temp S. tr	•		•		•	•		L	N
cris longiflora	Small shrub, many wiry stems; crowded foliage, bronze-red new growth; many scarlet and white-tipped long bells most of the year. Regular pruning required.	60cm–1m	60cm–1m	Temp S. tr	•				•	•	2	L	N
cris microphylla	Dwarf to small upright shrub; tiny leaves, obscured by crowded dainty white campanulate flowers autumn–winter–spring. Container plant. Prune after flowering.	50cm–1m	30–50cm	Temp S. tr	•	•			•	•		L	N
cris pulchella	Dwarf shrub, crowded foliage; spikes of white to rose pink campanulate flowers most of the year, especially autumn and spring. Prune after flowering.	30–60cm	20–40cm	Temp S. tr	•				•	•		L	N
cris reclinata	Dwarf to small shrub, crowded foliage, massed cherry pink tubular bells autumn–winter–spring. Very beautiful plant. Prune after flowering.	50cm–1m	30–80cm	Temp S. tr	•	•			•	•		L	N
naea ufortioides	Small to medium many-branched shrub, crowded foliage, clusters of bright orange long-stamened flowers in spring. Prune after flowering.	80cm–2.5m	1–2m	W. te S. ar	•		•		•			L	N
naea violacea	Low spreading shrub, crowded furry foliage, dense clusters of showy violet-blue yellow-anthered flowers in spring. Best in sandy soils or container.	20–50cm	40–80cm	W. te S. ar	•		•		•	•		L	N
mophila riana	Dwarf to small spreading shrub, rigid crowded foliage, tubular lilac-purple flowers in spring. Drought resistant and hardy. Pruning beneficial.	15–50cm	30–70cm	W. te Arid S. ar	•		•		•	•		L	N
mophila oniiflora	Medium shrub or small tree, drooping linear leaves; tubular cream and red-tinged flowers, spotted inside, mostly winter–spring but also sporadic. Prune.	2–7m	1.5–3.5m	W. te Arid S. ar	•		•		•			L	N
mophila errata	Dense layering plant, toothed foliage; tubular flowers, yellow-green with purplish brown on upper lip, in spring. Adaptable and useful. Pruning beneficial.	prostrate	1–2.5m	W. te Arid S. ar	•		•	•	•			L	N

Temp — temperate L — light
W. te — warm temperate H — heavy
Trop — tropical N — nectar-feeding
S. tr — sub-tropical S — seed-eating
S. ar — semi-arid F — fruit-eating

		Height	Width	Climatic zones	Soil types							
					moist, well drained	wet	dry	dry limy	full sun	filtered sun	coastal regions	frosty regions
Eremophila bowmanii	Small spreading or upright shrub, silvery foliage; large tubular flowers of lavender-blue, spotted inside, winter–spring. Prune lightly.	30cm–2m	50cm–2m	W. te Arid S. ar	•		•	•	•			L
Eremophila calorhabdos	Small to medium upright shrub, lightly hairy crowded foliage, showy pinky red tubular flowers winter–spring–summer. Pruning beneficial.	1.5–2.5m	70cm–2m	W. te Arid S. ar	•		•	•	•	•		L
Eremophila decipiens	Small slightly sticky shrub, flat linear leaves; tubular red flowers in spring, also sporadic, much enjoyed by honeyeaters. Pruning beneficial.	1–1.5m	1–2m	W. te Arid S. ar	•		•	•	•	•		L
Eremophila densifolia	Spreading dwarf shrub, linear purplish green foliage, tubular blue-purple flowers winter–spring–summer. Hardy. Pruning beneficial.	prostrate–50cm	1–2.5m	Temp S. tr Arid S. ar	•		•		•	•	2	L
Eremophila denticulata	Small to medium shrub, sticky foliage; long tubular yellow flowers aging to red, loved by honeyeaters, spring–summer, also sporadic. Prune regularly.	1–2.2m	1–3m	Temp S. tr Arid S. ar	•		•	•	•		2	L
Eremophila divaricata	Small spreading shrub, spiny branches, narrow foliage, tubular blue-lilac flowers spring–summer. Grows well in heavy soils. Pruning beneficial.	80cm–1.5m	1–2.5m	Temp S. tr Arid S. ar	•		•		•	•		L
Eremophila gibbifolia	Dwarf to small shrub, tiny crowded leaves; massed tubular blue-lilac flowers spring–summer, also sporadic. Adaptable. Tip prune regularly.	25–90cm	20–90cm	Temp S. tr S. ar	•		•	•	•	•		H
Eremophila glabra	Prostrate to small variable shrub; grey or green foliage, sometimes toothed; tubular yellow, orange, red or green flowers spring–summer, also sporadic. Prune.	prostrate–1.5m	1–3m	Temp S. tr Arid S. ar	•		•	•	•	•		L
Eremophila laanii	Small to medium shrub, tangled branches, slightly hairy foliage; showy tubular white or pink flowers spring–summer, also sporadic. Pruning beneficial.	80cm–2.5m	1–3m	W. te Arid S. ar	•		•		•	•		H
Eremophila latrobei	Variable small to medium shrub; foliage linear to broad, green to silver; tubular cream, deep pink or red flowers winter–spring. Tip prune regularly.	1–3m	50cm–2m	W. te Arid S. ar	•		•	•	•	•		L
Eremophila lehmanniana	Small spreading shrub, broad hairy leaves with sticky new growth, white to violet-blue tubular flowers in spring. Prune lightly.	20cm–1.5m	40cm–2m	W. te Arid S. ar	•		•	•	•	•	2	L
Eremophila macdonnelli	Low spreading shrub with many forms in cultivation. Foliage variable, green to silver; tubular purple-violet flowers spring–summer, also sporadic. Prune.	50cm–1.5m	1–5m	W. te Arid S. ar	•		•	•	•	•		L

np — temperate	L — light
te — warm temperate	H — heavy
p — tropical	N — nectar-feeding
r — sub-tropical	S — seed-eating
r — semi-arid	F — fruit-eating

		Height	Width	Climatic zones	Soil types				full sun	filtered sun	coastal regions	frosty regions	bird attraction
					moist, well drained	wet	dry	dry limy					
mophila culata	Prostrate to medium variable shrub, green to grey foliage; tubular flowers of creamy yellow, orange, red or pink, spotted inside, most of year. Tip prune.	prostrate–3m	1–2.5m	Temp S.tr Arid S.ar	•		•	•	•	•	2	L	N
mophila yclada	Small to medium spreading tangled shrub, narrow scattered foliage; white, occasionally purple-tinged, tubular flowers spring–summer–autumn.	1–2.5m	50cm–3m	W.te Arid S.ar	•		•		•	•		L	N
mophila emosa	Small shrub, narrow pale green foliage; many very colourful orange, yellow, red and purple tubular flowers in spring. Well known in cultivation. Tip prune.	20cm–2m	30cm–1.5m	W.te S.ar	•		•		•	•		L	N
ostemon gustifolius . montanus	Small compact shrub; crowded tiny aromatic leaves, covered in pink buds opening to starry white flowers winter–spring. Beautiful container plant. Prune lightly.	60cm–1m	40–80cm	Temp S.ar	•		•		•	•		L	N
ostemon stralasius	Small to medium slender erect shrub, aromatic grey foliage, extremely showy large waxy pink flowers in spring. Excellent large container plant. Prune lightly.	1–2.2m	60cm–1.2m	Temp Trop S.tr	•		•		•	•			
ostemon xifolius	Small shrub, crowded leathery aromatic leaves, many pink buds opening to showy white or pale pink flowers in spring. Container plant. Prune lightly.	80cm–1.2m	1–2m	Temp S.tr	•				•	•		L	
ostemon arid 'Decumbent'	Compact dwarf shrub, crowded blue-green aromatic foliage, pink buds, pink-and-white flowers winter–spring. Container plant. Prune lightly.	45–60cm	60–80cm	Temp S.tr	•				•	•		L	
ostemon poroides	Small to large shrub, variable grey-green aromatic foliage, massed white or pale pink flowers autumn–winter–spring. Many forms. Prune regularly.	50cm–5m	50cm–3m	Temp Trop S.tr	•		•		•	•		L	
ostemon iflorus	Dwarf to small shrub, aromatic slightly hairy slender leaves, blue-mauve star flowers in clusters or spikes winter–spring. Prune lightly after flowering.	50cm–1m	30–80cm	Temp S.ar	•		•		•	•		L	
ostemon gens	Prostrate to dwarf shrub, narrow pointed aromatic foliage, dainty white star flowers in spring. Charming container plant. Light tip pruning recommended.	prostrate–50cm	30–90cm	Temp S.ar	•		•		•	•	2	L	
ostemon spicatus	Dwarf to small shrub, slightly hairy narrow aromatic leaves, deep blue-mauve star flowers in long racemes winter–spring. Container plant. Prune lightly.	20cm–1m	50cm–1m	Temp S.ar	•		•		•	•	2	L	
ostemon rucosus	Compact dwarf shrub, aromatic grey-green blunt warty foliage, massed pink-and-white waxy flowers winter–spring. Container plant. Prune after flowering.	30–60cm	40–60cm	Temp S.ar	•		•		•	•		L	

		Height	Width	Climatic zones	moist, well drained	wet	dry	dry limy	full sun	filtered sun	coastal regions	frosty regions

Temp — temperate
W. te — warm temperate
Trop — tropical
S. tr — sub-tropical
S. ar — semi-arid

L — light
H — heavy
N — nectar-feeding
S — seed-eating
F — fruit-eating

Soil types

Name	Description	Height	Width	Climatic zones	moist, well drained	wet	dry	dry limy	full sun	filtered sun	coastal regions	frosty regions
Eriostemon verrucosus double	Arching dwarf shrub, lightly suckering; aromatic foliage, shell pink buds, flowers like miniature water-lilies winter–spring. Container plant. Tip prune.	30–60cm	30–60cm	Temp S. ar	•		•		•	•		L
Eucalyptus acaciiformis	Medium to large tree, deeply fissured grey-brown bark, bright green peppermint-scented foliage, white flowers in spring. Very hardy, attractive shade tree.	10–20m	6–12m	Temp S. tr S. ar	•		•		•	•		H
Eucalyptus alba White Gum	Small to medium tree, smooth white powdery bark, bright green broad foliage, white flowers in spring. Beautiful tree for tropical regions.	4–15m	4–12m	W. te Trop S. tr	•				•	•		
Eucalyptus albens White Box	Medium to large spreading tree, fibrous bark, ovate bluish green foliage, white flowers autumn–winter. Tough shade tree for dry areas.	8–20m	6–15m	W. te S. ar	•		•		•	•		H
Eucalyptus alpina Grampians Gum	Small squat shrub or mallee, or tall tree; smooth bark, leathery dark leaves, warty buds and white flowers summer–autumn. Squat form attractive in gardens.	2–20m	3.5–8m	Temp S. tr	•		•		•	•		H
Eucalyptus amygdalina	Medium to tall tree, dark grey-brown bark, smooth narrow peppermint-scented leaves, cream flowers spring–summer. Attractive shade tree.	12–30m	6–20m	Temp S. tr	•				•	•		H
Eucalyptus anceps	Spreading mallee or small tree, smooth grey-brown bark, dark foliage, cream flowers summer–autumn.	3–7m	4–8m	W. te S. tr S. ar	•		•	•	•	•	1	L
Eucalyptus angulosa	Spreading mallee, smooth grey bark, leathery foliage, creamy yellow flowers spring–summer, cup-shaped ribbed capsules.	2–6m	3–8m	W. te S. ar	•		•	•	•	•	2	L
Eucalyptus annulata	Spreading mallee or small tree, smooth grey bark, dark narrow foliage; showy creamy yellow flowers spring-summer, producing copious nectar.	3–8m	5–7m	W. te S. ar	•		•	•	•			L
Eucalyptus argophloia	Tall tree, straight smooth grey-white trunk, bright green narrow foliage, creamy yellow flowers in winter. Excellent shade tree for inland areas.	20–35m	10–15m	W. te S. tr S. ar	•		•		•	•		H
Eucalyptus astringens	Small to large tree, smooth brown to grey trunk, dark shiny lanceolate foliage, creamy yellow flowers in spring. Excellent shade and shelter tree.	6–20m	5–12m	W. te S. ar	•		•		•	•		L
Eucalyptus bakeri	Small to medium mallee, smooth grey bark, narrow leathery leaves, white flowers in spring. Tough and drought hardy.	6–15m	5–10m	W. te S. tr S. ar	•		•		•	•		L

:GHT:
he vigorous *Hardenbergia
ʳiolacea* 'Happy Wanderer',
ɔvered in sprays of purple-mauve
ɇa flowers, forms a shade-casting
ɪrchway on this west-facing
ɇrandah. A slab of *Eucalyptus
ɪmaldulensis* bark hangs as a
ɇeder for numerous parrots.

LOW:
he inset close-up of *Clematis
ubescens* illustrates the fine detail
f this dainty climbing or
crambling shrub. Below, it
ombines with the purple
ɪardenbergia comptoniana* and
ɇ vivid coral *Kennedia coccinea*
climbing on and concealing an
d stump.

RIGHT:
Acacias, or wattles, are an important component of the Australian landscape. *Acacia cognata* is a softly weeping large shrub or small tree with foliage reaching to the ground. The delicate yellow flowers bloom in spring, and these, combined with the lightly perfumed foliage, make this a desirable plant for well-drained conditions.

BELOW:
Thryptomene saxicola arches over bold rock work, its pink flowers complementing similar tones in the rock. The upright silver-grey foliaged *Acacia flexifolia* behind is covered with lemon ball flowers. Both shrubs flower in winter and spring.

np — temperate L — light
te — warm temperate H — heavy
p — tropical N — nectar-feeding
— sub-tropical S — seed-eating
r — semi-arid F — fruit-eating

Species	Description	Height	Width	Climatic zones	moist, well drained	wet	dry	dry limy	full sun	filtered sun	coastal regions	frosty regions	L/H	bird attraction
...alyptus ...croftii	Medium to tall tree, smooth trunk with orange patches, spreading crown of leathery grey-green foliage, creamy white flowers spring–summer. Shade tree.	6–20m	3–12m	Temp S.tr S.ar	•	•	•		•	•			L	N S
...alyptus behriana	Small to medium mallee or tree; fibrous lower bark, upper limbs smooth grey to green; shiny foliage, cream flowers winter–spring–summer. Windbreak.	3–12m	2–10m	W.te S.ar	•		•	•	•	•			H	N S
...alyptus blakelyi	Medium to large tree, bark smooth with grey or cream patches, grey-green foliage, cream flowers spring–summer. Hardy rural shade tree.	8–20m	6–13m	Temp S.tr S.ar	•		•		•	•			H	N S
...alyptus ...ryoides	Medium to tall spreading tree, brown fibrous bark, glossy broad leaves, cream flowers in summer. Useful shade tree but often psyllid infested. Salt tolerant.	10–30m	10–25m	Temp Trop S.tr	•	•			•	•	1			N S
...alyptus ...ckwayi	Medium to tall upright tree, smooth white bark, dense crown of dark glossy foliage, cream flowers autumn–winter. Valuable shade and shelter tree.	10–25m	6–12m	W.te S.ar	•		•	•	•	•			L	N S
...alyptus ...dettiana	Spreading small mallee shrub or tree, smooth bark, glossy foliage, large bright yellow-green flowers winter–spring, clustered bell-shaped capsules.	1.5–8m	2.5–6m	W.te S.ar	•		•		•	•		1	L	N S
...alyptus ...racoppinensis	Small shrubby mallee, smooth bark, thick bluish green foliage; showy creamy yellow flowers in spring, attractive large capsules. Very ornamental.	2.5–6m	3–5m	W.te S.ar	•		•		•	•			L	N S
...alyptus caesia ...er Princess	Mallee or medium weeping tree, decorative peeling red bark, powdery white stems, pendulous grey foliage, rich pink flowers winter–spring. Spectacular.	4–10m	2.5–8m	Temp S.tr S.ar	•		•		•	•			L	N S
...alyptus caleyii	Medium to tall tree, hard furrowed very dark bark, silvery foliage, creamy yellow nectar-rich flowers autumn–winter–spring. A handsome ironbark.	15–25m	10–15m	W.te S.ar	•		•		•	•			H	N S
...alyptus ...ophylla ...ri	Tall spreading tree, rough bark, broad glossy leaves, pink or creamy showy flowers summer–autumn, large decorative capsules. Beautiful shade tree.	5–25m	2.5–15m	Temp	•				•	•		2	L	N S
...alyptus ...cogona	Medium mallee or small tree, smooth grey bark peeling in ribbons, narrow foliage, cream or pale pink flowers in spring. Drought tolerant windbreak.	2.5–8m	3–7m	W.te S.ar	•		•	•	•	•			H	N S
...alyptus ...aldulensis ...er Red Gum	Tall spreading tree, smooth grey-and-white bark, grey-green foliage, cream flowers in summer. Handsome broad landscape tree.	15–50m	15–35m	Temp Trop S.tr Arid S.ar	•	•	•	•	•	•			H	N S

Temp — temperate
W. te — warm temperate
Trop — tropical
S. tr — sub-tropical
S. ar — semi-arid

L — light
H — heavy
N — nectar-feeding
S — seed-eating
F — fruit-eating

		Height	Width	Climatic zones	Soil types				full sun	filtered sun	coastal regions	frosty regions
					moist, well drained	wet	dry	dry limy				
Eucalyptus cambageana	Medium to tall tree; grey tessellated bark on trunk, upper limbs white; grey-green foliage, cream flowers in summer. Attractive broad landscape tree.	15–25m	6–15m	W. te Trop S. tr	•				•	•		L
Eucalyptus campaspe	Small to medium tree; smooth coppery trunk, often fluted; silvery branchlets, grey-green foliage, creamy yellow flowers mostly spring–summer.	4–10m	3–8m	W. te Arid S. ar	•		•	•	•	•		H
Eucalyptus cephalocarpa	Medium to large tree, often crooked; grey-brown fibrous bark; pendulous grey-green foliage, glaucous new growth; white flowers in winter. Shade tree.	8–20m	6–18m	Temp S. tr	•				•	•		H
Eucalyptus cinerea	Small to medium tree, crooked trunk, grey fibrous bark; older leaves broad and tapered, rounded glaucous new foliage; cream flowers in spring.	6–15m	6–12m	Temp S. tr	•		•		•	•		H
Eucalyptus citriodora Lemon-scented Gum	Tall stately tree, pure white powdery bark, bright green lemon-scented pendulous foliage, white flowers winter–spring. Handsome in avenues.	15–30m	8–20m	Temp Trop S. tr S. ar	•		•		•	•	2	
Eucalyptus cladocalyx nana Bushy Sugar Gum	Small spreading tree, smooth grey-white bark, lanceolate foliage, cream flowers summer–autumn. Used for rural shelterbelts but generally inadequate.	5–8m	6–10m	Temp S. tr S. ar	•		•	•	•	•	2	H
Eucalyptus clelandii	Small to medium tree; bark rough at base, smooth above; narrow grey-green foliage, creamy yellow flowers spring–summer. Decorative tree.	8–13m	6–10m	W. te Arid S. ar	•		•	•	•	•	2	H
Eucalyptus cloeziana	Tall tree; flaky dark brown bark to upper limbs, then smooth grey-brown; lanceolate foliage, often purple in winter; white flowers in autumn. Broad landscape tree.	15–35m	8–20m	Temp Trop S. tr	•		•		•	•		L
Eucalyptus cneorifolia	Mallee shrub or medium tree; rough grey lower bark, then smooth and cream; narrow foliage, cream flowers summer–autumn. Coastal windbreak.	5–12m	4–12m	Temp S. tr S. ar	•		•	•	•	•	1	L
Eucalyptus coccifera Tasmanian Snow Gum	Small to large tree; smooth bark, pink when new; thick blue-grey leaves, profuse cream flowers in summer. Beautiful tree for cold climates.	2–25m	3–15m	Temp	•				•	•		H
Eucalyptus conferruminata Bushy Yate	Formerly *E. lehmannii*. Large shrub to medium tree, dark foliage, large clusters of green-yellow flowers spring–summer–autumn, ornamental capsules.	3–12m	4–12m	Temp S. tr	•		•	•	•		1	L
Eucalyptus cordata	Large shrub to tall tree, smooth bark; stem-clasping cordate silver juvenile foliage, lanceolate mature foliage; cream flowers in spring. Excellent for cut foliage.	5–30m	5–20m	Temp	•				•	•		L

					Soil types								
		Height	Width	Climatic zones	moist, well drained	wet	dry	dry limy	full sun	filtered sun	coastal regions	frosty regions	bird attraction
1p — temperate / e — warm temperate / p — tropical / — sub-tropical / r — semi-arid	L — light / H — heavy / N — nectar-feeding / S — seed-eating / F — fruit-eating												
alyptus cornuta e	Small shrub to tall upright tree; dark rough bark on trunk, then smooth and pale: lanceolate dark foliage, large clusters of pale yellow flowers in spring.	1.5–20m	2.5–10m	Temp S.tr S.ar	●	●	●		●	●	1	L	N S
alyptus coronata	Medium mallee, smooth grey bark, thick lanceolate foliage; large creamy yellow flowers winter–spring, decorative ribbed crowned capsules.	2.5m–5m	3–4m	W.te S.tr S.ar	●		●		●	●	1	L	N S
alyptus mophylla Gum	Tall mallee or small tree, grey-white patchy bark, dark foliage, massed showy cream buds and flowers autumn–winter–spring, cup-shaped capsules. Hardy.	4–8m	3–5m	Temp S.tr	●	●			●	●	2	L	N S
alyptus crebra	Medium to tall tree, hard furrowed grey bark, narrow blue-green foliage; white flowers winter–spring–summer, very rich in nectar.	15–30m	8–15m	W.te Trop S.tr	●		●		●	●	2	H	N S
alyptus ulata	Small to medium tree; lower bark rough and grey, upper limbs smooth; dense silver-grey foliage, cream flowers in spring. Fast growing and decorative.	4–15m	3–10m	Temp S.tr	●	●			●	●		L	N S
alyptus crucis	Mallee or small spreading tree, red-brown deciduous bark in curled strips, silvery branches and glaucous foliage, creamy yellow flowers spring–summer.	3–8m	5–9m	W.te Arid S.ar	●		●		●	●		L	N S
alyptus curtisii	Mallee or small tree, smooth grey-green bark, silvery branchlets, lanceolate foliage, profuse white flowers in spring. Fast growing and very attractive.	2–10m	3–7m	W.te Trop S.tr S.ar	●				●	●		L	N S
alyptus dawsonii	Medium to large tree, smooth mottled bark, grey-green lanceolate foliage, white flowers in spring. Excellent shade tree for rural or parkland use.	10–30m	8–20m	Temp S.tr S.ar	●		●		●	●		H	N S
alyptus mondensis	Pendulous mallee or small tree, smooth bark, silvery branchlets, thick grey-green foliage, pale yellow flowers autumn–winter–spring, bell-shaped capsules.	3–7m	2–6m	W.te Arid S.ar	●		●		●			L	N S
alyptus dielsii	Tall mallee or small tree, smooth grey-brown bark, narrow foliage, profuse yellow-green flowers spring–summer. Used for erosion control.	4–7m	5–7m	W.te S.ar	●		●	●	●	●		H	N S
alyptus diptera	Spreading mallee or small tree, fluted trunk, shiny brown bark, narrow glossy foliage; creamy green-yellow flowers autumn–winter, winged capsules.	3–8m	4–7m	W.te S.ar	●		●	●	●	●		H	N S
alyptus rsicolor i	Tall stately tree, creamy brown bark, broad-lanceolate foliage, white flowers spring–summer. Valuable hardwood tree; suitable for broad landscape.	40–70m	12–16m	Temp S.tr	●				●	●			N S

Temp — temperate
W. te — warm temperate
Trop — tropical
S. tr — sub-tropical
S. ar — semi-arid

L — light
H — heavy
N — nectar-feeding
S — seed-eating
F — fruit-eating

			Height	Width	Climatic zones	Soil types							
						moist, well drained	wet	dry	dry limy	full sun	filtered sun	coastal regions	frosty regions
Eucalyptus diversifolia	Mallee shrub or small spreading tree, smooth grey bark, grey-green foliage, cream flowers winter–spring–summer. Useful for coastal windbreaks.		2–10m	2.5–10m	Temp S.tr Arid S.ar	•		•	•	•	•	1	H
Eucalyptus dives 'Little Honey'	Small, often multi-stemmed tree; smooth bark on upper limbs; blue-grey foliage, plum new growth; profuse cream flowers winter–spring. Very attractive.		5–7m	3–4m	Temp S.tr S.ar	•		•		•	•		H
Eucalyptus doratoxylon	Medium mallee or small tree; cream bark, often purplish when new; bright green narrow foliage, profuse cream flowers in spring. Very decorative and useful.		3–7m	2–6m	Temp S.tr	•				•	•	1	
Eucalyptus drummondii	Mallee shrub or small tree, smooth white bark, lanceolate foliage, distinctive cream buds opening to a mass of cream flowers in spring.		2–6m	2.5–6m	W.te S.ar	•		•		•	•		
Eucalyptus dumosa	Medium mallee or small tree; bark mostly smooth, deciduous; grey-green foliage, cream flowers winter–spring–summer.		2.5–12m	3–10m	W.te S.tr S.ar	•		•	•	•	•		L
Eucalyptus dwyeri	Small tree, sometimes multi-stemmed; smooth cream-grey bark, lanceolate grey-green foliage, cream flowers winter–spring.		5–10m	3–8m	W.te S.ar	•		•			•		L
Eucalyptus elata River Peppermint	Tall tree, smooth white-grey bark, fine peppermint-scented foliage, clusters of small white flowers in spring. Graceful, fast growing; suitable for broad landscapes.		15–45m	10–20m	Temp S.tr	•				•	•		L
Eucalyptus eremophila Tall Sand Mallee	Mallee or small tree, smooth grey or pale brown bark, glossy narrow foliage, horn-capped buds, profuse large yellow or pink flowers winter–spring.		3–8m	4–6m	W.te Arid S.ar	•		•		•	•		L
Eucalyptus erythrocorys Illyarrie	Small tree, white to grey bark, leathery foliage, distinctive red-capped buds, vivid yellow flowers summer–autumn, decorative capsules. Spectacular.		4–8m	4–7m	W.te S.tr S.ar	•		•	•	•	•	2	L
Eucalyptus erythronema	Mallee or small fine tree, smooth white powdery bark, narrow glossy foliage, showy clusters of red flowers spring–summer. Particularly attractive.		3–8m	2.5–6m	W.te S.ar	•		•		•			L
Eucalyptus eximia	Small to medium spreading tree, tessellated yellow-brown bark, blue-green foliage, large clusters of thick creamy flowers in spring. Dwarf form in cultivation.		3–15m	2.5–12m	Temp S.tr	•		•		•	•	2	L
Eucalyptus fasciculosa	Tall shrub to medium tree, smooth grey and white bark, broad foliage, profuse cream flowers winter–spring–summer.		4–15m	4–12m	Temp S.tr S.ar	•		•	•	•	•	2	L

		Height	Width	Climatic zones	Soil types — moist, well drained	wet	dry	dry limy	full sun	filtered sun	coastal regions	frosty regions	bird attraction
p — temperate L — light													
e — warm temperate H — heavy													
) — tropical N — nectar-feeding													
— sub-tropical S — seed-eating													
— semi-arid F — fruit-eating													
...alyptus ficifolia ...Flowering ...m	Small to large tree, rough-barked trunk, dense broad foliage; massed orange, scarlet, crimson, pink or cream flowers in summer; large decorative capsules.	12–15m	10–18m	Temp S.tr	•				•		2		N S
...alyptus ...ktoniae	Tall mallee or small to medium tree, smooth bark, dark foliage, large clusters of pale yellow flowers in spring. Decorative and drought tolerant.	6–15m	4–9m	W.te S.ar	•		•	•	•	•	2	L	N S
...alyptus ...unda	Medium mallee or small tree, smooth grey to red bark, narrow glossy leaves, cream flowers in summer.	3–8m	3–8m	W.te S.tr S.ar	•		•	•	•	•	2	L	N S
...alyptus ...schiana	Small, often crooked tree; scaly brown bark, ovate foliage; conspicuous cream flowers spring–summer. Deciduous in the dry season.	8–10m	5–9m	Trop S.tr	•				•	•			N S
...alyptus formanii	Tall mallee or medium tree; rough lower bark, smooth upper limbs; crowded glaucous juvenile foliage, narrow mature leaves; white flowers in summer.	6–12m	6–10m	W.te Arid S.ar	•		•		•			L	N S
...alyptus ...estiana ...hsia Gum	Small tree, smooth grey bark, dense glossy foliage; decorative scarlet buds opening to yellow flowers summer–autumn, followed by attractive capsules.	3–8m	4–6m	W.te S.tr S.ar	•			•	•	•		L	N S
...alyptus gardneri	Mallee shrub or small tree, smooth grey bark; mauve-grey foliage, often purple; bright yellow flowers in winter. Decorative and hardy.	1.5–9m	2.5–8m	W.te S.tr S.ar	•		•		•	•		H	N S
...alyptus gillii ...ly Mallee	Mallee shrub or small tree, crooked trunk; grey, mostly smooth bark; waxy cordate silver foliage, profuse yellow flowers winter–spring–summer.	2–7m	3–8m	Arid S.ar	•		•	•	•	•		L	N S
...alyptus globulus ...manian Blue ...m	Tall stately tree, smooth bark; glaucous broad juvenile foliage, dark lanceolate mature leaves; cream flowers spring–summer, large button-like capsules.	15–50m	12–25m	Temp Trop S.tr	•				•	•	2	L	N S
...alyptus globulus globulus ...mpacta'	Small bushy tree, short trunk, many branches; juvenile broad glaucous foliage retained for a long time, cream flowers spring–summer, button-like capsules.	3–10m	4–8m	Temp Trop S.tr	•				•	•	2	L	N S
...alyptus ...phocephala ...rt	Tall tree, rough bark, thick grey-green leaves; large fragrant cream flowers summer–autumn, large bell-shaped capsules. Handsome coastal shade tree.	15–35m	10–15m	Temp Trop S.tr S.ar	•		•	•	•	•	2		N S
...alyptus gracilis	Mallee or small to medium tree, smooth upper bark, narrow glossy leaves, conspicuous white flowers autumn–winter–spring. Useful inland windbreak.	3–13m	4–8m	W.te S.tr S.ar	•		•	•	•	•		L	N S

		Height	Width	Climatic zones	Soil types							
					moist, well drained	wet	dry	dry limy	full sun	filtered sun	coastal regions	frosty regions
Temp — temperate W. te — warm temperate Trop — tropical S. tr — sub-tropical S. ar — semi-arid	L — light H — heavy N — nectar-feeding S — seed-eating F — fruit-eating											
Eucalyptus grandis Flooded Gum	Tall straight tree, smooth white to greenish bark, glossy lanceolate foliage, white flowers autumn–winter–spring. Handsome parkland tree.	20–45m	12–20m	Temp Trop S. tr	•				•	•		
Eucalyptus grossa	Spreading mallee shrub, smooth reddish upper bark, thick glossy rounded leaves, decorative buds, large yellow-green flowers in spring. Drought tolerant.	2–4m	3.5–5m	W. te S. tr S. ar	•		•		•			L
Eucalyptus gummifera	Medium to tall tree, often crooked branches, brown tessellated bark, bright green foliage, cream flowers summer–autumn, decorative capsules.	10–25m	8–15m	Temp S. tr	•		•		•	•	1	
Eucalyptus gunnii Cider Gum	Medium to tall tree, smooth white to pinkish bark; attractive silver juvenile foliage, grey-green mature leaves; cream flowers in summer. Cut foliage lasts well.	10–25m	6–15m	Temp S. tr	•	•			•	•		H
Eucalyptus haemastoma Scribbly Gum	Small to medium tree, smooth insect-scribbled bark, broad-lanceolate leaves, cream flowers autumn–winter–spring. Parkland tree.	5–15m	4–13m	Temp S. tr	•		•		•		2	L
Eucalyptus incrassata	Mallee or small tree, smooth deciduous bark, thick lanceolate leaves, pale yellow flowers in spring. Useful inland windbreak.	3–7m	4.5–6m	W. te S. tr S. ar	•		•	•	•	•	2	H
Eucalyptus intermedia	Medium to tall tree, grey-brown tessellated bark, lanceolate glossy foliage, very attractive massed cream flowers in summer. Ideal parkland tree.	15–30m	10–20m	W. te Trop S. tr	•		•		•	•	2	
Eucalyptus intertexta Gum-barked Coolibah	Small mallee to tall tree; rough persistent bark on most of tree, upper branches white; broad silvery leaves, white flowers in winter. Inland tree.	7–25m	4–15m	W. te S. ar	•		•		•	•		H
Eucalyptus kingsmillii	Medium mallee, smooth red-brown upper bark, lanceolate grey-green foliage, pale yellow or red flowers winter–spring, decorative ribbed capsules.	2.5–8m	3–7m	W. te Arid S. ar	•		•		•	•		L
Eucalyptus kitsoniana Bog Mallee	Tall mallee or slender tree, smooth pinkish brown bark, broad foliage, cream to pink flowers spring–summer–autumn. Very adaptable and hardy.	4–12m	3–6m	Temp S. tr	•	•			•	•	2	L
Eucalyptus kondinensis	Small to medium tree; dark bark on lower trunk, smooth above; narrow shining leaves, cream flowers in spring. Salt tolerant shade and shelter tree.	8–15m	5–12m	W. te S. ar	•		•	•			2	L
Eucalyptus kruseana	Small to medium spreading mallee, smooth bark, rounded silver leaves crowded along branches, showy yellow flowers autumn–winter, silver capsules.	2–6m	4–6m	W. te Arid S. ar	•		•		•			L

np — temperate   L — light
te — warm temperate   H — heavy
p — tropical   N — nectar-feeding
r — sub-tropical   S — seed-eating
r — semi-arid   F — fruit-eating

Name	Description	Height	Width	Climatic zones	Soil types: moist, well drained	wet	dry	dry limy	full sun	filtered sun	coastal regions	frosty regions	bird attraction
calyptus e-poolei	Small to medium tree; bark both rough and smooth, new bark often pinky white; dense foliage, cream flowers winter–spring. Attractive shade tree.	8–12m	5–10m	W. te S. ar	•				•	•	2	L	N S
calyptus sdowneana	Mallee to medium tree, often crooked trunk, smooth white to brown bark, lanceolate grey-green foliage, cream to purple-pink flowers spring–summer.	3–12m	2–8m	Temp S. ar	•		•	•	•	•	2	L	N S
calyptus giflorens ck Box	Medium to large tree, dark rough bark, grey-green foliage; tiny white and pink flowers on same umbel spring–summer. Excellent shade tree.	8–20m	6–15m	W. te S. ar	•	•		•	•	•		H	N S
calyptus mannii	Formerly E. lehmannii dwarf. Small mallee, smooth bark, lanceolate leaves, fused finger-like buds, bright yellow-green flowers winter–spring.	1.2–5m	2.2–5m	W. te S. tr S. ar	•		•		•	•	2	L	N S
calyptus lesouefii	Small to medium tree; base of trunk rough-barked, upper trunk smooth white; narrow leaves, ribbed buds, cream flowers in spring, ribbed capsules.	7–15m	5–9m	W. te Arid S. ar	•		•		•	•		L	N S
calyptus coxylon	Medium to tall tree, smooth bark, grey-green foliage, conspicuous cream or pink flowers winter–spring–summer. Hardy; very attractive to honeyeaters.	15–30m	12–20m	Temp S. tr S. ar	•		•	•	•	•		L	N S
calyptus coxylon arf	Small slender tree, smooth white to grey bark, lanceolate foliage; showy pink or cream flowers winter–spring–summer, very attractive to honeyeaters.	2.5–6m	3–5m	Temp S. tr S. ar	•		•	•	•	•	2	L	N S
alyptus coxylon ssp. galocarpa	Small to medium tree, smooth trunk, lanceolate foliage; cream, yellow, pink to deep pink flowers winter–spring–summer. Excellent coastal shelter tree.	4–8m	5–9m	Temp S. tr	•		•	•	•	•	1	L	N S
calyptus crandra	Tall mallee or small tree, smooth bark, glossy bluish green foliage, finger-like buds, clusters of fragrant bright yellow flowers in summer.	4–7m	4–6m	Temp S. tr S. ar	•		•	•	•	•	2	L	N S
calyptus crocarpa ttlecah	Sprawling mallee shrub, smooth grey bark, silver leaves along branches and stems, silver buds, large vivid pink flowers summer–autumn, decorative capsules.	3–4m	4–10m	W. te S. ar	•		•		•			L	N S
alyptus crorhyncha Stringybark	Tall tree, fibrous brown bark, blue-grey foliage, conspicuous cream flowers spring–summer–autumn. Excellent honey and rural shade tree.	15–30m	10–18m	Temp S. tr	•				•	•		L	N S
alyptus maculata tted Gum	Tall stately tree, beautiful grey-green mottled trunk, dark foliage, cream flowers winter–spring. Fast growing and hardy; handsome parkland tree.	20–35m	10–25m	Temp S. tr	•				•	•	2	L	N S

		Height	Width	Climatic zones	Soil types				full sun	filtered sun	coastal regions	frosty regions	bird attracting
					moist, well drained	wet	dry	dry limy					
Eucalyptus mannifera ssp. *maculosa*	Small to medium tree, powdery bark, grey-green foliage, cream flowers summer–autumn. This subspecies is common in Canberra.	8–14m	5–10m	Temp S.tr	•				•	•			H
Eucalyptus marginata Jarrah	Mallee to tall spreading tree, fibrous bark, dark lanceolate leaves, cream flowers spring–summer. Best known for its beautiful deep red timber.	3–40m	2–25m	Temp	•		•		•	•			L
Eucalyptus megacarpa Bullich	Mallee or tall tree, smooth cream bark, broad leaves, cream flowers in spring, decorative capsules.	3–25m	3–18m	Temp S.tr	•	•			•	•	2		
Eucalyptus megacornuta Warty Yate	Tall shrub or spreading tree, smooth bark, lanceolate foliage, long warty horn-like buds, large yellow-green flowers winter–spring, bell-shaped capsules.	5–13m	5–12m	W.te Arid S.ar	•		•	•	•	•	2		L
Eucalyptus melanophloia Silver-leaved Ironbark	Medium to large tree, black deeply ridged bark, striking crown of silver foliage, white flowers spring–summer. Excellent rural shade tree.	8–20m	5–12m	W.te S.ar	•		•		•	•			H
Eucalyptus melliodora Yellow Box	Small to large tree; rough lower bark, smooth above; blue-grey foliage, cream flowers (occasionally pink) spring–summer–autumn. Excellent honey tree.	6–30m	4–25m	Temp S.tr	•		•		•	•			H
Eucalyptus microcarpa Grey Box	Medium to tall tree, tessellated grey bark, narrow grey-green foliage, white flowers autumn–winter–spring. Excellent honey and rural shade tree.	8–20m	6–15m	W.te S.ar	•		•		•	•			H
Eucalyptus microcorys Tallow Wood	Large tree, red-brown fibrous bark, dark foliage, cream flowers winter–spring–summer. Important timber tree; handsome in northern parklands.	20–40m	10–15m	W.te Trop S.tr	•		•		•	•			L
Eucalyptus microtheca Coolibah	Medium to large, often sprawling tree; dark grey fibrous bark, smooth white upper branches; grey-green foliage, white flowers summer–autumn.	10–20m	8–15m	W.te Arid S.ar	•	•	•	•	•	•			H
Eucalyptus miniata Darwin Woollybutt	Medium to large tree; black lower bark, white above; lanceolate foliage, glaucous ribbed buds, vivid orange flowers winter–spring, large ribbed capsules.	15–25m	10–20m	Trop	•		•		•	•			
Eucalyptus moluccana Grey Box	Medium to tall tree; pale grey tessellated lower bark, upper branches smooth; lanceolate foliage, white flowers summer–autumn. Rural shelter tree.	15–25m	10–20m	S.tr W.te	•		•		•	•			H
Eucalyptus moorei Little Sallee	Medium shrub or small tree, smooth grey-white bark, narrow dark foliage, white flowers in summer. Useful small landscape tree.	3–6m	1–4m	Temp	•	•			•	•			H

Temp — temperate
W. te — warm temperate
Trop — tropical
S. tr — sub-tropical
S. ar — semi-arid

L — light
H — heavy
N — nectar-feeding
S — seed-eating
F — fruit-eating

							Height	Width		Soil types								

Legend:
-) — temperate
- — warm temperate
- — tropical
- — sub-tropical
- — semi-arid
- L — light
- H — heavy
- N — nectar-feeding
- S — seed-eating
- F — fruit-eating

Species	Description	Height	Width	Climatic zones	moist, well drained	wet	dry	dry limy	full sun	filtered sun	coastal regions	frosty regions	bird attraction
…lyptus caulis ...stick Mallee	Tall mallee or small tree, smooth grey bark; pale grey foliage, plum new growth; glaucous buds, cream flowers in winter. Beautiful small landscape tree.	3–10m	3–8m	Temp S.tr	•				•	•	2	L	N S
…lyptus nicholii ...w Peppermint	Medium tree, yellow-brown fibrous bark, peppermint-scented fine blue-grey foliage, white flowers summer–autumn. Fast-growing shade tree.	12–16m	5–12m	Temp S.tr	•		•		•	•		H	N S
…lyptus nutans ...ding Gum	Mallee shrub, smooth grey bark, glossy dark foliage, profuse clusters of red or creamy yellow flowers in spring. Decorative small species.	2.5–4m	3–5m	W.te Arid S.ar	•		•	•	•	•		L	N S
…lyptus obliqua ...smate ...ngybark	Small to large tree, brown fibrous bark, glossy broad foliage, cream flowers summer–autumn. Useful rural and honey tree.	7–50m	6–30m	Temp S.tr	•		•		•	•		H	N S
…lyptus …dentalis ...mp Yate	Medium to tall upright tree; dark rough lower bark, smooth white above; lanceolate foliage; bright creamy yellow flowers autumn–winter, attractive to honeyeaters.	8–20m	5–10m	W.te S.ar Arid	•	•	•	•	•	•	2	L	N S
…lyptus …ophloia ...nyah	Medium to tall tree; dark bark on trunk, lower branches; smooth creamy upper branches; narrow foliage, cream flowers winter–spring–summer. Shade tree.	15–20m	5–15m	W.te S.ar	•		•		•	•		L	N S
…lyptus oldfieldii	Mallee or small tree, smooth grey-brown bark, grey-green foliage, creamy yellow flowers in spring. Attractive and drought tolerant.	3–8m	4–8m	W.te Arid S.ar	•		•		•	•		L	N S
…lyptus oleosa	Tall mallee or medium tree; rough lower bark, smooth upper limbs; narrow glossy foliage, profuse pale yellow-green flowers spring–summer.	5–12m	4–8m	W.te Arid S.ar	•		•	•	•	•		L	N S
…lyptus orbifolia ...nd-leaf Mallee	Small to medium mallee shrub, smooth curling red-brown bark, round silvery grey leaves, bright yellow flowers winter–spring. Decorative and drought tolerant.	2.5–6m	3–8m	W.te Arid S.ar	•		•		•	•		L	N S
…lyptus …dophila	Medium tree; fibrous grey lower bark, smooth and pale above; dense lanceolate foliage, white flowers autumn–winter–spring. Shade and shelter tree.	10–15m	5–12m	W.te S.tr	•		•		•	•		L	N S
…lyptus ovata ...mp Gum	Medium to large tree, smooth grey-white bark above rough base, wavy dark shiny foliage, cream flowers autumn–winter. Excellent in poorly drained soils.	8–30m	5–20m	Temp S.tr	•	•			•	•	2	H	N S
…lyptus …yphylla ...budded Mallee	Mallee shrub, smooth grey bark, leathery grey foliage, distinctive red ribbed buds; creamy yellow flowers winter–spring, followed by decorative capsules.	1–5m	2–6m	W.te Arid S.ar	•		•		•	•		L	N S

Temp — temperate
W. te — warm temperate
Trop — tropical
S. tr — sub-tropical
S. ar — semi-arid

L — light
H — heavy
N — nectar-feeding
S — seed-eating
F — fruit-eating

		Height	Width	Climatic zones	moist, well drained	wet	dry	dry limy	full sun	filtered sun	coastal regions	frosty regions
Eucalyptus papuana Ghost Gum	Medium to large tree, powdery white trunk and limbs, bright green foliage, white flowers spring–summer. Striking, graceful tree of inland Australia.	8–20m	8–15m	Trop S. tr Arid S. ar	●		●		●			L
Eucalyptus pauciflora Snow Gum	Small to large tree, smooth colourful bark, gleaming blue-grey foliage, cream flowers spring–summer. Beautiful and very adaptable.	6–20m	6–15m	Temp S. tr	●				●	●		H
Eucalyptus pauciflora 'Pendula'	Weeping medium tree, long pendulous powdery branches, grey leaves, cream flowers spring–summer. Graceful and hardy.	6–10m	4–8m	Temp S. tr	●				●	●		H
Eucalyptus peltata Rusty Jacket	Small to medium tree, shiny tessellated yellow to brown bark, peltate foliage, white flowers summer–autumn. Ornamental.	6–12m	3–8m	W. te S. tr S. ar	●		●		●	●		L
Eucalyptus perriniana Spinning Gum	Mallee or small tree, smooth bark; silvery round juvenile leaves drying as spinning circles, lanceolate mature foliage; cream flowers in summer.	4–10m	4–10m	Temp S. tr	●				●	●		H
Eucalyptus phoenicea Scarlet Gum	Small to medium tree, scaly fibrous gold bark, shiny foliage, vivid orange flower clusters winter–spring. Magnificent tree for tropical gardens.	6–12m	3–10m	W. te Trop S. tr	●		●		●			
Eucalyptus pilligaensis Pilliga Grey Box	Medium tree, grey tessellated bark, narrow leaves, white flowers winter–spring. Attractive rural shade and shelter tree.	12–15m	6–12m	W. te S. ar	●				●	●		H
Eucalyptus pilularis Blackbutt	Tall tree; fibrous bark on trunk, smooth cream upper limbs; lanceolate foliage, white flowers spring–summer. Handsome; valuable timber tree.	24–40m	8–15m	W. te S. tr	●				●	●	2	L
Eucalyptus platypus Round-leaved Moort	Dense mallee or large shrub, smooth bark, thick glossy foliage to ground level, creamy yellow flowers spring–summer.	4–8m	4–8m	W. te S. ar	●		●		●	●	2	H
Eucalyptus platypus var. *heterophylla*	Similar to the above, but with narrow foliage. Both are ornamental, and excellent shelter-belt trees.	4–8m	4–8m	W. te S. ar	●		●	●	●	●	2	H
Eucalyptus plenissima Oil Mallee	Mallee to medium tree; dark flaky bark on trunk, smooth above; narrow foliage with high oil content, cream flowers in summer. Useful for windbreaks.	4–10m	4–10m	W. te Arid S. ar	●		●	●	●	●		H
Eucalyptus polyanthemos Red Box	Medium to large tree, grey bark, dense crown of rounded grey leaves, massed cream flowers mainly spring. Beautiful parkland tree; noted for honey production.	10–25m	5–15m	Temp S. tr	●		●		●	●		H

		Height	Width	Climatic zones	Soil types								bird attraction
					moist, well drained	wet	dry	dry limy	full sun	filtered sun	coastal regions	frosty regions	

Legend:

p — temperate	L — light
e — warm temperate	H — heavy
— tropical	N — nectar-feeding
— sub-tropical	S — seed-eating
— semi-arid	F — fruit-eating

Name	Description	Height	Width	Climatic zones	moist, well drained	wet	dry	dry limy	full sun	filtered sun	coastal regions	frosty regions	bird attraction
lyptus bractea Mallee	Mallee or small tree, narrow blue-grey foliage, cream flowers summer–autumn–winter. Used for eucalyptus oil extraction.	4–10m	4–6m	Temp S. ar	•		•		•	•		H	N S
alyptus ulnea ar Box	Medium to large tree, flaky grey bark, dense glossy leaves, cream flowers in bundles summer–autumn. Excellent shade and shelter tree.	10–20m	5–12m	W. te S. ar	•		•		•	•		H	N S
alyptus ssiana fruited Mallee	Spreading mallee shrub, smooth bark, broad leathery grey leaves, red-capped buds, clusters of vivid yellow flowers winter–spring, attractive bell-shaped capsules.	1.5–5m	3–10m	Temp S. ar	•		•		•	•	2	L	N S
alyptus hocarpa mp Bloodwood	Small to large tree, rough bark, broad leathery leaves; showy pink, red, apricot or white flowers mainly autumn and spring, decorative capsules. Striking.	8–15m	3–10m	W. te Trop S. tr	•	•			•	•			N S
alyptus pulchella	Medium to large upright tree, smooth grey-white bark, narrow dark foliage, white flowers summer–autumn. Particularly attractive street tree.	9–20m	6–12m	Temp S. tr					•	•		L	N S
alyptus verulenta er-leaved ountain Gum	Small to medium tree, crooked smooth trunk, round silver juvenile foliage generally covering tree, white flowers in spring. Excellent for cut foliage.	6–10m	2–5m	Temp	•		•		•	•		H	N S
alyptus formis r-fruited Mallee	Spreading shrub or small tree, thick lanceolate foliage, large ribbed buds, showy cream to pink-red flowers winter–spring, decorative capsules.	2–5m	3–5m	W. te Arid S. ar	•		•		•			L	N S
alyptus radiata row-leaved ppermint	Medium to large tree, rough brown bark on most of tree, strongly peppermint-scented foliage, white flowers spring–summer. Rural shade tree.	10–30m	6–20m	Temp S. ar	•		•		•	•		H	N S
alyptus dantha e Mallee	Spreading mallee shrub, smooth grey-brown bark, powdery glaucous broad foliage, silver buds, large pink-red flowers most of year, decorative capsules.	2.5–4m	3–6m	W. te S. ar			•		•			L	N S
alyptus risdonii don Peppermint	Mallee to medium tree, trunk sometimes twisted, smooth bark; silver stem-clasping juvenile foliage, mature foliage rare; cream flowers in spring.	3–20m	5–10m	Temp	•				•	•	1	L	N S
alyptus robusta amp Mahogany	Tall straight tree, fibrous brown bark, broad glossy leaves, clusters of conspicuous cream flowers most of the year. Useful parkland tree.	20–25m	10–20m	W. te S. tr	•	•			•	•	1		N S
alyptus rossii ibbly Gum	Medium to large tree, smooth scribbled bark, lanceolate leaves, white flowers in summer. Common in Canberra's National Botanic Gardens.	15–20m	8–15m	Temp S. ar	•				•	•		H	N S

	Height	Width	Climatic zones	Soil types							
				moist, well drained	wet	dry	dry limy	full sun	filtered sun	coastal regions	frosty regions
Eucalyptus rubida Candlebark	15–30m	10–20m	Temp S.tr	•		•		•	•		H
Eucalyptus rugosa Kingscote Mallee	3–10m	4–10m	W.te S.ar	•		•	•	•	•	1	L
Eucalyptus rupicola Cliff Mallee Ash	1–5m	2–4m	Temp	•				•	•		H
Eucalyptus saligna Sydney Blue Gum	20–45m	10–25m	Temp S.tr	•				•	•	2	
Eucalyptus salmonophloia Salmon Gum	10–30m	8–20m	W.te Arid S.ar	•		•		•	•		H
Eucalyptus salubris Gimlet Gum	6–20m	5–10m	W.te Arid S.ar	•		•	•	•	•		H
Eucalyptus sargentii Salt River Mallet	6–12m	5–8m	W.te S.ar	•		•	•	•			L
Eucalyptus scoparia Wallangarra White Gum	8–12m	5–10m	Temp S.tr	•				•	•		L
Eucalyptus sepulcralis Blue Weeping Gum	3–6m	1–3m	Temp S.ar	•				•	•		
Eucalyptus sessilis Finke River Mallee	2–4m	2–5m	W.te Arid S.ar	•		•		•			H
Eucalyptus setosa Rough-leaved Bloodwood	5–10m	3–6m	Trop S.tr	•		•		•			
Eucalyptus shirleyi	7–12m	3–6m	W.te Trop S.tr	•		•		•	•		H

Legend:
- Temp — temperate
- W.te — warm temperate
- Trop — tropical
- S.tr — sub-tropical
- S.ar — semi-arid
- L — light
- H — heavy
- N — nectar-feeding
- S — seed-eating
- F — fruit-eating

Descriptions:

Eucalyptus rubida Candlebark: Medium to tall tree; colourful smooth bark, often brilliant red in summer; blue-grey foliage, cream flowers summer–autumn. Lovely broad landscape tree.

Eucalyptus rugosa Kingscote Mallee: Mallee or small tree, smooth grey bark, thick grey-green foliage, cream flowers in summer. Excellent coastal windbreak.

Eucalyptus rupicola Cliff Mallee Ash: Small to medium mallee shrub, smooth pale brown bark, narrow glossy foliage, cream flowers autumn–winter. Attractive for the small landscape.

Eucalyptus saligna Sydney Blue Gum: Tall stately tree, powdery white-grey bark, broad leaves, profuse white flowers summer–autumn. Handsome, fast-growing parkland tree.

Eucalyptus salmonophloia Salmon Gum: Medium to tall tree, smooth gleaming pale to deep brown bark, glossy foliage, small white flowers spring–summer–autumn. Very beautiful trunk.

Eucalyptus salubris Gimlet Gum: Small to tall tree, fluted trunk, shiny smooth coppery bark, narrow glossy leaves, cream flowers spring–summer–autumn. Very striking.

Eucalyptus sargentii Salt River Mallet: Small tree; dark rough-barked trunk, smooth upper branches; narrow foliage, massed cream flowers in spring. Valued for its salt tolerance.

Eucalyptus scoparia Wallangarra White Gum: Medium tree, smooth white bark, narrow dark foliage, white flowers spring–summer. Beautiful landscape tree, graceful and hardy.

Eucalyptus sepulcralis Blue Weeping Gum: Slender mallee, fine powdery pendulous branches, sparse foliage, creamy yellow flowers spring–summer, attractive capsules. Plant of rare beauty.

Eucalyptus sessilis Finke River Mallee: Small mallee; flaky lower bark, smooth above; thick foliage, ribbed buds, cream flowers winter–spring–summer, bunched ribbed capsules.

Eucalyptus setosa Rough-leaved Bloodwood: Medium shrub or small crooked tree, bristly leaves, hairy pear-shaped buds; large white, pink or apricot flowers spring–summer, round capsules. Ornamental.

Eucalyptus shirleyi: Small to medium crooked tree, dark fissured bark, broad rounded silver foliage on weeping branches, creamy yellow flowers spring and autumn.

np — temperate   L — light
te — warm temperate   H — heavy
p — tropical   N — nectar-feeding
r — sub-tropical   S — seed-eating
r — semi-arid   F — fruit-eating

Species	Description	Height	Width	Climatic zones	moist, well drained	wet	dry	dry limy	full sun	filtered sun	coastal regions	frosty regions	soil	bird attraction
alyptus eroxylon rosea, d Ironbark	Medium to tall tree, black deeply furrowed bark, blue-grey foliage, cream to deep pink flowers winter–spring. Striking broad landscape tree for dry areas.	10–30m	8–20m	Temp S.ar	•		•		•	•		2	H	N S
calyptus socialis	Mallee or slender tree, smooth grey-brown bark, lanceolate grey-green foliage, profuse cream flowers spring–summer. Adaptable and hardy.	2–10m	2.5–10m	W.te S.ar	•		•	•	•	•		2	H	N S
calyptus thulata amp Mallet	Small spreading tree, smooth pale brown bark, narrow blue-grey foliage, cream flowers winter–spring–summer. Adaptable, attractive, salt tolerant.	6–10m	6–8m	Temp S.tr S.ar	•	•	•		•	•			H	N S
calyptus thulata . grandiflora	Mallee form of the above; dense fine foliage, massed flowering, larger capsules. Not salt tolerant.	3–5m	4–6m	Temp S.tr S.ar	•	•	•		•	•			H	N S
calyptus igerana non-scented onbark	Medium to large tree, dark deeply fissured bark, lemon-scented pale foliage, white to pale pink flowers summer–autumn–winter.	10–20m	5–10m	Trop S.tr	•				•					N S
calyptus edmanii	Medium shrub or small tree, smooth shiny bark, dark foliage, winged buds, creamy yellow flowers (occasionally pink) in summer, winged capsules.	4–10m	3–10m	W.te S.ar	•		•		•	•			L	N S
calyptus stellulata ck Sallee	Small compact spreading tree, smooth green upper bark, dense leathery foliage, conspicuous cream flowers winter–spring. Excellent cold climate tree.	6–10m	5–10m	Temp	•	•			•	•		2	H	N S
calyptus wardii	Mallee or small tree, smooth pinkish grey bark, bright glossy foliage, long ribbed buds, creamy yellow flowers winter–spring, large ribbed capsules.	3–8m	4–6m	W.te S.ar	•		•	•	•				H	N S
calyptus cklandii	Small to medium tree; rough bark at base, smooth above; grey-green foliage, bright yellow flowers spring–summer–autumn. Useful and attractive.	6–10m	5–8m	W.Te Arid S.ar	•		•	•	•	•			H	N S
calyptus uiramis ver Peppermint	Small to large tree, smooth pale bark, broad glaucous to green foliage, white flowers spring–summer. Very attractive cold climate tree.	8–25m	6–20m	Temp	•				•	•			H	N S
calyptus eticornis est Red Gum	Tall spreading tree, white to grey patchy bark, bright green foliage, cream flowers winter–spring. Attractive, hardy rural landscape tree.	20–30m	10–20m	Temp Trop S.tr	•		•		•	•		2	H	N S
calyptus sellaris rbeen	Medium to tall tree; dark tessellated bark stocking, white above; grey-green foliage, cream flowers spring–summer–autumn. Striking.	10–25m	8–15m	W.te S.tr	•		•		•	•		2	L	N S

		Height	Width	Climatic zones	Soil types							
	Temp — temperate W. te — warm temperate Trop — tropical S. tr — sub-tropical S. ar — semi-arid L — light H — heavy N — nectar-feeding S — seed-eating F — fruit-eating				moist, well drained	wet	dry	dry limy	full sun	filtered sun	coastal regions	frosty regions
Eucalyptus tetragona Tallerack	Spreading mallee shrub, smooth grey bark, large silver leaves, silver buds, creamy flowers spring–summer, attractive capsules. Very decorative.	2.5–8m	3–8m	W. te S. ar	•		•		•		2	
Eucalyptus tetraptera Four-winged Mallee	Sprawling open shrub, smooth bark, thick grey-green leathery leaves, bright red buds, yellow flowers in spring, large woody 4-winged capsules. Decorative.	2–4m	3–5m	W. te S. ar	•		•	•	•		2	
Eucalyptus todtiana Pricklybark	Mallee to medium compact tree, fibrous prickly grey-brown bark, bright green lanceolate foliage, profuse cream flowers in summer. Shade and shelter tree.	5–15m	6–10m	W. te S. ar	•		•		•		2	
Eucalyptus torelliana Cadaghi	Medium to tall tree; tessellated dark bark on lower trunk, smooth green above; dense bright green ovate foliage, profuse white flowers spring–summer.	15–30m	5–12m	Trop S. tr	•				•	•		
Eucalyptus torquata Coral Gum	Small to medium tree, fibrous bark, grey foliage, decorative ribbed buds; clusters of cream, pink or red flowers spring–summer; distinctive capsules.	5–10m	4–8m	W. te S. ar	•		•	•	•	•		L
Eucalyptus 'Torwood'	Hybrid between *E. torquata* and *E. woodwardii*. Small tree, grey-blue foliage, glaucous buds, golden or red flowers spring–summer. Attractive but unstable.	5–8m	3–6m	W. te S. ar	•		•		•			L
Eucalyptus urnigera	Small to large tree, smooth grey bark, silvery grey foliage, glaucous buds, white flowers summer–autumn, glaucous capsules. Very pretty.	6–40m	6–20m	Temp	•				•	•		H
Eucalyptus vernicosa Varnished Gum	Small shrub or small tree, smooth grey bark, shiny crowded foliage, small cream flowers in summer. Seed germinates poorly, plants difficult to obtain.	1–6m	2–8m	Temp	•				•	•		H
Eucalyptus viminalis Manna Gum	Medium to tall tree, grey-white bark often peeling in long ribbons, dark lanceolate foliage, cream flowers summer–autumn. Graceful, rural landscape tree.	10–50m	8–15m	Temp S. tr	•	•			•	•	2	H
Eucalyptus viridis Green Mallee	Mallee or small tree, smooth grey bark, fine dark foliage, small white flowers spring–summer. Attractive and adaptable.	5–12m	3–6m	Temp S. ar	•		•		•	•		H
Eucalyptus wandoo Wandoo	Small to tall tree, mottled creamy white bark, grey-green foliage, cream flowers spring–summer–autumn. Very attractive in large gardens or parklands.	8–30m	6–20m	W. te S. ar	•		•	•	•	•		L
Eucalyptus websteriana	Medium to large spreading shrub, curling dark red-brown bark, rounded silvery grey foliage, creamy yellow flowers winter–spring, silvery capsules.	3–6m	3–6m	W. te S. ar	•		•		•			L

mp — temperate	L — light
te — warm temperate	H — heavy
ap — tropical	N — nectar-feeding
r — sub-tropical	S — seed-eating
ar — semi-arid	F — fruit-eating

			Climatic zones	Soil types								
	Height	Width		moist, well drained	wet	dry	dry limy	full sun	filtered sun	coastal regions	frosty regions	bird attraction
alyptus willisii — Mallee or mostly medium tree, smooth grey-white bark, aromatic foliage, cream flowers spring–summer. Decorative, hardy and adaptable.	4–15m	5–10m	Temp	•		•		•	•	2	H	N S
calyptus odwardii non-flowered um — Small to medium tree, silvery bark, pendulous branches, grey foliage, glaucous buds, large bright yellow flowers winter–spring, silver bell-shaped capsules.	6–15m	3–8m	W.te Arid S.ar	•		•	•	•			H	N S
calyptus ungiana — Spreading mallee shrub, rough lower bark, smooth above; leathery foliage, large ribbed buds, showy red or yellow flowers winter–spring, attractive capsules.	4–12m	5–12m	W.te Arid S.ar	•		•		•			L	N S
ryphia lucida smanian eatherwood — Medium to tall straight tree, open crown of shiny oblong leaves, large pale pink or white flowers spring–summer. Source of the famous Leatherwood Honey.	8–20m	5–15m	Temp S.tr	•				•	•		L	N
genia wardtiana ch Cherry — Small to large bushy shrub, smooth bark, dark foliage, 4-petalled multi-stamened white flowers winter–spring–summer, edible red berries.	1–6m	50cm–2m	W.te Trop S.tr	•				•	•	1	L	F
dia elleryana — Medium to tall rainforest tree, pale fissured bark, trifoliolate leaves eaten by Ulysses Butterfly larvae, massed pink flowers summer–autumn. Fast growing.	12–20m	10–20m	W.te Trop S.tr	•				•	•		L	N
omatia laurina per Laurel — Large shrub or medium tree, corky bark, glossy coppery ovate leaves, sweetly scented white flowers spring–summer, edible fruit. Beautiful foliage.	4–10m	1–2m	Temp Trop S.tr	•				•	•		L	F
axia cuneata — Small many-branched shrub, neatly decussate foliage, showy spikes of glowing pink-red-and-orange pea flowers in spring. Regular pruning essential.	1–2m	50cm–1.5m	Temp S.tr	•		•		•	•		L	
axia microphylla — Dwarf groundcovering shrub, spiny branchlets, tiny linear leaves, yellow-and-red pea flowers in spring. Tolerant of dry periods. Container plant.	prostrate–30cm	50cm–1.5m	Temp S.ar	•		•		•	•		L	
axia obovata — Small to medium compact shrub, crowded decussate foliage, yellow-and-red pea flowers spring–summer. Ideal low screen. Prune regularly.	1–2.5m	1.5–3m	Temp S.tr	•		•		•	•	2	L	
adaya splendida — Climbing rainforest plant, shiny dark foliage, clusters of highly perfumed white flowers spring–summer.	climber	vigorous	Trop S.tr	•					•			
us benjamina eping Fig — Small to medium dense weeping tree, shiny leathery leaves, fleshy red receptacles (fruit) winter–spring–summer. Attractive indoor plant.	8–15m	5–15m	W.te Trop S.tr	•					•		L	F

		Height	Width	Climatic zones	Soil types				full sun	filtered sun	coastal regions	frosty regions
	Temp — temperate / W. te — warm temperate / Trop — tropical / S. tr — sub-tropical / S. ar — semi-arid	L — light / H — heavy / N — nectar-feeding / S — seed-eating / F — fruit-eating			moist, well drained	wet	dry	dry limy				
Ficus rubiginosa Port Jackson Fig	Medium to large bushy tree, dark leaves hairy beneath, fleshy yellowish receptacles (fruit) autumn–winter–spring. Variegated form also grown.	10–20m	10–20m	Temp Trop S. tr	•					•		L
Flindersia australis	Medium to large rainforest tree, pinnate foliage, cream flowers in panicles spring–summer, decorative open woody seed capsules. Valuable timber tree.	10–20m	4–12m	Temp Trop S. tr	•	•			•	•		L
Frankenia pauciflora	Dwarf matting plant, small grey foliage, massed pink flowers spring–summer. Several forms. Salt tolerant, hardy, attractive. Light pruning recommended.	prostrate–30cm	50cm–1.2m	Temp Arid S. ar	•		•	•	•		1	H
Gastrolobium truncatum	Compact matting plant, notched rounded foliage, yellow-and-red pea flowers spring–early summer. Container or basket plant. Tip prune lightly.	prostrate	50–90cm	Temp S. ar	•		•		•	•		L
Geijera salicifolia	Medium to large tree, willow-like leaves, loose panicles of creamy white flowers spring–early summer. Slow growing, useful and attractive shade tree.	12–20m	6–12m	W. te S. tr S. ar	•		•	•	•	•		H
Geissois benthamii Red Carabeen	Medium to large rainforest tree; handsome trifoliolate leaves, brilliant red new growth; yellow flowers in summer. Beautiful indoor tub specimen.	10–18m	5–12m	W. te Trop S. tr	•					•		
Glischrocaryon behrii	Herbaceous small plant, fine stems, small foliage, massed clusters of yellow or occasionally orange flowers spring–early summer.	30–80cm	30–45cm	Temp S. ar	•		•	•	•		2	L
Gompholobium ecostatum	Dwarf to small shrub, fine grey leaves, large cream-and-yellow or coral-and-yellow pea flowers spring–summer. Container plant.	10–45cm	20–40cm	Temp S. tr	•		•	•	•	•		L
Gompholobium grandiflorum	Small to medium upright shrub, trifoliolate leaves, bright creamy yellow pea flowers spring–early summer. Light tip pruning recommended after flowering.	80cm–1.5m	50cm–1m	Temp S. tr	•		•		•	•		L
Gompholobium huegelii	Dwarf to small shrub, fine foliage, large buttercup yellow pea flowers spring–summer. Container plant. Tip prune after flowering.	50cm–1m	50cm–1m	Temp S. tr	•		•		•	•		L
Goodenia amplexans	Dwarf to small upright shrub, stem-clasping leaves, bright yellow flowers spring–summer. Prune regularly to promote bushy growth.	40cm–1m	30–90cm	Temp Arid S. ar	•		•	•	•			L
Goodenia hederacea var. *alpestris*	Layering carpeting plant, shiny rounded leaves, yellow to orange-yellow flowers late spring–summer. Container plant. Light tip pruning recommended.	prostrate	1–2m	Temp S. tr	•		•		•	•		H

LEFT
Trees retained on rural land provide shade relief for stock, stability for soil, resting and feeding places for numerous birds, and a reminder of the wonderful bushland we have inherited. This particular group is *Eucalyptus papuana* (*Corymbia paracolpica*), a handsome tree of Central Australia.

BELOW:
'Australflora Euky Dwarf'

A selected small form of *Eucalyptus leucoxylon* suitable for private gardens, streetscapes and parklands in a wide range of climates and soils. The upper trunk and branches are white, and the fine dense foliage is massed with colour from late autumn to early summer.

Eucalypts are a major element of the natural landscape. *Eucalyptus dives*, one of the peppermints, is a small, lightly barked tree with blue-grey foliage, and large sprays of cream flowers in winter and spring. It is the perfect size for small gardens, where it provides copious nectar for insect and honey-eating birds.

These two forms of *Pandorea jasminoides* not only have exotically different flowers, but contrast in growth habits. 'Southern Belle' (pink) is shrubby with an occasional climbing tendril, and 'Lady Di' is an elegant climber, beautifying verandas, pergolas and walls. What a combination they make when planted together.

		Height	Width	Climatic zones	Soil types				full sun	filtered sun	coastal regions	frosty regions	bird attraction
					moist, well drained	wet	dry	dry limy					

Legend:

np — temperate
te — warm temperate
p — tropical
r — sub-tropical
r — semi-arid

L — light
H — heavy
N — nectar-feeding
S — seed-eating
F — fruit-eating

Plant	Description	Height	Width	Climatic zones	moist, well drained	wet	dry	dry limy	full sun	filtered sun	coastal regions	frosty regions	bird attraction
odenia humilis	Dwarf suckering tufted plant, linear to ovate leaves, panicles of yellow or cream flowers late spring–summer–autumn. Container or bog margin plant.	10–20cm	10–20cm	Temp S.tr	•	•			•	•		L	
odenia lanata	Trailing carpeting plant which layers; glossy flat leaves, bright yellow flowers spring–summer. Suitable for rockery or container. Prune lightly.	prostrate	60cm–1m	Temp S.tr	•				•	•		L	
odenia varia	Dwarf suckering shrub, toothed foliage, long-stalked yellow flowers spring–summer. Container or basket plant. Prune lightly.	10–60cm	50cm–1m	Temp S.ar	•		•	•	•	•		L	
odenia vernicosa	Small rounded shrub, stiff shiny toothed leaves, sticky new growth; yellow flowers spring–summer and sporadic. Prune after flowering.	60cm–1m	80cm–1m	Temp S.ar	•		•		•	•		L	
dia lotifolia	Open medium shrub, round grey trifoliolate leaves, sprays of perfumed creamy yellow pea flowers in spring. Prune to encourage bushiness.	1.5–2.5m	2–2.5m	Temp Trop S.tr	•				•	•		L	
sypium tianum t's Desert Rose	Medium shrub, smooth blue-grey rounded foliage, pink to lilac hibiscus-like flowers with red centres most of the year. Prune lightly.	90cm–2m	90cm–1.2m	S.tr Arid S.ar	•		•		•				N
otophyllum elsum	Small erect shrub, shiny obovate foliage, brilliant waxy crimson flowers in summer. Regular pruning recommended.	1–3m	1.5–2m	Trop S.tr S.ar	•				•	•		L	N
otophyllum igerum	Small compact shrub, shiny foliage, white flowers along the stems most of the year. Light pruning recommended.	80cm–1m	60cm–1m	Trop S.tr					•	•		L	N
villea thifolia	Low spreading arching rigid shrub, prickly lobed foliage, pink toothbrush flowers winter–spring–early summer. Suited to poorly drained sites. Prune.	60cm–1.5m	1.5–3m	Temp Trop S.tr	•	•			•	•		L	N
villea alpina dfields Apricot'	Dwarf to small shrub, soft furry leaves, bunches of apricot flowers winter–spring–summer. Red, white and yellow forms. Regular pruning essential.	30–80cm	50cm–1m	Temp S.ar	•				•	•	•	L	N
villea alpina mpians low	Low arching shrub; neat, often crowded foliage; bright gold-and-red flowers late winter–spring. Rockery or container. Light pruning essential.	prostrate–20cm	30–60cm	Temp	•				•	•		L	N
villea alpina Dandenong	Small shrub, soft hairy foliage and stems, red-and-white flowers autumn–winter–spring. Light pruning essential.	80cm–1.5m	1–2m	Temp	•		•		•	•		L	N

		Height	Width	Climatic zones	Soil types moist, well drained	wet	dry	dry limy	full sun	filtered sun	coastal regions	frosty regions
Temp — temperate	L — light											
W. te — warm temperate	H — heavy											
Trop — tropical	N — nectar-feeding											
S. tr — sub-tropical	S — seed-eating											
S. ar — semi-arid	F — fruit-eating											
Grevillea alpina Mt Ida	Small dense shrub, crowded foliage, bunches of woolly red-and-yellow flowers winter–spring. Very showy. Prune after flowering.	60cm–1m	40–60cm	Temp S. ar	•		•		•	•		L
Grevillea alpina Mt Zero	Small erect narrow shrub, small grey leaves, large waxy red-and-gold flowers winter–spring–early summer. Prune lightly after flowering.	80cm–1.5m	50–80cm	Temp	•		•		•	•		L
Grevillea alpina Tooborac	Compact dwarf shrub, small hairy foliage, tight bunches of red-and-gold flowers winter–spring. Very beautiful; showy container plant. Tip prune.	30–60cm	45–75cm	Temp S. ar	•		•		•	•		L
Grevillea anethifolia	Small shrub, fine foliage, white flowers winter–spring. Tolerates extended dry periods. Prune after flowering.	80cm–1.5m	1–1.2m	Temp S. ar	•		•		•	•		L
Grevillea apiciloba	Medium shrub, finely divided foliage, unusual green-and-black toothbrush flowers autumn–winter–spring and occasionally summer. Prune lightly.	1–2m	1.2–2.2m	W. te S. ar	•		•	•	•	•		L
Grevillea aquifolium	Variable small to medium shrub, grey-green holly-like foliage, red toothbrush flowers spring–summer–autumn. Prune regularly.	30cm–2m	1–2.2m	Temp S. tr	•				•	•		H
Grevillea aquifolium prostrate	Ground-covering form of the above, usually smaller in foliage. Very useful for banks. Carpenter's Rocks (S.A.) form suited to limy soils.	prostrate–20cm	1.5–2m	Temp S. tr	•				•	•		H
Grevillea arenaria	Variable small to medium shrub, grey or grey-green velvety foliage, red or sulphur yellow flowers winter–spring–summer. Prune regularly.	1–2.5m	1.5–2m	Temp S. tr	•				•	•		L
Grevillea asparagoides	Small shrub, intricately lobed grey foliage, pendulous racemes of pink flowers spring–late summer. Prune lightly after flowering.	60–90cm	40–90cm	Temp S. ar	•		•		•	•		L
Grevillea aspera	Small shrub, stiff linear leaves, bunches of unusual red-and-green flowers winter–spring. Hardy. Tip prune after flowering.	60cm–1.2m	45cm–1m	Temp S. ar	•		•		•	•		L
Grevillea aspleniifolia	Large spreading shrub, linear grey foliage, rich burgundy toothbrush flowers spring–summer–autumn. Attractive screen. Prune regularly.	2–3m	2–3m	Temp S. ar	•				•	•		L
Grevillea 'Audrey'	Medium shrub, crowded dark foliage, red spider flowers most of the year. Hardy; excellent screen. Prune regularly.	2–2.5m	2.5–3m	Temp S. tr	•				•	•		L

	p — temperate	L — light
	e — warm temperate	H — heavy
	o — tropical	N — nectar-feeding
	— sub-tropical	S — seed-eating
	r — semi-arid	F — fruit-eating

		Height	Width	Climatic zones	Soil types				full sun	filtered sun	coastal regions	frosty regions	bird attraction
					moist, well drained	wet	dry	dry limy					
villea straflora Bon ord'	Erect medium shrub, deeply divided foliage with bronze new growth, large bunches of brilliant red flowers spring–summer. Outstanding cultivar.	1–2m	80cm–2m	Temp S. ar	•		•		•	•		L	N
villea straflora terbury Gold'	Low spreading shrub, soft linear grey foliage, bunches of gold flowers winter–spring–summer. Adaptable, hardy; useful low hedge. Prune regularly.	1–1.5m	2–3m	Temp S. tr	•				•	•	2	H	N
villea straflora Copper st'	Spreading groundcover, divided foliage with coppery bronze new growth; soft pink toothbrush flowers spring–summer, also sporadic. Prune regularly.	prostrate	2–3m	Temp S. tr	•	•			•	•		L	N
villea straflora Fanfare'	Carpeting groundcover, large deeply lobed green foliage with rich red new growth, wine red toothbrush flowers spring–summer–autumn. Tip prune.	prostrate	2–3m	Temp S. tr	•				•	•		L	N
villea straflora Jubilee'	Small upright shrub, fine foliage, waxy gold-and-red flowers winter–spring. Adaptable and hardy. Prune regularly.	80cm–1m	60–80cm	Temp S. ar	•		•		•	•		L	N
villea straflora ebird'	Small shrub, outwardly arching branches, finely divided feathery grey-green leaves, many orange toothbrush flowers autumn–winter–spring. Tip prune.	1–2m	1.5–2m	Temp S. tr	•				•	•		L	N
villea straflora Donald Park'	Compact dwarf shrub, crowded linear leaves, massed bunches of red-and-gold flowers autumn–winter–spring. Container plant. Tip prune after flowering.	30–60cm	30–60cm	Temp S. ar	•		•		•	•		L	N
villea straflora Old d'	Low mounding shrub, golden green foliage with gold new growth, coral pink flowers most of the year. Hardy and adaptable. Pruning recommended.	45–65cm	1–1.5m	Temp S. tr	•		•		•	•		H	N
villea straflora Pendent sters'	Small to medium upright shrub, fine foliage, greenish cream flowers most of the year. Particularly useful nectar plant for birds. Prune lightly.	1.5–2m	1–2m	Temp S. tr	•				•	•		L	N
villea australis	Low spreading mound, fine crowded foliage, small strongly perfumed cream flowers in summer. Hardy and adaptable. Prune after flowering.	prostrate–60cm	90cm–1.2m	Temp	•				•	•		H	N
villea banksii	Medium to large shrub, soft grey pinnate foliage, erect racemes of large red or white flowers most of the year. Pruning recommended.	2–3m	1.5–2m	W. te Trop S. tr	•					•		L	N
villea banksii strate red	Prostrate red-flowering coastal form of the above, forming an attractive dense carpet. Tip prune lightly.	prostrate	1.5m	W. te Trop S. tr	•					•	1	L	N

Temp — temperate
W. te — warm temperate
Trop — tropical
S. tr — sub-tropical
S. ar — semi-arid

L — light
H — heavy
N — nectar-feeding
S — seed-eating
F — fruit-eating

	Height	Width	Climatic zones	Soil types				full sun	filtered sun	coastal regions	frosty regions
				moist, well drained	wet	dry	dry limy				
Grevillea barklyana ssp. *barklyana* — Large shrub or medium tree; handsome, mostly lobed leaves; pink toothbrush flowers spring–early summer. Particularly useful in shady gardens.	4–10m	3–7m	Temp S. tr	•	•			•	•		L
Grevillea barklyana ssp. *macleayana* 'Jervis Bay' — Small to medium compact shrub, mostly entire leaves; deep pink toothbrush flowers spring–summer, also sporadic. Light pruning recommended.	1–2.5cm	1.5–3m	Temp S. tr	•		•		•	•	1	L
Grevillea baueri — Low dense spreading shrub, smooth foliage with bronze new growth, pink flowers winter–spring. Prune regularly.	30cm–1m	1–1.2m	Temp S. tr	•		•		•	•		L
Grevillea bedggoodiana — Spreading groundcover, dense holly-like leaves, pink-and-yellow toothbrush flowers spring–early summer. Excellent in dry shady sites. Prune lightly.	prostrate	1.5–2.5m	Temp S. ar	•		•		•	•		L
Grevillea bipinnatifida — Small compact shrub, deeply divided stiff large leaves, bunches of orange-red flowers most of the year. Exceptional bird-attracting plant. Prune.	80cm–1.2m	1–1.5m	Temp S. tr	•		•		•	•		L
Grevillea 'Bonnie Prince Charlie' — Compact dwarf shrub, crowded linear leaves, bunches of waxy vivid gold-and-red flowers spring–summer. Container plant. Prune after flowering.	40–60cm	80cm–1m	Temp S. ar	•		•		•	•		L
Grevillea 'Boondooma' — Large upright shrub, finely divided foliage, beautiful large bunches of lemon yellow flowers most of the year. Prune regularly.	3–4m	1.5–2m	W. te Trop S. tr	•				•	•		L
Grevillea 'Boongala Spinebill' — Small compact shrub, divided foliage, red toothbrush flowers autumn–winter–spring and occasionally summer. Regular pruning essential.	60cm–1m	1–1.5m	Temp S. tr	•				•	•		L
Grevillea brachystylis — Dwarf to small shrub, linear foliage, bright crimson flowers with dark blue styles spring–summer. Container plant. Tip pruning essential.	10cm–1m	45–65cm	Temp S. tr	•	•			•	•		L
Grevillea bracteosa — Small to medium open shrub, fine narrow foliage, rounded golf-ball size pink flowers in spring. Very attractive. Light pruning recommended.	1.5–2.5m	1.5–2m	Temp S. ar	•		•	•	•			L
Grevillea 'Bronze Rambler' — Spreading groundcover, divided net-like bronze-and-green foliage, burgundy-pink toothbrush flowers in spring, also sporadic. Pruning recommended.	prostrate	2–4m	Temp S. tr	•				•	•		L
Grevillea 'Bush Carpet' — Spreading groundcover, pink-tipped foliage, cherry red toothbrush flowers mainly in spring, also sporadic. Light pruning recommended.	prostrate	2–3m	Temp S. tr	•				•	•		L

				Soil types								
	Height	Width	Climatic zones	moist, well drained	wet	dry	dry limy	full sun	filtered sun	coastal regions	frosty regions	bird attraction

Legend:
- p — temperate
- e — warm temperate
- — tropical
- — sub-tropical
- — semi-arid
- L — light
- H — heavy
- N — nectar-feeding
- S — seed-eating
- F — fruit-eating

		Height	Width	Climatic zones	moist, well drained	wet	dry	dry limy	full sun	filtered sun	coastal regions	frosty regions	bird attraction
illea buxifolia	Small upright shrub, grey-green linear leaves, silver grey spider flowers winter–spring–summer. Good screening plant. Tip prune to encourage bushiness.	80cm–1.5m	1–2m	Temp S.tr	•				•	•		L	N
illea caleyii	Arching open medium shrub, deeply divided soft foliage, burgundy-pink toothbrush flowers winter–spring. Light pruning recommended.	2–2.5m	2–3m	Temp S.tr	•		•		•	•		L	N
illea berra Gem'	Dense rounded medium shrub, dense needle foliage, clusters of pink flowers spring–summer and occasionally winter. Good screening plant. Prune regularly.	2–2.5m	2–3m	Temp S.tr	•		•		•	•		H	N
illea delabroides	Medium to large upright shrub, fine foliage, candle-like racemes of creamy white flowers spring–summer. Pruning recommended after flowering.	2–4m	1.5–3m	W.te S.tr S.ar	•		•		•	•		L	N
illea sophaea	Dwarf to small shrub, blunt linear foliage, gold or red-and-gold flowers winter–spring. Suitable for dry sites. Prune after flowering.	30cm–1.2m	45cm–1.2m	Temp S.tr	•		•		•	•		L	N
illea ire Dee'	Medium to large shrub, deeply divided foliage, large bunches of red-orange flowers most of the year. Regular pruning recommended.	2.5–3.5m	3–3.5m	Temp S.tr	•				•	•		L	N
illea arview David'	Medium shrub, dense needle foliage, scarlet flowers winter–spring. Ideal for hedge and screening. Regular pruning recommended.	2–3m	2.2m–3.5m	Temp S.tr	•				•	•	2	H	N
illea arview Robin'	Medium shrub, dense grey foliage, bright red-pink flowers winter–spring. Attractive foliage contrast; useful screening and hedge plant. Prune regularly.	2–2.5m	2.5–3m	Temp S.tr S.ar	•		•		•	•		L	N
illea stal Glow'	Spreading medium shrub, attractive grey-green foliage, plentiful purple-red toothbrush flowers spring–summer. Prune to encourage bushiness.	2–3m	1.5–3m	Temp Trop S.tr	•				•	•	1	L	N
illea conut Ice'	Medium shrub, soft pinnate foliage, large pink-and-orange brushes most of the year. Attractive and showy. Prune regularly.	1–1.5m	1.5–2m	W.te Trop S.tr	•				•	•		L	N
illea concinna	Low to medium spreading shrub, soft grey linear foliage, red or orange toothbrush flowers spring–summer. Useful screen plant. Pruning recommended.	90cm–2m	1–2.5m	Temp S.tr S.ar	•		•		•	•	1	L	N
illea ertifolia	Prostrate or small shrub, crowded needle leaves, bright pink or raspberry pink flowers spring–summer. Hardy and adaptable. Prune after flowering.	prostrate–1m	40–90cm	Temp S.tr	•	•			•	•		L	N

		Height	Width	Climatic zones	Soil types — moist, well drained	wet	dry	dry limy	full sun	filtered sun	coastal regions	frosty regions
Grevillea 'Copper Rocket'	Large spreading shrub, deeply lobed green foliage with copper tips, pink toothbrush flowers spring–summer. Vigorous and hardy. Prune regularly.	2–3m	2–3.5m	Temp Trop S. tr	•				•	•		L
Grevillea crithmifolia	Groundcovering or small to medium shrub, divided grey foliage, pink-and-white brushes winter–spring. Prune regularly.	prostrate–2m	90cm–2m	Temp S. tr	•		•	•	•	•	1	L
Grevillea 'Crosbie Morrison'	Small to medium weeping shrub, fine soft grey foliage, deep red flowers winter–spring. Extremely adaptable. Regular pruning recommended.	1.5–2m	1.5–2.5m	Temp S. tr	•				•	•		L
Grevillea curviloba (syn. *G. tridentifera*)	Spreading groundcover with some upright stems; crowded bright green foliage, massed cream flowers spring–summer. Handsome. Prune regularly.	prostrate–1m	2–4m	Temp S. tr	•		•		•	•	2	H
Grevillea 'Dallachiana'	Small dense shrub, crowded grey-green leaves, red-and-cream flowers in spring. Hardy, useful screening plant. Responds to pruning.	1–2m	1–2m	Temp S. tr	•		•		•	•		L
Grevillea 'Dargan Hill'	Medium shrub, dense grey-green leaves, pink-and-red flowers winter–spring–summer. Useful for screening. Pruning recommended.	2–2.5m	2–2.5m	Temp S. tr	•				•	•		L
Grevillea deflexa	Small compact shrub, needle foliage, bright red flowers spring–summer. Useful low hedging plant. Prune lightly after flowering.	75cm–1m	80cm–90cm	W. te S. ar	•		•		•	•		L
Grevillea depauperata (syn. *G. brownii*)	Dwarf shrub or trailing plant, rounded small leaves, numerous orange-red flowers autumn–winter–spring. Container plant. Prune lightly.	10–30cm	60cm–1m	Temp S. tr	•				•	•		L
Grevillea dielsiana	Small upright open shrub, narrow divided foliage; pendent brushes of red, pink or orange flowers winter–spring. Very showy. Prune lightly.	1–1.2m	60–90cm	Temp S. tr S. ar	•		•		•	•		L
Grevillea diffusa (syn. *G. capitellata* Holdsworthy)	Compact dwarf shrub, silvery grey foliage and stems, wine red spider flowers winter–spring. Light pruning beneficial.	10–60cm	30cm–1m	Temp S. tr	•		•		•	•		L
Grevillea diffusa ssp. *evansiana*	Small shrub, dark rounded foliage, pendent bunches of wine red flowers in spring. Prune lightly after flowering.	60cm–1.2m	75cm–1.2m	Temp S. tr	•				•	•		L
Grevillea diminuta	Low spreading shrub, rounded leaves, small bunches of pendent red flowers in summer. Hardy; a useful groundcover in tough conditions. Prune regularly.	30–60cm	1.5–2m	Temp S. tr	•				•	•		H

mp — temperate
te — warm temperate
op — tropical
r — sub-tropical
ar — semi-arid

L — light
H — heavy
N — nectar-feeding
S — seed-eating
F — fruit-eating

Name	Description	Height	Width	Climatic zones	moist, well drained	wet	dry	dry limy	full sun	filtered sun	coastal regions	frosty regions	bird attraction
evillea ummondii	Small to medium shrub, soft hairy foliage, small groups of golden yellow flowers in spring. Prune lightly after flowering.	90cm–3m	1–2m	Temp S. tr	•				•	•		L	N
evillea dryandrii	Low arching shrub, grey pinnate foliage, very long racemes of pink-and-red flowers winter–spring. Very showy. Prune lightly after flowering.	prostrate–50cm	90cm–1.2m	W. te Trop S. tr S. ar	•		•		•			L	N
evillea dryophylla	Low sprawling shrub, grey holly-like foliage, compact racemes of buff or red-and-green flowers in spring. Light pruning encourages compact habit.	60cm–1m	90cm–1.2m	Temp S. tr S. ar	•		•		•	•		L	N
evillea dlicheriana	Compact rounded medium shrub, fine silver foliage, long graceful stems bearing pink-and-white flowers autumn and spring. Lovely foliage contrast. Prune.	1.5–3m	1.5–2.5m	Temp S. tr	•		•		•	•		L	N
evillea ostachya ssp. celsior	Small to large spreading shrub, woolly stems, finely divided hairy foliage, prominent racemes of bright orange flowers winter–spring–summer. Spectacular.	1.5–5m	2–4m	Arid S. ar	•		•		•			L	N
evillea elyn's Coronet'	Upright medium shrub, grey-green soft foliage, compact heads of pink-and-grey spider flowers winter–spring. Hardy, attractive. Prune after flowering.	1.5–2.5m	1.5–2m	Temp S. tr	•		•		•	•	2	L	N
evillea fasciculata	Dwarf shrub; fine grey-green, sometimes silver foliage; groups of orange-red flowers autumn–winter–spring. Prune regularly.	prostrate–60cm	60–90cm	Temp S. tr	•		•		•	•	1	L	N
evillea fistulosa	Upright medium shrub, velvety leaves, groups of bright orange flowers summer–autumn. Prune lightly to encourage bushiness.	1.5–2.5m	1.5–2m	Temp S. tr	•		•		•	•	2	L	N
evillea floribunda	Dwarf to small shrub, grey soft foliage, massed golden flowers sprinkled with brown hairs, most of the year. Very beautiful and unusual. Prune lightly.	50cm–1.2m	60cm–1.2m	W. te S. tr S. ar	•		•		•	•		L	N
evillea ipendula	Spreading groundcover, attractive lobed leaves, compact racemes of yellow-and-red or buff-and-maroon flowers in spring.	prostrate	1.5–4m	Temp S. tr	•		•		•	•		L	N
evillea formosa	Formerly G. Mt Brockman. Low spreading shrub, finely divided grey foliage, bright green buds, large racemes of orange flowers summer–autumn.	60–90cm	1.5–2.5m	W. te Trop S. tr	•		•		•	•			N
evillea mpton's Hybrid'	Large shrub, lobed foliage, pink-red toothbrush flowers spring–summer. Hardy and useful screening plant. Prune regularly.	2.5–3m	2–3m	Temp S. tr	•				•	•		L	N

		Height	Width	Climatic zones	Soil types							
					moist, well drained	wet	dry	dry limy	full sun	filtered sun	coastal regions	frosty regions

Temp — temperate
W. te — warm temperate
Trop — tropical
S. tr — sub-tropical
S. ar — semi-arid

L — light
H — heavy
N — nectar-feeding
S — seed-eating
F — fruit-eating

		Height	Width	Climatic zones	moist, well drained	wet	dry	dry limy	full sun	filtered sun	coastal regions	frosty regions
Grevillea fulgens	Open spreading medium shrub, fine slightly lobed foliage, lilac flowers in spring. Light pruning recommended.	1–2m	1–2m	Temp S. tr S. ar	•		•		•	•		L
Grevillea x gaudichaudii	Groundcovering plant, maroon-tipped lobed dark green foliage, showy burgundy toothbrush flowers spring–summer. Light tip pruning recommended.	prostrate	2–3m	Temp Trop S. tr	•				•	•		H
Grevillea glabrata	Large spreading shrub, broadly or narrowly divided foliage, lacy white flowers in most seasons. Adaptable, attractive screen. Prune regularly.	2–3m	2.5–3.5m	Temp S. tr	•				•	•	2	H
Grevillea glossadenia	Dense medium shrub, broad foliage, striking red-orange flowers in clusters winter–spring. Light pruning recommended.	1.5–2m	1–1.5m	W. te Trop S. tr	•				•	•		L
Grevillea 'Golden Lyre'	Small dense shrub, linear foliage, groups of apricot-yellow flowers winter–spring. Useful screening plant. Regular pruning recommended.	1.2–1.5m	1.2–2m	Temp S. tr	•				•	•		L
Grevillea goodii ssp. *decora*	Large, sometimes open shrub; elliptical grey leaves, many loose racemes of pink-red flowers winter–spring.	2–5m	2–4m	W. te Trop S. tr S. ar	•		•		•	•		L
Grevillea 'Grass Fire'	Spreading groundcover, deeply lobed foliage, rich red toothbrush flowers most of the year. Excellent for large areas requiring cover.	prostrate	1.5–2.5m	Temp S. tr	•				•	•		L
Grevillea 'Green Glow'	Slightly mounding groundcover, bright green lobed foliage, burgundy toothbrush flowers most of the year but peaking in spring.	15–40cm	1.5–2.2m	Temp Trop S. tr	•				•	•		L
Grevillea hilliana White Silky Oak	Tall shafting tree, pendulous undulate deeply lobed foliage, large candle-like bunches of creamy white flowers spring–summer.	8–20m	4–9m	W. te Trop S. tr	•				•	•		
Grevillea 'Honeycomb'	Large upright shrub, deeply lobed dark foliage, upright bunches of creamy yellow flowers all year. Pruning will encourage more compact habit.	3–4m	1–2m	W. te Trop S. tr	•				•	•		L
Grevillea 'Honey Gem'	Large dense shrub, finely divided foliage, golden-orange brushes all year. Pruning will encourage more compact habit.	3–5m	2–3.5m	W. te Trop S. tr	•				•	•		L
Grevillea 'Hookeriana x hybrid'	Large spreading shrub, deeply divided fern-like foliage, bright scarlet toothbrush flowers winter–spring–summer. Hardy. Regular pruning essential.	2.5–4m	2–3.5m	Temp S. tr	•		•		•	•		L

		Height	Width	Climatic zones	Soil types							frosty regions	bird attraction
					moist, well drained	wet	dry	dry limy	full sun	filtered sun	coastal regions		
..p — temperate	L — light												
e — warm temperate	H — heavy												
ɔ — tropical	N — nectar-feeding												
— sub-tropical	S — seed-eating												
ʳ — semi-arid	F — fruit-eating												
villea huegelii	Low spreading or small shrub, prickly foliage, groups of purple-pink or sulphur yellow flowers winter–spring. Light pruning beneficial.	10cm–1m	30–80cm	W. te Arid S. ar	•		•	•	•	•		L	N
villea iaspicula e Jasper	Compact medium shrub, crowded bright green foliage, plentiful pendent groups of pink flowers winter–spring. Hardy and very showy. Pruning beneficial.	1.5–2m	1–1.5m	Temp S. tr	•		•	•	•	•		H	N
villea ilicifolia	Prostrate to dwarf shrub, small holly-like leaves, squash-yellow or pink toothbrush flowers winter–spring. Prune lightly after flowering.	prostrate–60cm	1–1.5m	W. te S. tr S. ar	•		•	•	•	•		L	N
villea insignis	Spreading medium shrub, stiff holly-like foliage, groups of large waxy pink flowers in spring. Very showy. Prune after flowering.	2–3m	1.5–2m	W. te S. tr S. ar	•		•		•			L	N
villea intricata	Small to medium shrub, fine intricate densely interwoven foliage, upright candles of white flowers in spring. Very beautiful. Requires only light pruning.	1–2m	1.5–2.5m	Temp S. tr S. ar			•	•	•	•		L	N
villea involucrata	Low spreading shrub, small but deeply divided leaves, pink bracts surrounding mauve flowers winter–spring. Light pruning recommended.	20–40cm	1–2m	W. te S. tr S. ar	•				•	•		L	N
villea nhoe'	Large spreading shrub; fern-like foliage, bronze new growth; red toothbrush flowers spring–summer. Fast-growing screen. Regular pruning essential.	2–4m	2.5–4m	Temp S. tr	•				•	•		L	N
villea jephcottii	Upright medium shrub, hairy oval foliage, clusters of green flowers with red styles autumn–winter–spring. Particularly attractive to honeyeaters. Prune regularly.	1.5–3m	1–2m	Temp S. tr	•		•		•	•		L	N
villea johnsonii	Medium to large shrub, dense fine foliage, waxy pink-and-orange flowers winter–spring. Handsome, very showy screening plant. Pruning beneficial.	2–3.5m	1.5–3m	Temp S. tr	•		•		•	•		L	N
villea ly Swagman'	Matting plant, lobed leaves with pinky bronze new growth, dark red toothbrush flowers mainly in spring. Hardy and adaptable.	prostrate	2–3m	W. te S. tr	•				•	•		L	N
villea juncifolia	Medium shrub, fine foliage, brilliant orange racemes of flowers spring–summer and occasionally at other times. Prune regularly.	2–2.5m	1.5–2m	W. te Arid S. ar	•		•		•			L	N
villea juniperina	Large spreading shrub, dense needle foliage, bright red (occasionally yellow) flowers winter–spring–summer. Hardy screening plant. Prune.	2–3m	2–3m	Temp S. tr	•		•		•	•	2	H	N

		Height	Width	Climatic zones	Soil types							
					moist, well drained	wet	dry	dry limy	full sun	filtered sun	coastal regions	frosty regions

Temp — temperate L — light
W. te — warm temperate H — heavy
Trop — tropical N — nectar-feeding
S. tr — sub-tropical S — seed-eating
S. ar — semi-arid F — fruit-eating

Plant	Description	Height	Width	Climatic zones	moist, well drained	wet	dry	dry limy	full sun	filtered sun	coastal regions	frosty regions
Grevillea juniperina 'Molonglo'	Spreading groundcover, flattened crowded linear foliage, apricot flowers winter–spring–summer. Regular pruning recommended.	10–30cm	1.5–3m	Temp S. tr	•		•		•	•		H
Grevillea juniperina prostrate	Spreading groundcover, crowded needle foliage, red or sulphur yellow flowers in winter–spring–summer. Regular pruning recommended.	10–30cm	1.5–3m	Temp S. tr	•		•		•	•		H
Grevillea lanigera	Small to medium shrub, crowded woolly foliage, shell pink or pink-and-white flowers winter–spring–summer. Hardy and adaptable. Prune regularly.	1–1.5m	1–1.5m	Temp S. tr	•		•		•	•	1	L
Grevillea lanigera prostrate	Dense matting groundcover, crowded woolly foliage, showy bunches of pink flowers winter–spring–summer. Container or rockery plant. Prune lightly.	prostrate	60cm–1m	Temp S. tr	•		•		•	•	1	L
Grevillea laurifolia	Carpeting groundcover, bright green foliage with bronze new growth, maroon-red toothbrush flowers spring–summer. Light pruning beneficial.	prostrate	2–3m	Temp S. tr S. ar	•		•		•	•		L
Grevillea lavandulacea Billywing cascading	Small spreading shrub, narrow grey foliage, vivid pink flowers winter–spring–summer. Very showy container or rockery plant. Tip pruning recommended.	60–90cm	80cm–1m	Temp S. tr S. ar	•				•	•		L
Grevillea lavandulacea Billywing compact	Compact mounding dwarf shrub, grey-green linear foliage, massed glowing pink flowers winter–spring–summer. Container plant. Tip pruning recommended.	30–60cm	50–80cm	Temp S. tr S. ar	•				•	•		L
Grevillea lavandulacea Penola	Small spreading shrub, dark linear foliage, bright pink flowers winter–spring. Regular pruning recommended.	80cm–1m	1–1.5m	Temp S. tr S. ar	•		•		•	•		L
Grevillea lavandulacea Tanunda	Low spreading shrub, grey soft foliage, deep pink flowers winter–spring. Attractive colour combination, and foliage contrast. Prune regularly.	50–80cm	80cm–1.2m	Temp S. tr S. ar	•		•		•	•		H
Grevillea leptobotrys	Dwarf mounding shrub; tangled fine lobed foliage, silvery grey tinged with mauve; lacy pink flowers summer–autumn. Container plant or sand mound.	10–30cm	20–50cm	Temp S. ar	•		•		•	•		L
Grevillea leucopteris	Rounded medium shrub, deeply lobed grey foliage, large heads of perfumed cream flowers held on leafless stems above the foliage spring–summer. Dramatic.	2–2.5m	1.5–2.5m	W. te S. ar	•		•	•	•	•	2	L
Grevillea 'Lillian'	Low spreading shrub, fine foliage, groups of pendent red flowers autumn–winter. Useful low hedging plant. Regular pruning recommended.	50cm–1m	90cm–1.5m	W. te Trop S. tr	•				•	•		L

ɔ — temperate	L — light
— warm temperate	H — heavy
— tropical	N — nectar-feeding
— sub-tropical	S — seed-eating
— semi-arid	F — fruit-eating

Name	Description	Height	Width	Climatic zones	Soil types: moist, well drained	wet	dry	dry limy	full sun	filtered sun	coastal regions	frosty regions	bird attraction
illea linearifolia (G. parviflora)	Extremely variable prostrate to medium shrub; fine, often silvery foliage; perfumed white or pink flowers spring–summer. Prune lightly.	prostrate–2.5m	30cm–2m	Temp S. tr	•				•	•	2	L	N
illea longifolia	Medium to large spreading shrub, long slightly lobed dark foliage, pink-red toothbrush flowers winter–spring. Screen plant. Prune regularly.	2–4m	2–4m	Temp Trop S. tr	•				•	•	2	L	N
illea longistyla	Medium to large shrub, finely lobed dark foliage; showy waxy pink-and-red flowers winter–spring, also sporadic. Handsome and hardy. Prune regularly.	2.5–4m	2–3.5m	Temp S. tr S. ar	•		•		•	•	2	L	N
illea 'estic'	Large bushy shrub, bright green broadly lobed foliage, large cylindrical brushes of red-and-cream flowers all year. Regular pruning recommended.	3–4m	1.5–2.5m	W. te Trop S. tr	•				•	•		L	N
illea glesioides	Upright medium shrub, attractive lobed foliage, groups of creamy white flowers winter–spring. Useful screening plant. Regular pruning recommended.	2–3m	1–2.5m	W. te S. tr	•				•	•		L	N
illea ostegia	Spreading groundcover, tangled fine net foliage with red new growth, squat racemes of crimson flowers in spring. Hardy. Light pruning recommended.	30cm–1m	2–3m	Temp S. tr	•		•		•	•		L	N
illea 'ty Pink'	Bushy medium shrub, large grey-green divided foliage, spectacular cylindrical pink-and-cream flowers most of the year. Light pruning beneficial.	2–3m	2–2.5m	Temp Trop S. tr	•				•	•		L	N
illea molyneuxii	Dwarf mounding shrub, fine pointed foliage, showy clusters of crimson flowers summer–autumn. Particularly useful in moist sites. Prune lightly.	30–60cm	60–90cm	Temp S. tr	•	•			•	•		L	N
illea tiscole	Low spreading shrub, bright green holly-like leaves, crimson toothbrush flowers winter–spring. Excellent in moist shaded sites. Prune regularly.	20cm–1m	1–1.2m	Temp S. tr	•	•			•	•		L	N
illea ronulata (G. cinerea)	Variable small to medium shrub; rounded, often hairy foliage; pale green flowers winter–spring–summer. Particularly attractive to honeyeaters.	1–2.2m	1–2.5m	Temp S. tr	•				•	•	2	L	N
illea 'Kelly'	Small to medium shrub, large irregularly lobed foliage, pendent bunches of orange-red flowers all year. Very attractive landscape plant. Requires regular pruning.	1.5–2.2m	1.5–2.5m	Temp Trop S. tr	•				•	•		L	N
illea nudiflora	Low sprawling shrub, fine foliage, red-and-yellow flowers on long leafless stems winter–spring. Very graceful and unusual; suits banks and walls.	10–40cm	1–3cm	Temp S. tr	•		•		•	•		L	N

		Height	Width	Climatic zones	Soil types						coastal regions	frosty regions
					moist, well drained	wet	dry	dry limy	full sun	filtered sun		

Temp — temperate
W. te — warm temperate
Trop — tropical
S. tr — sub-tropical
S. ar — semi-arid

L — light
H — heavy
N — nectar-feeding
S — seed-eating
F — fruit-eating

Species	Description	Height	Width	Climatic zones	moist, well drained	wet	dry	dry limy	full sun	filtered sun	coastal regions	frosty regions
Grevillea obtecta	Small carpeting plant with several leaf forms, yellow or buff nectar-rich flowers spring–summer. Excellent in dry shady sites. Requires only light pruning.	prostrate–20cm	1–2m	Temp S. ar	•		•		•	•		L
Grevillea occidentalis	Small to medium upright shrub, stiff linear leaves, interesting silver-grey spider flowers most of the year. Regular pruning recommended.	1–2m	80cm–1.2m	Temp S. tr	•		•		•	•		L
Grevillea oldei	Small shrub, pointed leaves, clusters of wine red flowers winter–spring. Useful low hedging plant. Requires regular pruning.	60cm–1m	90cm–1.2m	Temp S. tr	•				•	•		L
Grevillea olivacea	Large shrub, dense silvery linear foliage, loose clusters of red or yellow spider flowers in spring. Excellent coastal windbreak. Regular pruning recommended.	2–3.5m	1.5–2.5m	Temp S. ar	•		•	•	•	•	1	L
Grevillea paniculata (syn. *G. biternata*)	Low or erect open shrub, fine foliage, white-and-pink upright cones of flowers winter–spring. Responds to regular pruning.	40cm–1.5m	60cm–1.2m	Temp S. tr S. ar	•		•		•	•		L
Grevillea pauciflora	Small compact shrub, oblanceo-late leaves, small clusters of red-and-yellow flowers winter–spring–summer. Hardy and adaptable. Prune lightly.	60cm–1m	40cm–1m	Temp S. tr S. ar	•		•	•	•	•	1	L
Grevillea petrophiloides	Small to medium shrub, finely divided foliage, pink-and-green flower spikes on long leafless branches extending from foliage late winter–spring. Spectacular.	1–3m	2–3m	W. te S. ar	•		•		•	•		L
Grevillea phanerophlebia	Low dense spreading shrub, prickly foliage, clusters of white flowers spring–early summer. Hardy and useful landscape plant. Prune regularly.	60–90cm	1–2.2m	Temp S. tr S. ar	•		•		•	•		L
Grevillea pilosa	Small arching shrub, hairy grey holly-like foliage, woolly bright pink flowers spring–summer. Very attractive. Light pruning beneficial.	60cm–1m	1–1.5m	Temp S. tr S. ar	•		•		•	•		L
Grevillea pilulifera	Dwarf to small shrub, small blunt leaves; pretty woolly white flowers tipped orange, yellow or red winter–spring. Container or rockery plant. Tip prune only.	60cm–1m	60cm–1m	Temp S. ar	•		•		•	•		L
Grevillea 'Pinkie'	Small compact shrub, fine crowded foliage, waxy pink flowers mainly winter–spring. Hardy and adaptable. Regular pruning recommended.	1–1.5m	1–1.5m	Temp Trop S. tr	•		•		•	•		H
Grevillea 'Pink Lady'	Low spreading shrub, needle foliage, shell pink flowers winter–spring–summer. Extremely hardy. Prune to control spread.	15–90cm	1.5–2m	Temp S. tr S. ar	•				•	•		L

		temperate		L — light

Top-left key:

- ıp — temperate
- e — warm temperate
- o — tropical
- — sub-tropical
- r — semi-arid

- L — light
- H — heavy
- N — nectar-feeding
- S — seed-eating
- F — fruit-eating

		Height	Width	Climatic zones	moist, well drained	wet	dry	dry limy	full sun	filtered sun	coastal regions	frosty regions	bird attraction
villea k Parfait'	Medium to large shrub, grey pinnate foliage, showy watermelon pink terminal flowers most of the year. Light pruning recommended.	2–3m	1–1.5m	Temp Trop S.tr	•				•	•		L	N
villea k Pearl'	Medium to large compact shrub, crowded needle foliage, bright pink flowers winter–spring–summer. Hedge or screen. Withstands heavy pruning.	1.5–3m	2–3m	Temp Trop S.tr S.ar	•		•		•	•	2	H	N
villea k Star'	Compact medium shrub, neat crowded foliage, clusters of pink-and-cream flowers spring–summer–autumn. Attractive screen or hedge. Prune regularly.	1.5–2m	1–1.5m	Temp S.tr	•		•		•	•		L	N
villea k Surprise'	Medium to large shrub, ferny foliage, pink-and-cream terminal candle flowers mainly in autumn, also sporadic. Light pruning beneficial.	2–5m	1.5–3m	Temp Trop S.tr	•				•	•		L	N
villea pinnatifida	Small to medium tree, broadly lobed dark green leaves with a bronze undersurface, white terminal flowers spring–summer.	5–9m	4–8m	W.te Trop S.tr	•					•			N
villea platypoda	Small spreading shrub, rigid divided prickly foliage, showy red flowers mainly in spring. Hardy; useful on banks. Regular pruning recommended.	60cm–1m	1–1.5m	Temp S.tr S.ar	•		•		•	•		L	N
villea bractea	Medium shrub, hairy foliage, tight clusters of gold-and-red woolly spider flowers in spring. Very showy. Tip pruning recommended.	1.5–2.5m	1–2m	Temp S.tr S.ar	•		•		•	•		L	N
villea rinda Beauty'	Medium shrub, dense grey-green foliage, scarlet flowers spring–summer. Useful for screen or hedge. Prune regularly.	1.2–2m	1.5–2m	Temp S.tr S.ar	•		•		•	•		L	N
villea rinda Blondie'	Medium to large shrub, lobed foliage, creamy apricot toothbrush flowers spring–summer. Screen or hedge plant. Regular pruning required.	2–3m	1.5–3m	Temp Trop S.tr S.ar	•		•		•	•		L	N
villea rinda stance'	Medium to large shrub, dense glossy short linear leaves, scarlet spider flowers all year. Ideal for screen or hedge. Withstands heavy pruning.	1.5–3.5m	2–2.5m	Temp Trop S.tr	•		•		•	•		L	N
villea rinda Diadem'	Small shrub, crowded foliage, bright yellow flowers winter–spring. Hardy and adaptable. Withstands heavy pruning.	1–1.5m	1–1.5m	Temp S.tr	•		•		•	•		L	N
villea rinda Elegance'	Rounded medium shrub, glossy blunt foliage, apricot flowers with red styles winter–spring. Excellent screen or hedge plant. Regular pruning essential.	2–2.5m	2–2.5m	Temp S.tr	•		•		•	•		L	N

		Height	Width	Climatic zones	Soil types				full sun	filtered sun	coastal regions	frosty regions
					moist, well drained	wet	dry	dry limy				
Grevillea 'Poorinda Firebird'	Small to medium shrub, grey linear foliage, bright scarlet spider flowers late winter–spring. Useful screen or hedge plant. Regular pruning essential.	1–2.5m	1.2–2m	Temp S. tr	•		•		•	•		H
Grevillea 'Poorinda Golden Lyre'	Compact medium shrub, crowded linear foliage, creamy yellow flowers late winter–spring. Useful screen or hedge plant. Regular pruning essential.	1.2–2m	1–2m	Temp S. tr	•		•		•	•		L
Grevillea 'Poorinda Hula'	Small spreading shrub, arching branches, fine foliage, mauve flowers all year. Light pruning beneficial.	1–1.5m	1–1.5m	Temp S. tr	•				•	•		L
Grevillea 'Poorinda Illumina'	Small shrub, grey-green soft foliage, bright pink flowers winter–spring. Light pruning beneficial.	90cm–1.2m	1–1.2m	Temp S. tr S. ar	•		•		•	•		L
Grevillea 'Poorinda Julie'	Small to medium shrub, dark foliage, bright red spider flowers spring–summer. Suited to narrow areas. Regular pruning beneficial.	1.5–2m	1–1.5m	Temp S. tr S. ar	•		•		•	•		L
Grevillea 'Poorinda Peter'	Medium to large shrub, arching branches, red-tipped serrated foliage, salmon pink toothbrush flowers spring–summer. Hardy. Withstands severe pruning.	2–3m	2–3m	Temp S. tr S. ar	•				•	•		L
Grevillea 'Poorinda Pink Coral'	Low spreading shrub, dense foliage, masses of deep pink flowers spring–summer. Hardy and showy. Regular pruning recommended.	80cm–1m	1.5–2m	Temp S. tr S. ar	•		•		•	•		L
Grevillea 'Poorinda Queen'	Medium to large shrub, dense blunt glossy leaves, apricot flowers winter–spring–summer. Hardy screen or hedge plant. Withstands severe pruning.	1.5–2.5m	2–2.5m	Temp S. tr S. ar	•		•		•	•		H
Grevillea 'Poorinda Refrain'	Medium shrub, grey velvety foliage, large showy clusters of multi-coloured (cream, apricot and pink) flowers winter–spring. Good drainage essential.	1.5–2.5m	1–2m	Temp S. tr	•		•		•	•		L
Grevillea 'Poorinda Rondeau'	Small spreading shrub, crowded foliage, masses of bright red flowers winter–spring. Hardy and adaptable. Withstands severe pruning.	80cm–1m	1–1.2m	Temp S. tr	•		•		•	•		L
Grevillea 'Poorinda Royal Mantle'	Carpeting groundcover, green and reddish bronze irregularly lobed leaves, dark red toothbrush flowers most of the year. Hardy and vigorous. Prune lightly.	prostrate	3–4m	Temp S. tr S. ar	•		•		•	•		L
Grevillea 'Poorinda Tranquillity'	Small rounded shrub, soft blue-grey foliage, pink spider flowers all year. Tip pruning recommended.	1–1.2m	1–1.2m	Temp S. tr S. ar	•		•		•	•		L

Temp — temperate
W. te — warm temperate
Trop — tropical
S. tr — sub-tropical
S. ar — semi-arid

L — light
H — heavy
N — nectar-feeding
S — seed-eating
F — fruit-feeding

						Soil types								
		Height	Width	Climatic zones	moist, well drained	wet	dry	dry limy	full sun	filtered sun	coastal regions	frosty regions	bird attraction
villea pteridifolia	Medium to large shrub or small open tree, finely divided ferny foliage, large bright orange toothbrush flowers winter–spring. Spectacular.	2–9m	3–7m	W. te Trop S. tr	•				•	•			N
villea pulchella	Small shrub, holly-like foliage, small cream flower spikes winter–spring. Dainty plant for small landscapes or container.	50–90cm	50–90cm	W. te S. ar	•		•		•	•		L	N
villea quercifolia	Variable dwarf to small shrub; grey oak-like foliage, bronze new growth; candy pink flowers spring–summer. Container or rockery plant. Prune lightly.	30–80cm	60cm–1.2m	Temp S. ar	•		•		•	•		L	N
villea repens	Carpeting groundcover, smooth holly-like foliage, red or orange-yellow toothbrush flowers spring–summer. Hardy, especially in dry shady sites.	prostrate	1.5–2.5m	Temp S. tr	•		•		•	•		L	N
villea rivularis	Spreading medium shrub, finely divided foliage, pinky blue flowers autumn–winter–spring. Tolerates wet soils; excellent bird habitat. Prune regularly.	1.5–2.5m	2.5–3m	Temp Trop S. tr	•	•			•	•		H	N
villea robusta y Oak	Small to large tree, ferny foliage, large brilliant orange racemes in summer. Vigorous and adaptable; hardy in a wide range of conditions.	6–20m	4–10m	Temp Trop S. tr	•				•	•		H	N
villea oyn Gordon'	Spreading medium shrub, large irregularly lobed foliage, large bunches of red flowers all year. Outstanding landscape plant. Regular pruning essential.	1–2.5m	2–3m	Temp S. tr	•				•	•		L	N
villea narinifolia rf green	Small compact shrub, fine foliage, yellow-green flowers winter–spring. Tip prune regularly.	60cm–1m	80cm–1m	Temp S. tr S. ar	•		•		•	•		H	N
villea narinifolia rf pink	Small compact shrub, narrow or broad foliage, pink to red flowers winter–spring. Adaptable and hardy. Regular pruning required.	30–80cm	60cm–1m	Temp S. tr S. ar	•		•		•	•		H	N
villea narinifolia en	Small to medium upright shrub, crowded needle foliage, greenish yellow flowers winter–spring. Excellent bird habitat. Regular pruning recommended.	1.5–2m	90cm–1.2m	Temp S. tr S. ar	•		•		•	•		H	N
villea narinifolia W.	Small to medium shrub, fine grey-green foliage, showy pink-red flowers winter–spring. Useful screening plant. Regular pruning recommended.	1–1.5m	1–2m	Temp S. tr S. ar	•				•	•		H	N
villea narinifolia	Large spreading shrub, dense needle foliage, clusters of pinky red flowers winter–spring. Very hardy; excellent bird habitat and screen. Prune regularly.	1–3m	1.5–3m	Temp S. tr S. ar	•		•		•	•		H	N

Legend (top left):

p — temperate
e — warm temperate
o — tropical
— sub-tropical
— semi-arid

L — light
H — heavy
N — nectar-feeding
S — seed-eating
F — fruit-eating

		Height	Width	Climatic zones	Soil types							
					moist, well drained	wet	dry	dry limy	full sun	filtered sun	coastal regions	frosty regions
Grevillea rosmarinifolia 'Rosy Posy'	Small compact shrub, crowded needle foliage, large pendulous racemes of pink flowers winter–spring. Very showy, hardy and adaptable. Prune regularly.	80cm–1.2m	1–1.2m	Temp S. tr S. ar	•		•		•	•		H
Grevillea saccata	Compact dwarf shrub, woolly grey foliage, scarlet flowers spring–summer. Container plant. Light tip pruning beneficial.	30–60cm	30–80cm	Temp S. ar	•		•		•	•		L
Grevillea 'Sandra Gordon'	Large spreading shrub, finely divided grey-green leaves, bright golden toothbrush flowers winter–spring. Spectacular. Light pruning beneficial.	2.5–4m	3–4m	W. te Trop S. tr S. ar	•		•		•	•		L
Grevillea sericea (syn. *G. leiophylla*)	Small shrub, fine foliage, mauve or bright pink spider flowers most of the year. White form also. Hardy and adaptable. Prune regularly.	1.5–2m	80cm–1.5m	Temp S. tr	•				•	•		L
Grevillea sessilis	Medium to large upright shrub, ferny silver foliage with rusty new tips, upright candles of cream flowers winter–spring. Spectacular. Prune lightly.	2–4m	1–2m	W. te Trop S. tr S. ar					•	•		L
Grevillea shiressii	Medium to large shrub, large undulate bronze-green leaves; inky blue flowers winter–spring, attractive to honeyeaters. Prune lightly.	3–4m	2–4m	Temp Trop S. tr	•	•			•	•		L
Grevillea 'Shirley Howie'	Small spreading shrub, fine foliage; deep pink spider flowers winter–spring, also sporadic. Hardy and attractive. Regular pruning recommended.	1–1.5m	1–1.5m	W. te S. tr	•				•	•		L
Grevillea 'Sid Cadwell'	Small spreading rigid shrub, deeply lobed grey-green foliage, pink-red toothbrush flowers autumn–winter–spring. Regular pruning required.	50–80cm	1.2–2m	Temp S. tr	•		•		•	•		L
Grevillea speciosa ssp. *dimorpha* broad leaf (syn. *G. dimorpha*)	Small upright shrub, broad smooth leaves, scarlet spider flowers along stems winter–spring. Prune after flowering.	1–1.5m	80cm–1.5m	Temp S. tr	•		•		•	•		L
Grevillea speciosa ssp. *dimorpha* fine leaf (syn. *G. dimorpha*)	Small shrub, very narrow long foliage, showy scarlet spider flowers along stems winter–spring. Prune after flowering.	60cm–1.5m	60cm–1m	Temp S. tr	•		•		•	•		L
Grevillea speciosa ssp. *oleoides* (syn. *G. oleoides*)	Upright medium shrub, long silver-backed leaves, brilliant scarlet spider flowers spring–summer. Prune after flowering.	1.5–2m	1–1.5m	Temp S. tr	•				•	•		L
Grevillea speciosa ssp. *speciosa*	Small to medium upright or spreading shrub, rounded grey-green foliage, dark red or pink spider flowers winter–spring–summer. Prune lightly.	1–3m	1.5–2m	Temp S. tr	•				•	•		L

Temp — temperate
W. te — warm temperate
Trop — tropical
S. tr — sub-tropical
S. ar — semi-arid

L — light
H — heavy
N — nectar-feeding
S — seed-eating
F — fruit-eating

		Height	Width	Climatic zones	Soil types								
					moist, well drained	wet	dry	dry limy	full sun	filtered sun	coastal regions	frosty regions	bird attraction
o — temperate / — warm temperate / — tropical / — sub-tropical / — semi-arid	L — light / H — heavy / N — nectar-feeding / S — seed-eating / F — fruit-feeding												
...illea 'fire'	Large shrub, finely divided silver-grey fern-like foliage, red upright candles with dark pink styles all year. Light pruning beneficial.	3–4m	1.5–2m	W. te Trop S. tr	•				•	•		L	N
...illea 'flame'	Bushy medium shrub, silver-green fern-like foliage, orange-red brushes all year. Light pruning beneficial.	2.5–3m	1.5–2.5m	W. te Trop S. tr	•				•	•		L	N
...illea ...litziana	Low sprawling shrub, holly-iike foliage, red-and-green toothbrush flowers winter–spring. Prune lightly after flowering.	50cm–1m	1–2.5m	Temp S. tr S. ar	•		•		•	•		L	N
...illea ...obotrya	Large shrub or upright small tree, fine foliage, white candle flowers late winter–spring, decorative seed capsules.	2–5m	2–3m	W. te S. tr S. ar	•		•		•	•		L	N
...illea stenomera	Low spreading or small upright shrub, finely divided grey foliage, clusters of bright red flowers most of the year. Hardy, useful landscape plant. Prune regularly.	30cm–2.2m	1.5–2m	Temp S. tr	•		•		•	•		L	N
...illea ...erb'	Small compact shrub, bright green lobed foliage, masses of pink-and-orange brushes most of the year. Very showy. Requires regular pruning.	1–1.5m	1.5–2m	Temp Trop S. tr	•					•		L	N
...illea ...ia'	Large bushy shrub, fine silver ferny foliage, deep pink brushes with gold styles most of the year. Spectacular. Light pruning beneficial.	3–5m	2.5–3.5m	W. te Trop S. tr	•		•		•	•		L	N
...illea synapheae	Low spreading shrub, blue-grey lobed foliage, clusters of cream flowers in spring. Attractive foliage contrast. Light pruning recommended.	15–45cm	1–2m	Temp S. tr S. ar	•		•		•			L	N
...illea tenuiloba ...d Glory'	Small spreading shrub, prickly divided foliage, loose racemes of golden flowers late winter–spring. Hardy; attractive foliage plant. Prune regularly.	90cm–1.2m	1–2m	W. te S. tr S. ar	•		•		•	•		L	N
...illea ...manniana ...thelemanniana	Variable shrub, silver-grey net foliage, bright pink or red clusters of flowers winter–spring. Showy, hardy and adaptable. Light pruning beneficial.	10–30cm	1.5–3m	Temp S. tr	•		•	•	•	•	2	L	N
...illea ...manniana ...obtusifolia (. G. obtusifolia)	Low spreading mounding shrub, crowded blunt leaves, soft pink-red flower clusters spring–summer. Hardy. Prune lightly.	prostrate–30cm	1–2m	Temp S. tr	•				•	•		L	N
...illea ...manniana ...pinaster (. G. pinaster)	Large dense shrub, fine grey foliage, loose clusters of scarlet flowers winter–spring. Hardy and adaptable. Regular pruning recommended.	1.5–3m	2–3m	Temp S. tr	•		•		•	•		L	N

		Height	Width	Climatic zones	Soil types							
					moist, well drained	wet	dry	dry limy	full sun	filtered sun	coastal regions	frosty regions
Grevillea thyrsoides	Low scrambling shrub, hairy silver-grey divided foliage, loose racemes of pink-red flowers spring–summer. Very attractive foliage plant. Prune lightly.	prostrate–20cm	60cm–1m	W. te S. tr S. ar	•		•		•			L
Grevillea trifida (syn. *G. muelleri* and *G. brevicuspis*)	Variable small shrub, dense pronged or divided foliage, clusters of pale yellow flowers spring–summer. Prune lightly.	60cm–1.5m	80cm–1.5m	Temp S. tr S. ar	•		•		•	•		L
Grevillea triloba	Medium shrub, dense grey trilobed foliage, clusters of white flowers in spring. Very hardy. Regular pruning recommended.	1.5–2.5m	2–2.5m	Temp S. tr	•				•	•		L
Grevillea tripartita (syn. *G. macrostylis*)	Medium to large rigid branching shrub, 3-pronged or shield-shaped foliage, clusters of large red-and-yellow flowers spring–summer. Prune lightly.	2.5–3.5m	2–3.5m	Temp S. tr S. ar	•		•		•	•		L
Grevillea triternata	Small shrub, fine foliage, clusters of white flowers late winter–spring. Prune lightly after flowering.	45cm–1m	90cm–1.2m	Temp S. ar	•		•		•	•		L
Grevillea umbellata (syn. *G. acerosa*)	Low spreading dense shrub, fine foliage, clusters of small woolly grey flowers winter–spring. Very attractive and hardy.	30–60cm	50–80cm	Temp S. tr S. ar	•		•		•	•		L
Grevillea venusta	Medium shrub, broadly lobed olive green foliage, deep yellow flowers with dark styles winter–spring. Light pruning beneficial.	2–2.5m	1.5–2m	W. te Trop S. tr	•				•	•		L
Grevillea vestita	Small to medium weeping shrub, broadly or narrowly lobed foliage, clusters of pink-and-white flowers in spring. Attractive and hardy.	1–2m	1.5–2.5m	Temp S. tr S. ar	•		•	•	•	•		L
Grevillea victoriae (syn. *G. miqueliana*)	Small to medium shrub; linear or rounded, grey or green foliage; red, pink or occasionally yellow flowers spring–summer. Prune after flowering.	1–3.5m	1.5–3m	Temp S. tr	•				•	•		H
Grevillea victoriae 'Genoa River'	Medium shrub, fine soft pink-tipped foliage, clusters of red flowers all year. Excellent bird habitat and screening plant. Withstands heavy pruning.	1–2.5m	1.5–2.5m	Temp S. tr S. ar	•		•		•	•		H
Grevillea whiteana	Formerly *G.* Coochin Hills or *G.* Mundubbera. Large shrub, finely divided foliage, upright creamy yellow or golden yellow flowers autumn–winter. Prune lightly.	3–5m	2–3m	W. te Trop S. tr S. ar	•		•		•	•		L
Grevillea 'White Wings'	Crowded narrow segmented leaves, clusters of lacy white flowers most of the year. Useful hedge plant. Withstands heavy pruning.	1.5–2.5m	2–3m	Temp S. tr	•				•	•		H

Temp — temperate
W. te — warm temperate
Trop — tropical
S. tr — sub-tropical
S. ar — semi-arid

L — light
H — heavy
N — nectar-feeding
S — seed-eating
F — fruit-eating

		Height	Width	Climatic zones	moist, well drained	wet	dry	dry limy	full sun	filtered sun	coastal regions	frosty regions	bird attraction

Legend:

p — temperate
e — warm temperate
▪ — tropical
— sub-tropical
— semi-arid

L — light
H — heavy
N — nectar-feeding
S — seed-eating
F — fruit-eating

Name	Description	Height	Width	Climatic zones	moist, well drained	wet	dry	dry limy	full sun	filtered sun	coastal regions	frosty regions	bird attraction
illea wickhamii	Medium to large open shrub, grey holly-like foliage; clusters of brilliant crimson, pink or golden flowers winter–spring. Extremely attractive. Prune lightly.	2–4m	2–2.5m	Trop S.tr S.ar Arid	•		•	•	•	•		L	N
illea willisii	Medium to large spreading shrub, rigid prickly lobed foliage, woolly stems, cream toothbrush flowers spring–summer. Hardy; excellent bird habitat. Prune.	2–3.5m	2.5–3.5m	Temp S.tr	•		•		•	•		L	N
illea willisii pachylostyla	Small to medium spreading shrub, arching branches, finely divided foliage; pendulous cream-and-deep-pink flowers in spring, also sporadic. Prune.	90cm–2m	2–3m	Temp S.tr S.ar	•		•		•	•		L	N
illea wilsonii	Small shrub, dense intricate fine foliage, showy bunches of waxy crimson flowers in spring. Handsome flower and foliage combination. Prune lightly.	1–1.5m	1–2m	Temp S.ar	•		•		•	•		L	N
illea ▪para Gem'	Upright medium shrub, finely divided grey-green foliage, pink-orange spider flowers winter–spring. Attractive screening or hedge plant. Prune regularly.	1.5–2.5m	1–2m	Temp S.tr S.ar	•		•	•	•	•	2	L	N
illea ▪para Gold'	Upright medium shrub, finely divided grey-green foliage, golden spider flowers winter–spring. Attractive screening or hedge plant. Prune regularly.	1.5–2.5m	1–2m	Temp S.tr S.ar	•		•	•	•	•	2	L	N
chenotia ▪rantha	Small open shrub, fine woolly grey foliage, large mauve bell flowers winter–spring. Container or rockery plant. Regular tip pruning essential.	90cm–1.2m	80cm–1m	Temp S.tr S.ar	•		•		•	•		L	
ea ambigua	Small to medium compact shrub, stiff linear grey-green leaves, profuse white or pink flowers in spring.	1–2m	1–1.8m	W.te S.ar	•		•		•			L	N
ea baxteri	Upright open medium shrub; distinctive rigid fan-shaped foliage, sharply toothed; white flowers in small clusters in spring.	2.5–3m	1–1.8m	W.te S.ar	•		•		•	•	2	L	N
ea bucculenta	Large erect shrub, long narrow leaves, showy spikes of brilliant pink-red flowers along old wood in winter.	1.8–4m	2–2.5m	W.te S.ar	•		•		•		2	L	N
ea ceratophylla	Small upright shrub, attractive lobed leaves, rusty brown flowers in small clusters in summer.	50cm–1m	60–80cm	W.te S.ar	•		•		•	•		L	N
ea conchifolia	Small upright shrub, stiff shell-like leaves along stems, pink-and-white flowers in winter.	90cm–1.5m	60cm–1.2m	W.te S.ar	•		•		•	•	2	L	N

					Height	Width	Climatic zones	Soil types							

Legend:
Temp — temperate
W. te — warm temperate
Trop — tropical
S. tr — sub-tropical
S. ar — semi-arid

L — light
H — heavy
N — nectar-feeding
S — seed-eating
F — fruit-eating

		Height	Width	Climatic zones	moist, well drained	wet	dry	dry limy	full sun	filtered sun	coastal regions	frosty regions
Hakea coriacea	Large erect shrub, grey linear leaves, long spikes of vivid pink flowers late winter–spring.	3–5m	2–4m	W. te S. ar	•		•		•		2	L
Hakea corymbosa Cauliflower Hakea	Small to medium solid compact shrub, rigid linear pointed leaves, extremely showy large heads of cream flowers winter–spring.	1–2m	1.5–2m	W. te S. ar	•		•		•		2	L
Hakea costata	Upright medium shrub, short pungent narrow leaves, massed small white flowers along upper stems in a showy display in spring.	1.5–2.2m	1–2m	W. te S. ar	•		•	•	•			L
Hakea cucullata Scallops	Small to large shrub, stems closely covered with regular scalloped leaves, bright pink flower clusters in leaf axils winter–spring.	3–5m	1–2.2m	W. te S. ar	•				•		2	L
Hakea dactyloides	Small to large shrub, lanceolate foliage, massed pink-and-white sweetly fragrant flowers clustered along stems in spring.	1.5–7m	1–5m	Temp S. tr	•		•		•	•	2	L
Hakea elliptica	Large bushy shrub, large oval bright green leaves with bronze new growth, cream flowers in clusters winter–spring. Hardy and useful screening plant.	2.5–4m	2–4m	Temp S. tr	•		•		•	•	2	L
Hakea eriantha	Medium to large upright shrub, narrow lanceolate foliage, showy display of creamy flowers with red styles along stems winter–spring. Hardy screening plant.	3–7m	1.5–5m	Temp S. tr	•		•		•	•		L
Hakea erinacea	Small to medium compact shrub, short rigid intricate grey foliage, massed white to rose pink flowers winter–spring.	1–1.8m	1.5–2.5m	Temp S. tr S. ar	•				•	•		L
Hakea francisiana	Upright medium shrub, long flat linear leaves, long spikes of showy red flowers in spring.	2.5–3.5m	2–3m	W. te S. ar	•		•		•		2	L
Hakea gibbosa	Medium to large upright shrub; needle foliage, silky when new; clusters of cream flowers in spring, followed by large capsules.	2–4m	1.8–3m	Temp S. tr	•		•		•	•		L
Hakea hookerana	Medium to large shrub, oblong leaves, red flowers clustered along stems in spring, followed by distinctive large capsules.	2–3.5m	2–3m	W. te S. ar	•		•		•		1	L
Hakea invaginata	Small upright shrub, long narrow leaves, small clusters of pink flowers in spring.	50–90cm	40–80cm	W. te S. ar	•		•		•		2	L

				Soil types								
p — temperate L — light e — warm temperate H — heavy — tropical N — nectar-feeding — sub-tropical S — seed-eating — semi-arid F — fruit-eating		**Height**	**Width**	**Climatic zones**	moist, well drained	wet	dry	dry limy	full sun	filtered sun	coastal regions	frosty regions	bird attraction
ea lasianthoides	Medium to large shapely shrub, pale green linear leaves, profuse cream fragrant flowers in spring. Will tolerate seasonally wet soils.	3–5m	2–5m	Temp S.tr	●	●			●	●		L	N
ea laurina ushion Hakea	Large shrub or small tree, occasionally pendulous; dark elliptical foliage, massed clusters of cream-and-rose-pink pincushions summer–autumn.	3–6m	3–7m	Temp S.tr S.ar	●		●		●	●	2	L	N
ea lehmanniana	Small compact shrub, fine needle foliage, unusual blue-green flowers winter–spring.	50–80cm	60cm–1m	Temp S.ar	●		●		●		2	L	N
ea leucoptera dlewood	Medium to large spreading or upright shrub, narrow foliage, showy clusters of white flowers in summer.	2–5m	2–3m	W.te Arid S.ar	●		●	●	●			H	N
ea lissocarpha	Low spreading shrub, divided foliage, clusters of white flowers in winter.	60–90cm	90cm–1.2m	Temp S.ar	●		●		●	●		L	N
ea macraeana	Large shrub or small tree, rough fibrous bark, fine pendulous foliage, white flowers in spring. Hardy, adaptable and very graceful.	4–8m	2–4m	Temp Trop S.tr	●				●	●	2	L	N
ea multilineata	Large upright shrub, stiff grey linear foliage, long spikes of vivid pink flowers (occasionally white) winter–spring.	3–4m	2–3m	W.te S.ar	●		●		●			L	N
ea myrtoides	Dwarf mounding shrub; stiff, sharply pointed elliptical foliage; vivid purple-pink flowers clustered along stems late winter–spring. Container plant.	30–60cm	1–1.5m	Temp S.tr S.ar	●		●		●			L	N
ea nodosa	Upright or rounded medium shrub, fine dense grey-green foliage, showy display of lemon yellow scented flowers clustered along stems summer–autumn.	2–2.5m	1–2m	Temp S.tr	●	●			●	●		H	N
ea obtusa	Small to medium compact shrub, attractive ovate foliage, profuse globular clusters of cherry pink flowers winter–early spring.	1.5–2.2m	1–1.5m	Temp S.ar	●		●		●			L	N
ea oleifolia	Large dense shrub or occasionally small tree, grey-brown rough bark, short oblong leaves forming dense crown, white flowers in spring.	3–5m	2–3m	Temp S.tr	●		●		●	●		L	N
ea orrhyncha	Small to medium spreading shrub; narrow, sometimes divided foliage; profusion of bright crimson flowers on older wood in winter.	90cm–1.8m	1–2m	W.te S.ar	●		●		●	●	2	L	N

		Height	Width	Climatic zones	Soil types						coastal regions	frosty regions
					moist, well drained	wet	dry	dry limy	full sun	filtered sun		
Hakea pandanicarpa	Upright open medium shrub, oblanceolate leaves; clusters of rusty brown-and-cream flowers in spring, followed by decorative large woody rough capsules.	1.2–1.8m	1–1.5m	W. te S. ar	•		•		•		2	L
Hakea petiolaris Sea-urchin Hakea	Large shrub or small tree, silvery grey stiff foliage; massed creamy purplish pincushion flowers, often on old wood, autumn–winter. Excellent bird habitat.	4–6m	2–5m	Temp S. tr S. ar	•		•		•	•	2	L
Hakea platysperma	Small to medium upright shrub, stiff narrow leaves; clusters of white flowers in spring, followed by very decorative large round woody capsules.	90cm–1.8m	1–1.5m	W. te S. ar	•		•		•	•		L
Hakea propinqua	Medium to large open shrub, sometimes arching; narrow rigid leaves, white to yellow flower clusters autumn–winter, distinctive grey woody capsules.	3–7m	1.5–3m	Temp S. tr	•		•		•	•	2	L
Hakea prostrata	Large compact shrub, occasionally prostrate; bright green stiff oval toothed leaves, white flowers in spring.	60cm–2.5m	2–3m	Temp S. tr S. ar	•		•		•	•	2	L
Hakea purpurea	Small to medium rounded shrub, narrow divided leaves, clusters of bright red flowers winter–spring.	90cm–1.8m	1–1.5m	Temp S. tr	•		•		•	•		L
Hakea pycnoneura	Spreading rounded medium shrub, long thin flattened and curved leaves, clusters of creamy pink flowers in winter.	1.8–3m	2–3.5m	W. te S. ar	•		•		•	•		L
Hakea rostrata Beaked Hakea	Small to medium compact shrub, long narrow foliage, clusters of white flowers in spring, large woody beaked capsules.	90cm–1.8m	1–1.5m	W. te S. ar	•		•		•	•	2	L
Hakea ruscifolia	Small to medium open shrub, dense elliptical leaves, profuse clusters of perfumed pinkish white flowers spring–summer.	1.5–2m	1–1.5m	W. te S. ar	•		•		•	•		L
Hakea salicifolia	Large shrub or small tree; dense dark smooth foliage, bronze-purple new growth; clusters of white perfumed flowers spring–summer. Screen or shade tree.	5–12m	4–8m	Temp Trop S. tr	•				•	•	2	L
Hakea scoparia	Small to medium upright shrub, long fine channelled leaves, clusters of pink-red flowers late winter–spring.	1.8–3m	1.5–2.5m	Temp S. ar	•		•		•			L
Hakea sericea	Small to medium upright shrub, stiff needle foliage; massed cream to deep pink flowers, sweetly scented, late winter–spring. Excellent bird habitat.	1–4m	1–2.5m	Temp S. tr	•	•	•		•	•	1	L

Temp — temperate
W. te — warm temperate
Trop — tropical
S. tr — sub-tropical
S. ar — semi-arid

L — light
H — heavy
N — nectar-feeding
S — seed-eating
F — fruit-eating

					Soil types								
		Height	Width	Climatic zones	moist, well drained	wet	dry	dry limy	full sun	filtered sun	coastal regions	frosty regions	bird attraction

Legend:
- ıp — temperate
- e — warm temperate
- p — tropical
- — sub-tropical
- r — semi-arid
- L — light
- H — heavy
- N — nectar-feeding
- S — seed-eating
- F — fruit-eating

Name	Description	Height	Width	Climatic zones	moist, well drained	wet	dry	dry limy	full sun	filtered sun	coastal regions	frosty regions	bird attraction
ea stenocarpa	Small to medium weeping shrub, attractive curly linear leaves, dainty clusters of cream flowers along the stems in spring.	1.4–2.5m	1–2.2m	Temp S.tr	•	•			•	•		L	N
ea suaveolens	Dense large shrub or small tree, rigid narrowly divided foliage, profuse clusters of creamy white flowers autumn–winter. Excellent screen and bird habitat.	3–6m	2–6m	Temp S.tr S.ar	•		•		•	•	1	H	N
ea subsulcata	Bushy medium shrub, long grooved leaves, creamy pink flower clusters in spring.	1.8–3m	1.5–2.5m	W.te S.ar	•		•		•			L	N
kea sulcata	Small to medium rounded shrub, long channelled leaves, white to pink flowers in spring.	90cm–1.8m	1–1.5m	W.te S.ar	•		•		•			L	N
kea teretifolia	Small to medium open shrub, long needle foliage, clusters of white flowers spring–summer. Excellent bird habitat.	1–1.8m	80cm–1.5m	Temp S.tr	•	•			•	•	2	H	N
kea trifurcata	Small to medium bushy shrub. Two leaf types on same plant: one long, narrow, often divided; the other flat and lanceolate. White flowers autumn–winter.	1.8m–3m	2–2.5m	Temp S.tr	•				•	•	2	L	N
kea undulata	Small to medium dense upright shrub, oval leaves with wavy prickly margins, white flowers in spring.	90cm–3m	80cm–2.2m	Temp S.tr	•				•	•	2	L	N
kea varia	Dense medium shrub with variable foliage: narrow to broad, toothed or lobed; white flowers in clusters spring–summer.	1.8m–3m	1.5m–3m	W.te S.tr S.ar	•				•	•	2	L	N
kea verrucosa	Small to medium compact shrub, dense needle foliage, clusters of white to purple-red flowers in winter.	30cm–2m	1–2m	Temp S.tr S.ar	•		•	•	•		1	L	N
kea victoriae yal Hakea	Erect medium shrub; large prickly-edged shell-like leaves, multi-coloured in gold, bronze, red and green; white flowers in spring. Dramatic.	2–3.5m	40cm–1m	W.te S.ar	•		•		•		1	L	N
gania cyanea	Dwarf suckering herbaceous plant, grey-green slightly toothed foliage, open-petalled china blue flowers spring–summer. Rockery plant.	20–60cm	40–90cm	Temp S.ar	•		•		•			L	
gania preissiana	Dwarf suckering erect shrub, strong grey-green stems and foliage, brilliant china blue open-petalled flowers spring–summer. Rockery plant.	30–60cm	20–30cm	Temp S.ar	•		•		•			L	

Temp — temperate L — light													
W. te — warm temperate H — heavy													
Trop — tropical N — nectar-feeding													
S. tr — sub-tropical S — seed-eating													
S. ar — semi-arid F — fruit-eating													

		Height	Width	Climatic zones	Soil types							
					moist, well drained	wet	dry	dry limy	full sun	filtered sun	coastal regions	frosty regions
Hardenbergia comptoniana W. A. Sarsaparilla	Climber or creeper, bright green trifoliolate leaves, festoons of vivid purple pea flowers spring–early summer. Handsome and very hardy.	climber or creeper	medium	Temp S. tr	•		•		•	•	1	L
Hardenbergia violacea Sarsaparilla	Variable climber or creeper, broad leaves, showy clusters of deep purple pea flowers late winter–spring. Hardy and attractive.	climber or creeper	light–medium	Temp S. tr S. ar	•		•		•	•		H
Hardenbergia violacea 'Austraflora Aspiration'	Twining climber or creeper, broad leaves, clusters of musk pink pea flowers late winter–spring. Unusual and very showy.	climber or creeper	light	Temp S. tr	•				•	•		L
Hardenbergia violacea bushy	Small to medium dense shrub, broad foliage; clusters of white, pink, mauve or purple pea flowers late winter–spring. May also climb lightly.	80cm–1.2m	60cm–1.8m	Temp Trop S. tr S. ar	•		•		•	•	2	H
Hardenbergia violacea 'Happy Wanderer'	Vigorous cultivar form, broad dense foliage, massed clusters of bright purple-mauve pea flowers winter–spring. Hardy and showy; excellent landscape plant.	climber	vigorous	Temp Trop S. tr	•		•		•	•		L
Harpullia alata Winged Tulip	Small to large rainforest shrub, winged stems and toothed leaves (its outstanding feature), white flowers in spring, red seeds. Useful undershrub or tub plant.	1–4m	1–2m	W. Te Trop S. tr	•					•		
Harpullia pendula Tulipwood	Small to medium rainforest tree, smooth foliage, white flowers in spring, orange seed capsules. Shady ornamental tree in warm climates, attractive tub plant.	6–10m	4–6m	W. te Trop S. tr	•				•	•		L
Helichrysum apiculatum	Spreading groundcover, velvety silver foliage; many small golden everlasting flowerheads on long stems all year, excellent as cut flowers. Hardy. Prune regularly.	prostrate–60cm	90cm–1.5m	Temp S. tr	•		•		•	•		L
Helichrysum argophyllum	Dwarf shrub, pale silvery grey-green foliage, profuse pale pink-and-white everlasting flowers spring–summer. Light tip pruning recommended.	30–50cm	20–60cm	W. te	•		•		•			L
Helichrysum baxteri	Compact dwarf plant, silver stems, dark linear leaves, massed white yellow-centred everlasting flowers spring–summer. Container plant. Prune after flowering.	20–40cm	40–60cm	Temp S. tr	•		•		•	•		L
Helichrysum bracteatum	Small shrub, soft leaves; showy everlasting flowers of white, cream, gold, pink or bronze-red spring–summer. Numerous cultivars. Pruning essential.	30cm–1m	60–80cm	Temp S. tr	•				•	•	2	L
Helichrysum bracteatum 'Dargan Hill Monarch'	Selected cultivar form; soft grey-green leaves; large vivid yellow everlasting flowers most of the year, especially spring–summer. Regular pruning essential.	60cm–1m	1–1.5m	Temp S. tr	•				•	•		L

		Height	Width	Climatic zones	Soil types				full sun	filtered sun	coastal regions	frosty regions	bird attraction
					moist, well drained	wet	dry	dry limy					
chrysum cteatum mond Head'	Spreading groundcover, narrow slightly furry leaves, bright golden everlasting flowers most of year. Container or rockery. Prune regularly.	10–30cm	60cm–1m	Temp S. tr	•		•		•		1		L
chrysum ordatum	Small upright shrub, rounded dark glossy leaves, groups of bright yellow everlasting flowers topping each stem in spring. Prune regularly.	90cm–1.5m	50–90cm	Temp Trop S. tr	•		•		•	•			L
chrysum usifolium	Upright dwarf shrub, silvery woolly leaves, white everlasting flowers with gold outer bracts spring–summer. Light tip pruning recommended.	20–50cm	30–50cm	Temp	•		•		•	•			L
chrysum osissimum	Suckering mounding dwarf plant, silvery to pale green soft narrow leaves, bright golden everlasting flowerheads all year. Rockery or container. Prune regularly.	10–15cm	50cm–1m	Temp Trop S. tr					•	•			L
chrysum ipapposum	Upright multi-stemmed dwarf shrub, silvery foliage; clusters of bright gold everlasting flowers most of the year, especially spring–summer. Prune lightly.	30–60cm	30–50cm	Temp S. tr					•	•			L
chrysum osum	Small upright slender shrub, sticky bright green linear foliage, gleaming gold everlasting flowers spring–summer. Prune regularly.	60cm–1m	30–60cm	Temp	•		•		•	•			L
pterum emoides	Dwarf mounding plant, silvery foliage, pink buds and white everlasting flowers most of the year. Rockery or container. Prune regularly to retain compact habit.	30–50cm	20–35cm	Temp S. tr	•				•				L
pterum nglesii	Dwarf annual, small round leaves; large white, pale or deep pink everlasting flowers on each stem. Sow seed in autumn for massed display in spring.	10–30cm	10–15cm	Temp S. ar	•		•		•				L
pterum roseum	Dwarf annual, linear leaves; large white, pale or deep pink everlasting flowers on each stem. Sow seed in autumn for massed display in spring.	10–30cm	10–15cm	Temp S. ar	•		•		•				L
mholtzia rifolia am Lily	Upright spreading rainforest lily, long dark flax-like leaves, large compact spikes of small pale pink-and-white waxy flowers spring–summer–autumn.	1.2–2m	1–1.5m	Temp Trop S. tr	•	•					•		
mholtzia berrima am Lily	Upright spreading rainforest lily, long dark flax-like leaves, thick stems bear spikes of crowded waxy pink flowers late spring–summer.	1.2–2m	1–1.5m	Temp Trop S. tr	•	•					•		
niandra pungens	Dense spreading mat plant, crowded pointed narrow leaves; eye-catching display of mauve, pink or white flowers spring–summer. Container or rockery.	prostrate	1–4m	Temp S. tr S. ar	•		•	•	•				L

		Height	Width	Climatic zones	Soil types				full sun	filtered sun	coastal regions	frosty regions
					moist, well drained	wet	dry	dry limy				

Temp — temperate
W. te — warm temperate
Trop — tropical
S. tr — sub-tropical
S. ar — semi-arid

L — light
H — heavy
N — nectar-feeding
S — seed-eating
F — fruit-eating

Species	Description	Height	Width	Climatic zones	moist, well drained	wet	dry	dry limy	full sun	filtered sun	coastal regions	frosty regions
Hemigenia sericea	Prostrate or upright dwarf shrub, linear to oblong leaves, mauve-pink flowers in profusion winter–late spring. Container or rockery plant.	prostrate–90cm	50cm–1m	W. te S. ar	•		•		•	•		L
Hibbertia amplexicaulis	Low scrambling shrub, stem-clasping variable foliage, large yellow open flowers spring–summer. Container plant. Tip pruning recommended.	prostrate–30cm	80cm–1.2m	Temp S. tr	•				•	•		L
Hibbertia aspera	Small to medium rounded compact shrub, rough-textured oblong foliage, small but plentiful yellow flowers most of the year. Regular pruning recommended.	60cm–2m	60cm–1m	Temp S. tr	•				•	•	2	L
Hibbertia bracteata	Small erect bushy shrub, dark slightly hairy foliage, bright yellow terminal flowers spring–summer. Tip pruning recommended.	60cm–1m	30–60cm	Temp S. tr	•		•		•	•		L
Hibbertia bracteosa	Dwarf shrub; many stems, both upright and trailing; grey-green stem-hugging foliage, showy yellow flowers spring–summer. Container plant.	prostrate–50cm	80cm–1.2m	Temp S. tr	•		•		•			L
Hibbertia calycina	Dwarf shrub, crowded narrow short foliage, showy small yellow flowers late winter–spring. Rockery or container plant. Tip prune after flowering.	30–60cm	40–60cm	Temp	•		•		•	•		L
Hibbertia cuneiformis	Compact rounded medium shrub, dark glossy cuneate leaves, large yellow flowers most of the year. Ideal as low hedge. Prune regularly.	1–1.8m	1.2–1.5m	Temp S. tr	•		•		•		1	L
Hibbertia dentata	Twining light climber or creeper, red stems, dark glossy foliage with bronze new growth, large showy bright yellow flowers spring–summer. Container plant.	climber or creeper	light	Temp S. tr	•		•		•	•	2	L
Hibbertia empetrifolia	Low scrambling or twining shrub, tiny crowded leaves, massed bright yellow flowers spring–summer. Climbs if supported. Withstands clipping.	30–60cm	1–1.5m	Temp S. tr	•	•			•	•		L
Hibbertia humifusa	Small mounding groundcover, dense pale soft hairy foliage, open yellow flowers spring–summer. Container or rockery plant.	prostrate	60cm–1m	Temp S. tr	•				•			L
Hibbertia longifolia	Loose open dwarf shrub; smooth grey-green, often purplish foliage; large bright yellow flowers spring–summer–autumn. Container plant.	30–60cm	50–75cm	Temp Trop S. tr	•		•		•	•		L
Hibbertia microphylla	Dwarf shrub, dainty small leaves, decorative buds along stems open to profusion of bright yellow flowers mainly in spring. Rockery or container plant.	30–60cm	30–60cm	Temp S. tr	•				•	•		L

Species	Description	Height	Width	Climatic zones	moist, well drained	wet	dry	dry limy	full sun	filtered sun	coastal regions	frosty regions	bird attraction
...ertia obtusifolia	Dense matting groundcover, oblong shiny green foliage, large flat yellow flowers spring–summer. Rockery or container plant. Prune lightly.	prostrate	80cm–1.2m	Temp S.tr	•				•	•		L	
...ertia ...nculata	Dense matting groundcover, wiry stems covered in dark narrow foliage; profuse flat bright yellow flowers spring–summer, also sporadic. Rockery or container.	prostrate	60cm–1m	Temp S.tr	•				•	•		L	
...ertia perfoliata	Prostrate or compact shrub, shiny stem-clasping crinkly-edged foliage, large golden flowers spring–late summer. Container plant.	prostrate–30cm	60cm–1m	Temp S.tr	•		•		•	•	2	L	
...ertia scandens	Climber or creeper, smooth pale brown stems, fleshy leaves; large flat golden yellow flowers most of the year. May be pruned.	climber or creeper	medium	Temp Trop S.tr	•		•		•	•	1	L	
...ertia sericea	Twiggy dwarf shrub, silky grey to dark green small leaves, profusion of small golden flowers in spring. Rockery or container plant. Tip pruning recommended.	30–60cm	20–60cm	Temp S.tr	•				•	•		L	
...ertia ...yllifolia	Prostrate matting groundcover, tiny crowded narrow dark leaves; large flat bright golden flowers spring–summer, also sporadic. Container or rockery plant.	prostrate	60cm–1m	Temp S.tr	•				•	•		L	
...ertia stellaris	Compact dwarf shrub, orange-red stems, fine narrow foliage, vivid golden orange open flowers spring–summer. Container plant. Tip prune regularly.	20–30cm	10–30cm	Temp S.tr	•				•	•		L	
...ertia stricta	Open dwarf shrub, scattered linear leaves, large golden flowers late winter–spring. Rockery or container. Light tip pruning recommended.	30–60cm	30–60cm	Temp S.tr	•		•		•	•		L	
...ertia ...vaginata	Dwarf shrub, grey-green narrow stem-clasping leaves, yellow flowers spring–summer. Container or rockery plant. Light tip pruning recommended.	20–40cm	10–30cm	Temp S.ar	•		•		•	•		L	
...ertia vestita	Prostrate matting groundcover, attractive tiny glossy oblong leaves, large yellow flowers spring–summer. Very showy. Container plant.	prostrate	50–80cm	Temp S.tr	•		•		•	•	2	L	
...ertia virgata	Prostrate or dwarf twiggy shrub, shiny brown stems, scattered fine foliage, large yellow flowers spring–summer. Container or sand mound plant.	prostrate–30cm	20–60cm	Temp S.ar	•		•		•	•		L	
...scus ...rsifolius Swamp Hibiscus	Small open slender shrub, stems covered in tiny prickles, rough broad leaves, pale yellow purple-centred flowers autumn–winter. Prune hard after flowering.	1–1.8m	1–1.8m	W.te S.tr	•	•			•			L	N

Temp — temperate
W. te — warm temperate
Trop — tropical
S. tr — sub-tropical
S. ar — semi-arid

L — light
H — heavy
N — nectar-feeding
S — seed-eating
F — fruit-eating

	Height	Width	Climatic zones	moist, well drained	wet	dry	dry limy	full sun	filtered sun	coastal regions	frosty regions
Hibiscus heterophyllus — Medium to large upright open pyramidal shrub, prickly stems; long pointed, often lobed leaves; large white red-centred flowers in autumn. Prune after flowering.	3–6m	2–5m	W. te S. tr	•		•		•			L
Hibiscus splendens — Large shrub or small tree; broad bright green leaves, often lobed; very large decorative pink flowers spring–summer. Prune hard after flowering.	1.5–2.5m	2–3m	Temp S. tr	•		•		•			L
Hibiscus tiliaceus Cotton Tree — Small spreading tree, broad smooth leaves, decorative large yellow dark-centred flowers in summer. Useful northern coastal shade tree.	4–8m	3–6m	W. te Trop S. tr	•	•			•		1	
Hicksbeachia pinnatifolia Red Boppel Nut — Large multi-stemmed shrub, deeply divided foliage; purplish spikes of flowers on old wood in spring, followed by edible red-cased seeds.	2–7m	1.5–4m	W. te Trop S. tr	•				•	•		L
Homoranthus darwinioides — Small upright shrub, strongly aromatic grey-green foliage; dainty pendulous fringed flowers of pink and yellow, in pairs, spring–summer. Prune lightly.	60cm–1m	60–90cm	Temp S. tr	•		•		•	•		L
Homoranthus flavescens — Arching dwarf shrub, fine short aromatic leaves crowded along stems, cascading layers of tiny yellow perfumed flowers spring–summer. Container plant.	20–60cm	60–80cm	Temp S. tr	•		•		•	•		L
Homoranthus papillatus — Small, horizontally layered shrub; aromatic fine grey foliage, large sprays of honey-gold honey-scented flowers in spring. Regular pruning recommended.	60cm–1m	1–1.2m	Temp S. tr	•		•		•	•		L
Hovea acutifolia — Small upright bushy shrub, elliptical leaves, massed deep purple pea flowers along the stems in spring. Very showy. Light pruning recommended.	1–1.8m	60cm–1m	Temp S. tr	•					•		L
Hovea chorizemifolia — Dwarf to small open shrub, holly-like leaves, vivid purple pea flowers in spring. Showy container or rockery plant.	60cm–1m	60cm–1m	W. te	•		•		•	•		L
Hovea elliptica — Upright open medium shrub, soft elliptical leaves, massed purple pea flowers along the stems in spring. Very showy. Light pruning recommended.	2–3m	1–1.5m	Temp S. tr	•					•		L
Hovea heterophylla — Dwarf scrambler, few stems, sparse grey-green linear leaves, soft mauve pea flowers late winter–spring. Container plant.	10–30cm	5–10cm	Temp	•		•			•		L
Hovea lanceolata — Open medium shrub, slightly leathery lanceolate foliage, blue-mauve pea flowers late winter–spring. Light pruning recommended.	2–3m	1–2m	Temp	•					•		L

					Height	Width	Climatic zones	Soil types				full sun	filtered sun	coastal regions	frosty regions	bird attraction
								moist, well drained	wet	dry	dry limy					

Legend:

np — temperate   L — light
te — warm temperate   H — heavy
p — tropical   N — nectar-feeding
r — sub-tropical   S — seed-eating
r — semi-arid   F — fruit-eating

Name	Description	Height	Width	Climatic zones	moist, well drained	wet	dry	dry limy	full sun	filtered sun	coastal regions	frosty regions	bird attraction
vea pungens	Small erect shrub, linear pointed leaves, vivid blue-purple pea flowers along the stems late winter–early spring. Container plant. Tip prune lightly.	60cm–1.5m	30–90cm	Temp	•		•		•	•		L	
vea trisperma	Loose dwarf shrub, soft elliptical leaves scattered along the stems, blue-mauve pea flowers winter–spring. Container plant. Tip prune lightly.	30–60cm	20–60cm	Temp	•				•	•		L	
wittia trilocularis	Soft dense medium shrub, hairy foliage, clusters of open-petalled mauve-blue flowers late winter–spring–summer. Useful screen for shady areas.	1.5–3m	2–3m	Temp S.tr	•					•		L	N
va australis	Twining rooting climber, thick fleshy rounded leaves, highly perfumed clusters of waxy pale pink or white flowers in spring. May be grown indoors.	climber	medium	W.te Trop S.tr	•				•	•	1		
va macgillivrayii	Twining rooting climber, broad bright green leaves, spectacular clusters of large fragrant dark red waxy flowers in spring. Fast growing.	climber	medium	W.te Trop S.tr	•					•			
va nicholsoniae	Twining rooting climber, broad silvery-veined leaves, clusters of creamy yellow waxy flowers in spring. May be grown indoors.	climber	medium	W.te Trop S.tr	•					•			
va rubida	Twining rooting climber, hairy bright green rounded leaves, clusters of waxy dark red flowers in spring.	climber	medium	W.te Trop S.tr	•					•			
nenosporum um ive Frangipani	Large slender upright shrub or medium tree, bright green glossy foliage; large clusters of fragrant flowers, cream aging to gold, spring–summer. Handsome.	3–8m	2–5m	Temp Trop S.tr	•				•	•		L	N
ocalymma ustifolium	Small compact to arching shrub, fine aromatic foliage, massed dainty white to deep rose pink flowers late winter–spring. Container plant. Prune lightly.	60cm–1m	40cm–1m	Temp S.tr	•				•	•		L	N
ocalymma difolium	Small dense shrub, crowded heart-shaped aromatic foliage with bronze new growth, white flowers in spring. Miniature form also. Prune after flowering.	30–90cm	50cm–1.8m	Temp S.tr	•				•	•		L	N
ocalymma difolium 'Iden Veil'	Small compact shrub, crowded heart-shaped aromatic variegated foliage, small white flowers in spring. Foliage contrast. Prune after flowering.	60–90cm	1–1.8m	Temp S.tr	•				•	•		L	N
ocalymma rtifolium	Dwarf shrub, bronze-green aromatic foliage, strongly fragrant cream flowers winter–spring. Sandy soil or container. Tip prune lightly.	30–60cm	50–90cm	Temp	•		•		•			L	N

		Height	Width	Climatic zones	Soil types							
					moist, well drained	wet	dry	dry limy	full sun	filtered sun	coastal regions	frosty regions
Hypocalymma puniceum	Small upright shrub, fine aromatic foliage, large deep pink flowers summer–autumn. Sandy soil or container. Tip prune after flowering.	60cm–1.2m	40–90cm	Temp S. ar	•		•		•			L
Hypocalymma robustum Swan River Myrtle	Dwarf to small upright shrub, narrow aromatic leaves, large deep pink flowers along stems in spring. Container plant. Tip prune after flowering.	50–90cm	40–60cm	Temp S. ar	•		•	•	•			L
Hypocalymma speciosum	Dwarf shrub, short blunt aromatic leaves, delicate pink flowers in spring. Container plant. Tip prune after flowering.	30–60cm	30–60cm	Temp S. ar	•		•		•			L
Hypocalymma strictum	Upright dwarf shrub, tiny heath-like aromatic foliage, dainty pink flowers in summer. Container plant. Tip prune after flowering.	30–60cm	20–50cm	Temp S. ar	•		•		•			L
Hypocalymma tetrapterum	Rounded dwarf shrub, broad oblong foliage, yellow flowers in spring. Container plant. Tip prune after flowering.	30–50cm	30–50cm	Temp S. ar	•		•		•			L
Hypocalymma xanthopetalum	Dwarf to small shrub, variable fine to broad foliage, showy yellow flowers winter–spring. Container plant. Tip prune after flowering.	20–90cm	30–70cm	Temp S. ar	•		•		•			L
Indigofera australis	Open medium shrub, rounded grey-green foliage, showy sprays of fragrant musk pink or white pea flowers late winter–spring. Light pruning beneficial.	2–2.5m	1–2m	Temp S. tr	•		•		•	•		L
Ipomoea brasiliensis	Climber or creeper, broad glabrous leaves, large deep pink trumpet flowers most of the year. Fast screen or sand-binding plant.	climber or creeper	vigorous	W. te Trop S. tr	•		•	•	•		1	L
Isopogon anemonifolius Drumsticks	Upright medium shrub, finely divided flattened leaves, showy yellow flowerheads on branch ends in spring. Dwarf forms also known.	2–2.5m	1–2m	Temp S. tr	•		•		•	•		L
Isopogon anethifolius	Erect medium shrub, narrowly divided foliage, yellow flowerheads on branch ends spring–summer.	2–3m	1–2m	Temp S. tr	•		•		•	•		L
Isopogon ceratophyllus	Dwarf to small mounding plant, rigid divided foliage, yellow flowerheads in spring. Hardy, adaptable groundcover.	30–45cm	60–75cm	Temp S. ar	•		•		•	•		L
Isopogon cuneatus	Small shrub, broad flat leaves, outstanding displays of large pink-mauve gold-tipped flowerheads late winter–spring. Requires sandy, gravelly soils.	1–1.5m	1–1.5m	W. te S. ar	•		•		•	•		L

Temp — temperate
W. te — warm temperate
Trop — tropical
S. tr — sub-tropical
S. ar — semi-arid

L — light
H — heavy
N — nectar-feeding
S — seed-eating
F — fruit-eating

Name	Description	Height	Width	Climatic zones	moist, well drained	wet	dry	dry limy	full sun	filtered sun	coastal regions	frosty regions	bird attraction
...ogon dubius, e Coneflower	Small to medium erect shrub, prickly divided leaves, dense silky rose pink flowerheads late winter–spring. Requires deep sandy, gravelly conditions.	1–2m	1–1.5m	W. te S. ar	•				•	•		L	N
...ogon formosus	Small rounded shrub, much-divided foliage, large silky deep pink flowerheads late winter–spring. Sandy soils essential.	1–1.5m	1–1.5m	W. te S. ar	•		•		•	•		L	N
...ogon latifolius	Small rounded shrub, large elliptical leaves, large silky mauve-pink flowerheads late winter–spring. Requires deep sandy, gravelly soils.	1–1.5m	1–1.5m	W. te S. ar	•		•		•	•		L	N
...oma fluviatalis	Flat creeping matting plant, small rounded leaves, pale blue star flowers most of the year. Excellent bog margin plant.	prostrate	1–2m	Temp S. tr	•	•			•	•		L	
...ia achillaeoides	Small slender erect shrub, few branches, sticky linear leaves, dense clusters of white papery flowers spring–summer which dry well. Prune regularly.	60cm–1m	30cm–1m	Temp S. ar	•					•		L	
...ksonia scoparia	Medium to large shrub, fine silver stems and foliage, showy masses of fragrant orange-lemon pea flowers in spring. Beautiful foliage and screening plant.	3–4m	2–3m	Temp S. tr	•		•		•	•		L	
...era pseudorhus, mbark	Small rainforest margin tree, ferny foliage with apricot-pink new growth, tiny flowers, yellowish brown fruit covered in irritating hairs spring–summer.	4–7m	2–5m	W. te Trop S. tr	•				•	•		L	
...ninum, vissimum	Slender fine-stemmed climber, dark narrow leaves, sweetly fragrant open white flowers spring–summer.	climber	light	Temp Trop S. tr	•				•	•		L	
...nedia beckxiana	Climber or creeper, large grey-green trifoliolate leaves, large showy brick red pea flowers spring–summer. Useful and hardy.	climber or creeper	medium	Temp S. tr	•				•	•		L	
...nedia carinata	Dainty ground creeper, soft rounded leaves, bright crimson pea flowers well displayed above foliage in spring.	prostrate	1–2m	Temp S. tr	•				•	•		L	
...nedia coccinea, Coral Pea	Climber or creeper, attractive trifoliolate leaves, showy clusters of coral-pink-and-orange pea flowers in spring.	climber or creeper	medium	Temp S. tr	•				•	•		L	
...nedia eximea	Ground creeper, dark textured trifoliolate leaves, deep crimson pea flowers in spring. Attractive on banks and walls.	prostrate	1–1.5m	Temp S. tr	•				•	•		L	

		Height	Width	Climatic zones	Soil types							
					moist, well drained	wet	dry	dry limy	full sun	filtered sun	coastal regions	frosty regions

Name	Description	Height	Width	Climatic zones	moist, well drained	wet	dry	dry limy	full sun	filtered sun	coastal regions	frosty regions
Kennedia glabrata	Dense ground creeper, shiny bright green trifoliolate leaves, vivid orange-red pea flowers well displayed above foliage spring–summer.	prostrate	1–1.5m	Temp S. tr	•				•	•		L
Kennedia macrophylla	Climber or groundcover, large round bright green trifoliolate leaves, clusters of orange pea flowers in spring. Attractive and hardy.	climber or creeper	vigorous	Temp S. tr S. ar	•		•		•	•		L
Kennedia microphylla	Tiny ground-creeping plant, minute dark trifoliolate leaves, dainty dark crimson pea flowers winter–spring. Container plant.	prostrate	60cm	Temp S. tr	•				•	•		L
Kennedia nigricans	Climber or groundcover, large single or trifoliolate leaves, striking yellow-and-black elongated pea flowers spring–summer. Very hardy.	climber or creeper	vigorous	Temp S. tr S. ar	•		•		•	•	2	L
Kennedia prorepens	Trailing ground creeper, slightly hairy grey-green leaves, purple pea flowers late winter–spring.	prostrate	1–2m	W. te S. ar	•		•		•	•		H
Kennedia prostrata Running Postman	Creeping groundcover, trifoliolate grey-green leaves, showy scarlet (occasionally white) pea flowers spring–summer.	prostrate	1–2m	Temp S. tr S. ar	•		•		•	•	2	L
Kennedia retrorsa	Climber or creeper, large soft grey-green trifoliolate leaves, large clusters of showy pink-purple pea flowers spring–summer.	climber or creeper	vigorous	S. tr S. ar	•				•	•		H
Kennedia rubicunda	Climber or groundcover, broad grey-green trifoliolate leaves, loose clusters of dusky red pea flowers spring–summer. Very hardy.	climber or creeper	vigorous	Temp S. tr	•		•		•	•	2	L
Kennedia stirlingii	Low scrambling shrub or prostrate creeper, fleshy foliage, yellow-orange pea flowers in spring.	30–60cm	60cm–1m	Temp S. tr S. ar	•		•		•	•		
Keraudrenia integrifolia	Small shrub, crinkly furry foliage, massed clusters of pink-mauve to deep lavender blue open-petalled flowers in spring. Grow in deep sand, or container.	60cm–1m	1–1.5m	W. te S. ar	•		•		•	•		L
Kunzea ambigua	Medium to large shrub, dense fine aromatic foliage, massed fluffy white or mauve-pink lightly fragrant flowers spring–summer. Tolerates heavy pruning.	2–4m	2–3m	Temp S. tr	•				•	•	2	L
Kunzea baxteri	Medium shrub, crowded grey to green aromatic foliage, very showy large scarlet gold-tipped brushes spring–summer. Prune.	2–3m	2–2.5m	Temp S. tr	•		•		•	•	1	L

					Soil types								
p — temperate L — light — warm temperate H — heavy — tropical N — nectar-feeding — sub-tropical S — seed-eating — semi-arid F — fruit-eating		Height	Width	Climatic zones	moist, well drained	wet	dry	dry limy	full sun	filtered sun	coastal regions	frosty regions	bird attraction
zea ericifolia (K. muelleri)	Ground-hugging alpine plant, crowded fine grey aromatic foliage, fluffy pale lemon flowers spring–summer. Container or rockery plant.	10–30cm	60cm–1m	Temp	●				●	●		H	N
zea ericoides (Leptospermum icoides)	Arching medium shrub or small tree, fine aromatic foliage; small white dark-centred flowers spring–summer, attractive to insect-eating birds.	2–5m	2–5m	Temp S.tr	●		●		●	●		H	N
zea parvifolia	Small to medium slender upright shrub, fine crowded grey aromatic foliage, showy clusters of mauve-pink pompom flowers in spring. Prune regularly.	1–2.5m	1–1.5m	Temp S.tr	●	●			●	●		H	N
zea parvifolia rf	Small round shrub, tiny aromatic leaves, very decorative mauve-pink pompom flowers in spring. Rockery or container plant. Tip pruning recommended.	30cm–1m	60cm–1m	Temp S.tr	●				●	●		H	N
zea pauciflora	Small to medium erect shrub, fine narrow aromatic leaves, deep pink pompom flowers in spring. Attractive light screen. Regular pruning recommended.	1–2.5m	1–2m	Temp S.tr	●				●	●		L	N
zea pomifera	Spreading ground-covering carpet, crisp curved aromatic foliage; massed fluffy cream flowers spring–early summer, followed by edible bluish berries.	prostrate	2–3m	Temp S.ar	●		●		●	●		H	N F
zea preissiana	Small to medium upright shrub, fine heath-like aromatic foliage, showy pink pompom flowers in spring. Light pruning beneficial.	1–2.5m	1–2m	Temp S.tr	●				●	●		L	N
zea pulchella	Small to medium erect shrub, obovate silvery aromatic foliage, brilliant scarlet-pink flower clusters spring–early summer. Very showy. Prune lightly.	1–2.5m	1–2m	Temp S.ar	●		●		●	●		L	N
zea recurva	Upright medium shrub, crowded small aromatic obovate leaves, mauve-pink pompom flowers spring–early summer. K. recurva var. montana has yellow flowers.	2–3m	1–1.5m	Temp S.tr	●				●	●		L	N
unaria patersonii folk Island iscus	Large dense pyramidal shrub or medium tree, soft elliptical grey-green leaves, open shell pink flowers spring–summer–autumn. Coastal street tree.	10–13m	3–4m	Temp Trop S.tr	●		●		●	●	1	L	
bertia ericifolia	Bushy medium shrub, long fine leaves, showy orange-red flower clusters autumn–winter–spring. Regular pruning recommended.	2–3m	2–2.5m	Temp S.ar	●		●		●	●		L	N
bertia formosa ntain Devil	Small to medium shrub, pointed linear leaves, upright flower clusters with scarlet-pink bracts most of the year, woody capsules shaped like a devil's head.	1–2.5m	1–1.5m	Temp S.tr	●				●	●	2	L	N

		Height	Width	Climatic zones	Soil types				full sun	filtered sun	coastal regions	frosty regions
					moist, well drained	wet	dry	dry limy				

Temp — temperate   L — light
W. te — warm temperate   H — heavy
Trop — tropical   N — nectar-feeding
S. tr — sub-tropical   S — seed-eating
S. ar — semi-arid   F — fruit-eating

Species	Description	Height	Width	Climatic zones	moist, well drained	wet	dry	dry limy	full sun	filtered sun	coastal regions	frosty regions
Lambertia inermis Chittick	Large shrub or small tree; small rounded leaves, felted beneath; buds enclosed in orange bracts, yellow to orange-red flower clusters winter–spring–summer.	2–8m	2–4.5m	Temp S. ar	•				•	•	2	L
Lambertia multiflora	Small bushy shrub, linear foliage, showy clusters of golden yellow or pink-red flowers late winter–spring. Light pruning recommended.	1–1.5m	1m	Temp S. ar	•		•		•	•		L
Lasiopetalum behrii	Small rounded shrub, felted stems, linear grey-green felted leaves, dainty dusty pink open flowers winter–spring. Prune after flowering.	1–1.5m	60cm–1m	Temp S. ar	•		•		•	•		L
Lasiopetalum macrophyllum	Prostrate or upright shrub; broad lanceolate leaves, woolly underneath; rusty cream cupped flowers in spring. Prostrate form excellent for coastal areas.	30cm–2m	1–2m	Temp S. ar	•		•		•	•	1	L
Lechenaultia biloba	Dwarf shrub, crowded linear leaves, vivid blue flowers spring–summer. Pale blue and white forms also. Container or rockery plant. Tip prune after flowering.	30–45cm	30–60cm	Temp S. ar	•		•		•	•		L
Lechenaultia floribunda	Compact dwarf shrub, tiny fleshy leaves, dense clusters of small pale blue flowers spring–early summer. Pretty container plant. Tip prune after flowering.	30–45cm	30–45cm	Temp S. ar	•				•	•		L
Lechenaultia formosa	Variable prostrate to dwarf shrub, tiny leaves; yellow, orange, scarlet or pink flowers spring–summer–autumn. Container or rockery plant. Prune lightly.	Prostrate–30cm	30–60cm	Temp S. ar	•		•		•	•	2	L
Lechenaultia hirsuta	Scrambling open dwarf shrub, hairy stems, sparse foliage, large brilliant scarlet flowers in spring. Sand mound or rockery plant.	10–30cm	30–60cm	Temp S. ar	•		•		•	•		L
Lechenaultia laricina	Dense dwarf shrub, very fine foliage, orange-red flowers in spring. Sand mound or rockery plant. Prune lightly after flowering.	30–45cm	30–60cm	Temp S. ar	•		•		•	•		L
Lechenaultia superba	Dwarf shrub, tiny fleshy leaves, large scarlet flowers most of the year. Rockery or container plant. Light pruning beneficial.	30–45cm	30–60cm	Temp S. ar	•		•		•	•		L
Lechenaultia tubiflora	Prostrate mat, minute foliage; erect tubular flowers may be yellow, scarlet, orange-red, cream or bicoloured, in spring. Container or sand mound plant.	prostrate	30–60cm	Temp S. ar	•		•		•	•		L
Leptospermum brachyandrum	Open medium shrub, soft linear foliage with coppery new growth, white flowers in spring. Hardy and attractive screening plant.	2–3m	2–2.5m	W. te Trop S. tr	•				•	•		L

p — temperate | L — light
e — warm temperate | H — heavy
— tropical | N — nectar-feeding
— sub-tropical | S — seed-eating
— semi-arid | F — fruit-feeding

Name	Description	Height	Width	Climatic zones	Soil types				full sun	filtered sun	coastal regions	frosty regions	bird attraction
					moist, well drained	wet	dry	dry limy					
ospermum ..ipes	Medium, gently arching shrub; linear silver-grey foliage with purple new growth, delicate sprays of white flowers in spring. Graceful screening plant.	2–3m	2–2.5m	Temp S.tr	•		•		•	•		L	S
ospermum ..per Sheen'	Low spreading mound, bronze-red foliage with red stems, strongly caramel-scented large creamy lime flowers in spring. Prune after flowering.	60cm–1.2m	1.5–2m	Temp S.tr	•				•	•		L	S
ospermum ..aceum	Bushy medium shrub, grey-green foliage, large white flowers spring–summer. Hardy, useful screening or hedge plant.	1.5–2m	1.5–2m	W.te S.ar	•		•		•	•		H	S
ospermum ..cia	Small to medium upright to spreading open shrub, bright green foliage, large showy golden flowers autumn–winter. Attractive screening plant.	1.5–2.5m	1.5–2m	W.te Trop S.tr	•				•	•		L	S
ospermum ..scens	Small to medium dense upright shrub, bright crowded foliage, massed creamy white flowers late spring–summer. Regular pruning recommended.	1–2.5m	1–1.5m	Temp Trop S.tr	•				•	•	2	L	S
ospermum ..scens ..dwell'	Low weeping shrub, soft narrow foliage with bronze new growth, profusion of white flowers cover the arching branches late winter–spring. Hardy landscape plant.	1–1.5m	1.5m	Temp Trop S.tr	•				•	•	2	L	S
ospermum ..scens ..fic Beauty'	Small spreading shrub, pendulous branches, fine foliage, massed white flowers in spring. Hardy and useful landscape plant.	50cm–1m	1.5–2m	Temp Trop S.tr	•				•	•	2	L	S
ospermum ..erinum ..izontalis'	Low spreading shrub, dense crowded dark foliage, masses of white flowers cover the arching branches in spring. Excellent bird habitat. Prune regularly.	60cm–1m	2–3m	Temp S.tr	•		•		•	•	1	L	S
ospermum ..gatum ..t Teatree	Medium shrub to small tree, grey-green foliage, white flowers spring–early summer. Excellent bird habitat (especially for seed and insect eaters).	4–6m	3–5m	Temp S.tr	•		•	•	•	•	1	L	S
ospermum ..erum ..lly Teatree	Variable medium to large shrub, erect or weeping; silky grey foliage, showy masses of white flowers in spring. Hardy; excellent bird habitat.	2.5–5m	1.2–3m	Temp S.tr	•	•			•	•		H	S
ospermum ..erum var. ..rocarpum	Small to medium rounded shrub, purplish green foliage, very large flowers with shell pink petals and green centres summer–autumn. Hardy. Prune regularly.	1–2m	60cm–1.5m	Temp S.tr	•	•			•	•		L	S
ospermum ..sidgei	Small shrub, strongly lemon-scented tiny foliage, creamy lemon (occasionally bright pink) flowers clustered along stems in spring. Prune regularly.	60cm–1.8m	60cm–1.2m	Temp Trop S.tr	•	•			•	•	2	L	S

Temp — temperate L — light
W. te — warm temperate H — heavy
Trop — tropical N — nectar-feeding
S. tr — sub-tropical S — seed-eating
S. ar — semi-arid F — fruit-eating

		Height	Width	Climatic zones	moist, well drained	wet	dry	dry limy	full sun	filtered sun	coastal regions	frosty regions
Leptospermum nitidum	Small to medium shrub, silky grey foliage, very large showy pure white flowers cover the bush in spring. Excellent bird habitat. Prune regularly.	1–2m	60cm–1.2m	Temp	•		•		•	•		H
Leptospermum obovatum	Large erect shrub or graceful small tree, dark purple foliage, masses of creamy lime small flowers late spring–summer. Especially beautiful in a copse.	2–7m	1–3.5m	Temp S. tr	•				•	•		L
Leptospermum petersenii Lemon-scented Teatree	Large shrub or small tree, pale green aromatic leaves with beautiful shiny coppery new growth, white flowers in spring. Hardy and attractive.	2–4m	1.5–2.5m	Temp S. tr	•				•	•	2	L
Leptospermum scoparium var. *rotundifolium*	Variable shrub, round dark leaves; very large well-displayed flowers of white to pink, mauve or lavender in spring. Prostrate forms in cultivation.	prostrate–2.2m	80cm–1.2m	Temp S. tr	•				•	•	2	L
Leptospermum sericeum	Small compact shrub, pale silvery green foliage, large shell pink flowers winter–spring. Prune regularly.	1–1.5m	1.5–2m	Temp	•		•		•	•	1	L
Leptospermum squarrosum	Small to medium upright shrub, dark prickly foliage, white to deep pink flowers closely massed along stems and old wood in spring. Prune regularly.	90cm–2.5m	50–90cm	Temp S. tr	•	•			•	•	2	L
Leucopogon virgatus Beard-heath	Wiry dwarf shrub, tiny stem-clasping leaves, dainty heads of woolly white flowers in spring. Container plant. Prune lightly after flowering.	30–60cm	30–50cm	Temp	•		•		•	•		L
Linospadix monostachya Walking Stick Palm	Small rainforest palm; white flowers in summer, followed by strings of red berries in winter. Ideal for small gardens and containers.	1–1.5m	80cm–1.2m	Temp Trop S. tr	•					•		
Linum marginale	Slender herb, scattered grey-green leaves, many pale blue open-petalled flowers in spring. Will self-sow, giving an ephemeral 'wildflower' effect.	20–90cm	5cm	Temp	•		•		•	•		L
Lobelia trigonocaulis	Scrambling rainforest herb, crinkly-edged dark leaves, spectacular china blue flowers spring–summer–autumn. Ideal basket plant, and in ferneries.	5–10cm	1–1.8m	Temp Trop S. tr	•	•				•		L
Lomandra longifolia	Upright to arching rush-foliaged clump; spikes of perfumed cream flowers in spring, followed by orange berries. Hardy and useful landscape plant.	30cm–1m	60cm–1m	Temp Trop S. tr	•		•		•	•		L
Lomandra obliqua	Small tangling clump of beautiful curly foliage, tight clusters of creamy gold flowers spring–summer. Unusual rockery or container plant.	30–60cm	30–60cm	Temp S. tr	•				•	•		L

np — temperate	L — light			
e — warm temperate	H — heavy			
p — tropical	N — nectar-feeding			
— sub-tropical	S — seed-eating			
r — semi-arid	F — fruit-eating			

Name	Description	Height	Width	Climatic zones	moist, well drained	wet	dry	dry limy	full sun	filtered sun	coastal regions	frosty regions	bird attraction
natia ilicifolia	Dwarf to small erect shrub, long lanceolate serrated leaves, showy sprays of cream flowers displayed above foliage in summer.	20–90cm	30–50cm	Temp S.tr	•					•		L	N
natia silaifolia	Upright medium shrub, variable divided foliage, showy long sprays of cream flowers held well above foliage in summer, attractive seed pods.	1.5–2.5m	1–2m	Temp S.tr	•				•	•	2	L	N
natia tinctoria	Small rounded shrub, beautiful divided foliage, large showy sprays of cream flowers in summer.	30–80cm	30–60cm	Temp S.tr	•				•	•		H	N
chocarpus ...ularis	Tropical climber, deciduous purple leaves which re-sprout in spring as the long bunches of pink-and-white pea flowers appear.	climber	vigorous	W.te Trop S.tr	•					•		L	S
hostemon ...fertus (m. *Tristania ...ferta*) ...sh Box	Large shrub or small to very large tree, beautiful smooth golden brown trunk, large dark leaves, clusters of white flowers in summer.	4.5–25m	3–15m	Temp Trop S.tr	•				•	•		L	N
iphyllum carronii (m. *Bauhinia ...onii*) ...eensland Bean	Large shrub or small to medium tree, 2-lobed dark leaves; red flowers in summer when tree is deciduous, also sporadic; decorative flat seed pods.	4–9m	5–10m	W.te Arid S.ar	•	•			•	•		L	N
cadamia ...aphylla ...cadamia Nut	Dense large shrub or tree, irregularly lobed leaves; white flowers in spring, followed by world-famous edible nuts. Hardy in many climates.	8–20m	4–10m	Temp Trop S.tr	•				•	•		L	S
caranga tanarius ...caranga	Large shrub or small tree, soft roundish leaves, yellow flowers in spring, yellowish seed capsules. Useful for regeneration, and as a tub plant.	3–5m	2–3m	W.te Trop S.tr	•					•		L	F
ckinlaya ...rosciadia ...ckinlaya	Small to medium rainforest shrub, broad glossy leaves, symmetrical sprays of yellow flowerheads spring–summer, fleshy blue-grey berries.	1.5–3m	1–2m	W.te Trop S.tr	•				•	•		L	
ropidia ...ginosa ...k Kangaroo Paw	Small plant, stout grey strap leaves, long stems bearing black-and-yellow kangaroo paw flowers in spring. Grow in deep sand or container.	40–60cm	30–50cm	W.te S.ar	•		•	•	•			L	N
crozamia spiralis ...rawang Palm	Small spreading palm-like plant, large deeply divided fronds, orange-red pineapple-like fruit on female plants. Slow growing; attractive container plant.	50–90cm	1.5–2.2m	W.te S.tr	•				•	•	2	L	S
reana brevifolia	Small rounded shrub, fleshy foliage, greenish red fruit most of the year. Very suited for arid area erosion control.	60cm–1m	80cm–1.2m	W.te Arid S.ar	•		•	•	•		2	H	S

		Height	Width	Climatic zones	moist, well drained	wet	dry	dry limy	full sun	filtered sun	coastal regions	frosty regions
					Soil types							
Mazus pumilio	Small matting herb; blue or white open flowers spring–summer, also sporadic. Attractive beside pools or bog margins.	prostrate	1–1.5m	Temp Trop S. tr	•	•			•	•		L
Melaleuca acerosa	Small to large dense sprawling shrub, fine crowded foliage, creamy yellow brushes winter–spring–early summer. Recommended for windbreaks.	1.5–3.5m	3–5m	Temp Trop S. tr	•		•	•	•		1	L
Melaleuca acuminata	Open medium shrub, short leaves, highly perfumed cream flowers along the stems spring–summer.	1–2m	60cm–1.8m	Temp S. ar	•		•		•			H
Melaleuca alternifolia	Large shrub, papery bark, fine linear foliage, white bottlebrush-like flowers in summer. Very hardy; valuable for oil extraction.	4–7m	2–4m	Temp Trop S. tr	•	•			•	•		L
Melaleuca argentea	Large shrub or small to large tree, papery bark, distinctive silvery foliage, lemon yellow brushes summer–autumn. Hardy and attractive in warm climates.	8–25m	3–10m	W. te Trop S. tr S. ar	•	•			•	•		L
Melaleuca armillaris Bracelet Honey Myrtle	Large spreading shrub or small tree, fine dense foliage, white brushes spring–summer. Excellent coastal or inland windbreak.	4–7m	6–8m	Temp S. tr	•		•		•	•	1	L
Melaleuca bracteata	Large shrub or small tree, fine crowded foliage, small white brushes along the stems in spring. Ideal shade and shelter tree for light to heavy soils.	4–7m	3–5m	Temp Trop S. tr S. ar	•		•		•	•		L
Melaleuca bracteata 'Golden Gem'	Low spreading shrub, dense fine golden foliage, white flowers in spring. Excellent bold feature plant. Regular pruning recommended.	1–1.5m	1.5–2.5m	Temp Trop S. tr	•				•	•		L
Melaleuca calothamnoides	Small to medium shrub, fine foliage, large orange-red brushes spring–summer. Very showy; hardy in dry conditions. Regular pruning recommended.	1.5–2.2m	1–2m	W. te S. ar	•		•		•		2	L
Melaleuca cardiophylla	Spreading dwarf shrub, stem-clasping heart-shaped leaves, deep pink or cream flowers spring–summer. Regular pruning recommended.	30–60cm	60cm–1m	Temp S. ar	•		•		•	•		L
Melaleuca citrina	Small to medium upright shrub, lemon-scented foliage, creamy yellow globular flowers spring–summer. Useful for coastal and dry areas. Prune regularly.	1.8–3.5m	1.2–2.5m	Temp S. ar	•		•		•		2	L
Melaleuca coccinea	Upright open medium shrub, attractive cordate foliage, brilliant scarlet bottlebrush-like flowers spring–summer. Regular pruning recommended.	1.5–2m	80cm–1.5m	Temp S. tr	•		•		•			L

Legend:

Temp — temperate
W. te — warm temperate
Trop — tropical
S. tr — sub-tropical
S. ar — semi-arid

L — light
H — heavy
N — nectar-feeding
S — seed-eating
F — fruit-eating

Legend:

- mp — temperate
- te — warm temperate
- p — tropical
- r — sub-tropical
- r — semi-arid
- L — light
- H — heavy
- N — nectar-feeding
- S — seed-eating
- F — fruit-eating

Name	Description	Height	Width	Climatic zones	moist, well drained	wet	dry	dry limy	full sun	filtered sun	coastal regions	frosty regions	bird attraction
laleuca nothamnoides	Low to medium spreading shrub, narrow elliptical leaves, rounded heads of purple flowers spring–summer. Attractive, hardy plant for well-drained soils.	50–90cm	1–1.2m	W. te S. ar	•		•		•			L	N
laleuca cuneata	Small rounded shrub, narrow grey foliage, pink flowers spring–summer. Prune after flowering.	60cm–1.5m	1–1.8m	W. te S. ar	•		•		•	•		L	N
laleuca icularis	Small to medium shrub, papery bark, bright green foliage, clusters of white flowers spring–summer. Very hardy; an attractive specimen plant.	1.5–3m	1–1.8m	Temp S. tr S. ar	•				•	•	1	L	N
laleuca decora	Large shrub or small tree, paperbark trunk, linear leaves, cream brushes in summer. Tolerates permanent moisture; useful screening plant.	4–7m	1.5–2.2m	Temp Trop S. tr	•	•			•	•		L	N
laleuca ussata	Medium shrub, neat grey foliage, soft pink or white brushes in spring. Very hardy, fast-growing screening plant. Prune regularly.	1.5–2m	1.5–2.2m	Temp Trop S. tr	•	•			•	•	2	H	N
laleuca densa	Dense medium shrub, dark stem-clasping foliage, small yellow-green brushes winter–spring–summer. Hardy, fast growing; useful for screening. Prune.	1.8–2.5m	1–2.2m	Temp Trop S. tr	•	•	•		•	•	1	L	N
laleuca smifolia	Large spreading shrub, neat regular dense foliage, bright green bottlebrush-like flowers in summer. Hardy, attractive screen. Regular pruning recommended.	2.5–4m	2.2–3.5m	Temp Trop S. tr	•				•	•	1	L	N
laleuca utherostachya	Rounded medium shrub, dense foliage, white brushes late spring–summer. Hardy, adaptable and drought tolerant.	1.5–2.5m	1.5–2.2m	Temp S. tr S. ar	•		•		•	•		L	N
laleuca elliptica	Upright medium shrub, stem-clasping rounded grey leaves, large burgundy brushes spring–summer. Hardy, distinctive plant. Prune regularly.	1.8–3m	1.5–2.5m	Temp S. tr S. ar	•		•		•	•		L	N
laleuca ericifolia	Suckering large shrub or small tree, fine foliage, small white brushes spring–summer. Hardy; very showy in flower. Excellent bird habitat.	3–6m	2–5m	Temp Trop S. tr	•	•			•	•	2	H	N
laleuca bescens	Small to medium rounded shrub, fine foliage, mauve flower spikes in summer. Hardy and useful screening plant. Regular pruning recommended.	1.5–2m	60cm–1m	Temp S. tr S. ar	•	•			•	•	2	L	N
laleuca fulgens	Medium shrub, fine grey-green foliage; deep pink, pale pink or salmon brushes in spring or summer. Hardy and attractive. Prune after flowering.	1.5–2.5m	1–2m	Temp S. tr S. ar	•		•		•		2	L	N

Temp — temperate
W. te — warm temperate
Trop — tropical
S. tr — sub-tropical
S. ar — semi-arid

L — light
H — heavy
N — nectar-feeding
S — seed-eating
F — fruit-eating

		Height	Width	Climatic zones	moist, well drained	wet	dry	dry limy	full sun	filtered sun	coastal regions	frosty regions
Melaleuca gibbosa	Small to medium shrub, minute crowded foliage, massed purple ball flowers late spring–summer. Very hardy and useful screening plant.	60cm–2m	40cm–1m	Temp S. tr	•	•			•	•	2	L
Melaleuca glaberrima	Small erect or arching shrub, fine foliage, soft pink brushes late spring–early summer. Excellent low hedging plant. Prune after flowering.	40–90cm	80cm–1.2m	Temp	•		•		•	•		L
Melaleuca halmaturorum	Large spreading shrub, papery bark, fine foliage, white flowers in spring. Useful coastal screening plant. Requires regular pruning.	3–6m	2.5–5m	Temp S. tr	•	•		•	•	•	1	L
Melaleuca huegelii	Medium to large upright shrub, fine foliage, fluffy cream brushes late spring–summer. Decorative, hardy and useful screen. Prune after flowering.	2–4m	1.5–2.5m	Temp S. tr	•		•		•	•	1	H
Melaleuca hypericifolia	Medium to large rounded shrub, bright green elliptical foliage, showy orange-red brushes spring–summer. Excellent screen or windbreak. Prune regularly.	2.5–4m	2.5–4m	Temp Trop S. tr	•		•		•	•	1	L
Melaleuca hypericifolia 'Ulladulla Beacon'	Prostrate or mounding low groundcover, bright green elliptical foliage, orange-red brushes above foliage spring–summer. Hardy and adaptable.	30–60cm	1–2m	Temp Trop S. tr	•		•		•	•	1	L
Melaleuca incana	Weeping medium shrub, silver-grey soft foliage, many small pale yellow flowers in spring. Smaller cultivar ('Velvet Cushion') suitable for temperate areas.	2–3m	2–2.5m	Temp S. tr	•				•	•	2	L
Melaleuca lanceolata	Large shrub, small dark heath-like foliage, white brushes in spring. Hardy, adaptable plant for dry to wet and saline soils. Regular pruning recommended.	4–6m	4–6m	Temp S. ar	•	•	•		•	•	1	L
Melaleuca lateritia Robin Red Breast	Small to medium shrub, soft fine foliage, lustrous orange-red brushes summer–autumn. Trim regularly to form beautiful hedge; prune single plants also.	1.5–3m	1–2m	Temp S. tr	•	•			•	•	2	L
Melaleuca laxiflora	Small to medium shrub, fine foliage, soft purple-pink brushes winter–late spring. Regular pruning required.	1–1.5m	1–1.5m	Temp S. tr	•		•	•	•		2	L
Melaleuca leucadendron	Large tree, long thick leaves, green or crimson brushes autumn–winter. Handsome and fast growing; particularly useful in swampy areas.	15–25m	6–10m	W. te Trop S. tr	•	•			•	•		L
Melaleuca linariifolia Snow in Summer	Large shrub or small tree, light green foliage, masses of fluffy white flowers in summer. Extremely showy and hardy; ideal street tree.	4–8m	2–5m	Temp Trop S. tr	•	•			•	•	2	L

		Height	Width	Climatic zones	Soil types				full sun	filtered sun	coastal regions	frosty regions	bird attraction
					moist, well drained	wet	dry	dry limy					
Jaleuca cronycha	Upright open medium shrub, lanceolate grey foliage, deep red brushes summer–autumn. Hardy and attractive. Requires regular pruning.	1.8–2.2m	1–1.5m	Temp S.tr S.ar	•		•		•	•		L	N
Jaleuca gacephala	Erect medium shrub, crowded ovate foliage, large yellow ball flowers spring–early summer. Attractive plant for dry areas. Requires regular pruning.	1.8–3m	2–3m	Temp S.ar	•		•		•	•		L	N
Jaleuca cromera	Small to medium conifer-like erect narrow shrub, minute crowded scale-like foliage, yellow pompom flowers in spring. Ideal for narrow areas. Prune regularly.	1–2.8m	60cm–2m	Temp S.tr	•		•		•	•		L	N
Jaleuca crophylla	Medium to large shrub, fine crowded foliage, cylindrical yellow flowers in spring. Hardy screening plant; salt tolerant. Requires regular pruning.	2.5–3m	1.5–2m	Temp S.tr	•	•		•	•	•	2	L	N
Jaleuca natophylla	Upright open medium shrub, long fine foliage, large deep pink ball flowers spring–early summer. Very showy. Prune lightly after flowering.	1.5–2.5m	1–2m	W.te S.ar	•		•		•			H	N
Jaleuca nesophila	Medium to large dense shrub, papery bark, elliptical foliage, strongly scented massed mauve ball flowers in summer. Hardy, salt tolerant. Prune regularly.	3–6m	3–5m	Temp Trop S.tr	•		•		•	•	1	L	N
Jaleuca yne's Hybrid'	Medium shrub, fine grey foliage, bright crimson brushes spring–summer–autumn. Showy, hardy and adaptable. Requires regular pruning.	1.5–2m	1.2–2m	Temp S.tr S.ar	•		•		•	•		L	N
Jaleuca tagona	Medium shrub, fine needle foliage, bright pink flowers spring–early summer. Graceful; grows well in deep sand. Light pruning recommended.	2–3m	1.5–2m	Temp S.ar	•		•		•	•		L	N
Jaleuca pulchella	Small compact shrub, neatly arranged small leaves, mauve claw flowers summer–autumn. Very decorative, hardy and adaptable. Prune lightly.	60cm–1m	60cm–1m	Temp S.tr S.ar	•		•		•	•		L	N
Jaleuca nquenervia	Large shrub or large tree, papery bark, large leaves, creamy white brushes autumn–winter. Very handsome parkland tree; suited to swampy areas.	12–25m	4–8m	Temp Trop S.tr	•	•			•	•	2		N
Jaleuca radula	Small to medium upright shrub, soft fine foliage, pink to mauve brushes winter–spring. Very hardy, attractive small screening plant. Prune regularly.	1–2.5m	1–2.2m	Temp S.ar	•		•		•	•		L	N
Jaleuca ohiophylla	Large spreading tree, papery bark, graceful soft linear foliage, highly perfumed fluffy white flowers spring–summer. Shady parkland tree.	8–25m	5–15m	Temp Trop S.tr	•	•			•	•		L	N

mp — temperate
te — warm temperate
p — tropical
r — sub-tropical
r — semi-arid

L — light
H — heavy
N — nectar-feeding
S — seed-eating
F — fruit-eating

		Height	Width	Climatic zones	Soil types				full sun	filtered sun	coastal regions	frosty regions
Temp — temperate / W. te — warm temperate / Trop — tropical / S. tr — sub-tropical / S. ar — semi-arid L — light / H — heavy / N — nectar-feeding / S — seed-eating / F — fruit-eating					moist, well drained	wet	dry	dry limy				
Melaleuca scabra	Dwarf to small shrub, fine soft hairy foliage, gold-tipped pink to purple flowers in spring. Distinctive and very pretty. Prune lightly after flowering.	30–60cm	50cm–1m	Temp S. ar	•		•		•	•		L
Melaleuca seriata	Small shrub, silvery foliage, bright pink flowers in spring. Hardy contrasting plant for dry areas. Prune lightly after flowering.	1–2m	80cm–1.5m	Temp S. tr S. ar	•		•		•			L
Melaleuca spathulata	Small to medium, often upright and narrow shrub; crowded foliage, pink ball flowers spring–summer. Hardy and attractive; useful in confined areas.	80cm–2m	50cm–1m	Temp S. tr	•				•	•		L
Melaleuca spicigera	Small shrub, blue-green ovate leaves, clusters of pink flowers spring–early summer. Requires very good drainage. Light pruning recommended.	60cm–1m	60cm–1m	Temp S. ar	•		•		•			L
Melaleuca squamea	Upright narrow medium shrub, crowded hairy foliage, pinky mauve brushes in spring. Excellent for constantly wet areas; useful as bird habitat.	2–2.5m	90cm–1.2m	Temp Trop S. tr	•	•			•	•	2	H
Melaleuca squarrosa	Upright medium shrub, neat crowded foliage, showy clusters of creamy yellow brushes spring–summer. Hardy screen for wet or dry areas.	2–3m	1–2m	Temp Trop S. tr	•	•	•		•	•	2	H
Melaleuca steedmanii	Small to medium shrub, smooth grey-green foliage, brilliant red brushes tipped with gold late winter–spring. Mauve form also. Light pruning recommended.	1–1.5m	1–1.5m	Temp S. tr S. ar	•		•		•		2	L
Melaleuca striata	Small spreading shrub; fine pointed foliage, almost covered with soft pink brushes spring–summer. Very showy and hardy. Light pruning recommended.	40cm–1m	70cm–1.5m	Temp S. ar	•		•		•	•	2	L
Melaleuca styphelioides	Medium to large shrub or small tree, papery bark, crowded short neat foliage, white flowers spring–summer. Good screen, windbreak and street tree.	5–10m	3–6m	Temp Trop S. tr	•	•			•	•	1	L
Melaleuca suberosa	Low spreading, sometimes straggling shrub; attractive corky bark, fine foliage, purple-red flowers on old wood spring–summer. Hardy and unusual.	50cm–1m	80cm–1.2m	W. te S. ar	•		•		•		2	L
Melaleuca tamarascina	Medium to large pendulous shrub, fine foliage, white or pink brushes in summer. Handsome and hardy; useful for screening and windbreaks.	2–4.5m	1.5–2m	W. te S. ar	•	•	•		•	•	2	L
Melaleuca thymifolia	Dwarf to small shrub, crowded grey-green foliage; pink, mauve or white claw flowers late spring–summer. Very hardy; ideal for a low hedge. Prune regularly.	50cm–1m	30–80cm	Temp Trop S. tr	•	•	•		•	•	2	L

	L — light
ıp — temperate	H — heavy
e — warm temperate	N — nectar-feeding
p — tropical	S — seed-eating
— sub-tropical	F — fruit-eating
r — semi-arid	

		Height	Width	Climatic zones	Soil types				full sun	filtered sun	coastal regions	frosty regions	bird attraction
					moist, well drained	wet	dry	dry limy					
aleuca hophylla	Medium shrub, soft hairy foliage, cream flowers aging to pink spring–summer. Attractive screen plant for dry regions; excellent bird habitat. Prune.	1.5–2m	2–2.5m	W. te S. ar	•		•		•		2	L	N
aleuca ostachya	Medium shrub, grey-green foliage with pink new growth, white brushes winter–spring. Very attractive. Regular pruning recommended.	1.5–2.5m	1–2m	W. te S. ar	•	•	•		•		2	L	N
aleuca violacea	Low spreading shrub which develops a layered appearance; papery bark, grey foliage, violet claw flowers spring–summer. Hardy; excellent landscape plant.	15–50cm	50cm–1.8m	Temp S. tr S. ar	•		•		•		2	L	N
aleuca viridiflora	Medium to large, often pendulous tree; papery bark, broad elliptical leaves, yellow-green or red spikes most of the year. Fast growing, handsome.	7–18m	5–8m	Temp Trop S. tr S. ar	•	•			•	•	2		N
aleuca wilsonii	Small to medium shrub, fine crowded foliage, cerise pink flowers in spring. Hardy, adaptable; excellent bird habitat. Prune regularly.	1–2m	1.5–2.5m	Temp S. tr S. ar	•	•			•	•	2	H	N
astoma affine n. M. abathricum)	Small to medium open shrub, distinctly veined dark leaves, large pink lasiandra-like flowers mainly in summer. Attractive foliage plant.	1–2.5m	1–2.5m	Temp Trop S. tr	•					•		L	S
ia azedarach ite Cedar	Small to large tree, pinnate foliage, sprays of lilac flowers in spring, followed by orange berries. Deciduous.	6–16m	3–12m	Temp Trop S. tr	•		•		•		2	L	N S
ntha gracilis	Scrambling herb, soft smooth strongly peppermint-scented leaves, tiny white or mauve flowers spring–summer. Grows well with ferns.	10–30cm	1–3m	Temp Trop S. tr	•	•			•	•		L	
trosideros eenslandicus	Large rainforest tree in natural habitat, smaller in cultivation. Shiny dense foliage, clusters of golden flowers autumn–winter, also sporadic. Indoor plant.	8–25m	6–15m	W. te Trop S. tr	•				•			L	
cromyrtus ciliata	Dwarf variable shrub, aromatic crowded foliage, massed small white to pink flowers in spring. Rockery or container. Tip prune after flowering.	30–60cm	30–75cm	Temp S. ar	•		•		•	•		H	
cromyrtus ammondii	Small upright shrub, tiny leaves, masses of white flowers spring–early summer. Rockery or container plant. Tip prune after flowering.	60cm–1m	60cm–1m	Temp S. ar	•		•		•	•		L	
lettia gasperma ive Wistaria	Vigorous liane, glossy pinnate leaves, showy sprays of large purple pea flowers summer–autumn. Very showy and fast growing.	climber	vigorous	Temp Trop S. tr	•	•			•	•		L	S

		Height	Width	Climatic zones	Soil types				full sun	filtered sun	coastal regions	frosty regions
					moist, well drained	wet	dry	dry limy				
Mirbelia dilatata	Erect medium shrub, stiff triangular prickly foliage, massed display of pink to purple pea flowers late spring–summer. Showy and fast growing.	2.5–3m	70cm–1m	Temp	•				•	•		
Mirbelia oxyloboides	Spreading medium shrub, small silver-grey foliage, bright yellow-orange pea flowers in spring. Showy, hardy and adaptable. Excellent screening plant.	1–2m	1–2m	Temp	•				•	•		
Muehlenbeckia adpressa	Dense tangled twining plant, broad heart-shaped leaves, insignificant flowers. Very useful for soil binding or for screening on a wire frame.	climber	medium	Temp S. ar	•		•		•	•	1	
Myoporum acuminatum Boobialla	Large dense shapely bush, lanceolate leaves, white flowers spotted with purple late spring–summer. Good coastal or dry area plant.	3–4m	2–3m	Temp S. ar	•		•	•	•	•	1	L
Myoporum debile	Creeping groundcover, long leaves; white flowers in spring, followed by pink berries. Very hardy.	prostrate	1–1.5m	Temp S. ar	•		•		•	•	2	L
Myoporum desertii	Large shrub, thick narrow leaves; white flowers winter–spring, followed by yellow berries. Very drought-hardy.	2–3m	1–2m	W. te S. ar	•		•	•	•	•		H
Myoporum ellipticum	Dense groundcovering plant, large leaves, small white flowers spring–summer, dark purple berries. Excellent for roadsides, coastal or general soil binding.	60cm–1m	2–3m	Temp S. ar	•		•		•	•	1	L
Myoporum floribundum	Spreading open medium shrub, fine foliage hanging gracefully from thin branches, white or occasionally pink flowers along stems in spring.	2–3m	2–3m	Temp S. tr	•		•		•	•	2	L
Myoporum insulare Boobialla	Large dense shrub, thick fleshy leaves, small white flowers spring–summer. Fast growing screen and coastal windbreak. Requires regular pruning.	3–4m	3–6m	Temp S. ar	•		•	•	•	•	1	L
Myoporum parvifolium	Densely layering groundcover; fine or broad foliage, variable in colour; pink or white flowers spring–summer. Hardy, vigorous sand or soil binder.	prostrate	1.5–2.5m	Temp S. ar	•		•	•	•	•	1	L
Nauclea orientalis Leichhardt Tree	Large spreading tree, glossy foliage, cream-and-gold golf-ball sized flowers spring–summer. Handsome parkland shade tree for warm, constantly moist areas.	15–20m	8–12m	W. te Trop S. tr	•	•			•	•		L
Nematolepis phebalioides	Dwarf to small shrub, shiny oblong leaves, pendent red tubular flowers in spring. Attractive container plant. Requires light tip pruning.	40cm–1m	60–80cm	W. te S. ar	•		•	•	•		2	L

Temp — temperate
W. te — warm temperate
Trop — tropical
S. tr — sub-tropical
S. ar — semi-arid

L — light
H — heavy
N — nectar-feeding
S — seed-eating
F — fruit-eating

		Height	Width	Climatic zones	Soil types								
					moist, well drained	wet	dry	dry limy	full sun	filtered sun	coastal regions	frosty regions	bird attraction
ɳp — temperate L — light													

Legend:
- ɳp — temperate
- e — warm temperate
- ɒ — tropical
- ʳ — sub-tropical
- ɹ — semi-arid
- L — light
- H — heavy
- N — nectar-feeding
- S — seed-eating
- F — fruit-eating

Name	Description	Height	Width	Climatic zones	moist, well drained	wet	dry	dry limy	full sun	filtered sun	coastal regions	frosty regions	bird attraction
olitsea dealbata	Large rainforest shrub or small to medium tree; large elliptical leaves, grey beneath; tiny flowers, globular dark red fruit in summer. Indoor plant.	6–10m	3–6m	W.te S.tr	•					•	2		
osepicaea unda	Vigorous liane, large shiny leaves, purple-red flowers late winter–spring.	climber	vigorous	Trop S.tr	•					•			
hofagus ninghamii uthern Myrtle eech	Tall tree, shiny crinkled foliage with gold to bronze new growth, insignificant flowers and fruit. Very handsome tree for cool moist areas.	8–25m	6–8m	Temp S.tr	•					•		L	
ytsia floribunda A. Christmas Tree	Small to medium tree which is parasitic. Long thick foliage, massed heads of golden flowers in summer. Difficult to establish.	3–9m	2–7m	W.te S.ar	•		•	•	•		2	L	N
aria axillaris	Small rounded shrub, silvery linear leaves, white daisy flowers in spring. Hardy, attractive foliage plant. Tolerant of salt spray. Prune lightly.	1–2m	1.5–2m	Temp S.ar	•		•	•	•		1		
aria ciliata	Dwarf shrub, crowded hairy foliage, bright purple daisy flowers on stalks above the foliage winter–spring. Light tip pruning improves shape.	15–30cm	10–20cm	Temp S.tr S.ar	•		•		•	•		L	
aria iodochroa	Small spreading shrub, dark shiny leaves with felted undersides, mauve daisy flowers in spring and sporadic. Regular tip pruning required.	60–90cm	60–90cm	Temp S.tr	•		•		•	•		L	
aria ogopappa	Small to medium upright shrub, grey oblong foliage, profuse mauve or pink daisy flowers in spring. Very showy. Regular pruning required.	1–1.5m	60–90cm	Temp S.tr	•		•		•	•		L	
aria picridifolia	Dwarf shrub, fine hairy foliage, large blue-mauve daisy flowers on long stalks in spring. Suited to dry areas and containers. Tip prune after flowering.	20–40cm	10–20cm	W.te S.ar	•		•		•	•		L	
aria ramulosa	Dwarf to small spreading scrambling shrub, linear or rounded leaves, blue daisy flowers in spring. Prune regularly.	40cm–2m	1–2m	Temp S.tr S.ar	•		•		•	•		L	
aria teretifolia . compacta	Dense dwarf plant; tight conifer-like foliage, covered in small white daisy flowers in spring. Interesting contrast plant for rockeries or borders. Tip prune.	30–50cm	20–50cm	Temp S.tr	•		•		•	•		L	
aria tomentosa	Small to medium shrub, scalloped leaves, large mauve or white flowers in spring. Low form is a useful coastal plant. Light pruning recommended.	20cm–2.2m	40–80cm	Temp S.tr					•	•	2	L	

		Height	Width	Climatic zones	Soil types				full sun	filtered sun	coastal regions	frosty regions
					moist, well drained	wet	dry	dry limy				
Omalanthus populifolius Bleeding Heart	Medium to large open shrub; large heart-shaped green leaves, blood red when old; insignificant flowers in spring. Attractive indoor tub plant.	2–5m	1–2.5m	Temp Trop S.tr	•				•	•		L
Oreocallis pinnata Dorrigo Waratah	Slender large shrub or small tree of rainforests, larger in natural habitat than in cultivation. Simple or divided leaves, spectacular red flowers spring–summer.	8–20m	4–7m	W.te Trop S.tr	•					•		
Oreocallis wickhamii Pink Silky Oak Tree Waratah	Large shrub or spreading tree of rainforests, smaller in cultivation than in natural habitat. Dark foliage, profuse clusters of scarlet flowers spring–summer.	10–25m	6–12m	Temp Trop S.tr	•				•	•		L
Orites excelsa Prickly Ash	Large rainforest shrub or tree, lobed or serrated foliage, spikes of creamy white flowers in spring. A good specimen tree for shaded sites.	3–10m	1–6m	W.te Trop S.tr	•					•		L
Orthrosanthus laxus	Dwarf lily, rush-like foliage, sky blue flowers autumn–winter–spring. Raised bed, rockery or container plant.	30–60cm	30–80cm	Temp S.tr	•				•	•		L
Orthrosanthus multiflorus	Small lily, rush-like foliage, long slender stems above foliage bearing massed sky blue flowers in spring. Hardy; an excellent landscape plant.	1–1.5m	1–1.5m	Temp S.tr	•				•	•	•	L
Oxylobium tricuspidatum	Carpeting groundcover, grey-green 3-pointed leaves, orange-yellow pea flowers covering foliage spring–summer. Excellent rockery plant.	prostrate	60–90cm	Temp S.ar	•		•		•			L
Pandorea jasminoides	Dense climber, glossy pinnate foliage, pale to deep pink trumpet flowers summer–late autumn. Very beautiful and hardy.	climber	vigorous	Temp Trop S.tr	•				•	•		L
Pandorea jasminoides 'Lady Di'	Dense climber, bright green glossy foliage, lightly perfumed white trumpet flowers with yellow throat summer–autumn. Hardy and very beautiful.	climber	vigorous	Temp Trop S.tr	•				•	•		L
Pandorea pandorana Wonga Vine	Dense climber; dark glossy pinnate foliage, occasionally with bronze new growth; clusters of cream purple-throated tubular flowers in spring. Very hardy.	climber	vigorous	Temp Trop S.tr S.ar	•		•		•	•		L
Pandorea pandorana 'Snow Bells'	Pure white form of the above. *P. pandorana* 'Golden Showers' is the golden form and has the same requirements.	climber	vigorous	Temp Trop S.tr S.ar	•		•		•	•		L
Parahebe perfoliata	Dwarf shrub, stem-clasping leaves in pairs, sprays of blue flowers on stems above foliage in summer. Contrast plant for shaded sites. Prune lightly.	30–60cm	60cm–1m	Temp	•		•				•	H

Temp — temperate   L — light
W. te — warm temperate   H — heavy
Trop — tropical   N — nectar-feeding
S. tr — sub-tropical   S — seed-eating
S. ar — semi-arid   F — fruit-eating

		Height	Width	Climatic zones	moist, well drained	wet	dry	dry limy	full sun	filtered sun	coastal regions	frosty regions	bird attraction
ersonia longifolia	Dwarf plant, rush-like short grey leaves, deep blue flag flowers spring–summer. Rockery or edging plant.	10–15cm	10cm	Temp S.tr	●		●		●	●		L	
ersonia dentalis ive Iris	Dwarf plant, rush-like foliage, masses of purple or white flag flowers spring–summer. Rockery or poolside plant.	30–60cm	30–60cm	Temp S.tr	●		●		●	●		L	
rsonia sericea	Dwarf plant, fine silky leaves, dainty blue-mauve flag flowers in spring. Rockery or poolside plant.	20–30cm	20–40cm	Temp S.tr	●		●		●	●		L	
rgonium eyanum	Small rosetted herb, rounded lobed foliage, pretty pink flowers on short stalks above the foliage spring–summer. Rockery or path-edging plant.	prostrate–10cm	10–20cm	Temp	●		●		●	●		L	
nisetum ecuroides	Vigorous grass, fine narrow leaves, fluffy pink purple-tinged flower plumes and seeds spring–summer–autumn. Hardy and very decorative.	40–80cm	50–80cm	Temp Trop S.tr	●	●			●	●		L	
soonia maepitys	Prostrate compact shrub, crowded fine light green leaves, bright yellow perfumed flowers late spring–summer. Prune after flowering.	prostrate	60cm–1.2m	Temp S.tr	●		●		●	●		L	N
soonia pinifolia	Medium to large shrub, fine soft foliage on pendulous branches, long racemes of golden perfumed flowers summer–autumn, attractive globular fruit. Hardy.	2.5–4m	2–3m	Temp Trop S.tr	●		●		●	●		L	N
ophile biloba	Small to medium shrub, attractive divided grey foliage, silky pink-and-grey flowers winter–spring. Prune lightly after flowering.	90cm–1.8m	60–90cm	W.te S.ar	●		●		●	●		L	N
ophile conifera	Small shrub, net foliage with red new growth, compact heads of highly perfumed creamy yellow flowers in spring. Decorative; suitable for moist sand.	1–1.5m	1–1.2m	Temp	●	●			●	●		L	N
ophile rsifolia	Medium shrub, deeply lobed foliage, creamy white flowers winter–spring. Prune lightly after flowering.	1.8–3m	1.2–2m	W.te S.ar	●		●		●	●		L	N
ophile ericifolia	Small bushy shrub, fine crowded foliage, heads of yellow flowers spring–summer. Prune lightly after flowering.	80cm–1m	1–1.2m	W.te S.ar	●		●		●	●		L	N
ophile fucifolia	Small erect shrub, narrowly divided foliage, terminal heads of yellow flowers in spring. Structurally interesting. Prune lightly after flowering.	1–2m	80cm–1m	Temp S.ar	●		●		●	●		L	N

		Height	Width	Climatic zones	moist, well drained	wet	dry	dry limy	full sun	filtered sun	coastal regions	frosty regions
Temp — temperate	L — light											
W. te — warm temperate	H — heavy											
Trop — tropical	N — nectar-feeding											
S. tr — sub-tropical	S — seed-eating											
S. ar — semi-arid	F — fruit-eating											

		Height	Width	Climatic zones	moist, well drained	wet	dry	dry limy	full sun	filtered sun	coastal regions	frosty regions
Petrophile linearis	Upright dwarf shrub, thick sickle-shaped grey leaves, woolly mop-head pink flowers spring–summer. Spectacular; grow in sand, raised bed or container.	30–50cm	10–30cm	W. te S. ar	•		•		•	•		L
Petrophile serruriae	Small to medium erect shrub, much-divided leaves, heads of creamy yellow flowers spring–summer. Decorative foliage plant.	90cm–3m	80cm–2m	W. te S. ar	•		•		•	•		L
Phebalium bilobum	Medium shrub, dense linear foliage lobed at the end, profuse white star flowers in spring. Suitable for heavy shade in moist soils. Light pruning beneficial.	1–2m	1–2m	Temp S. tr	•				•	•		L
Phebalium lamprophyllum	Small compact shrub, crowded small elliptical leaves, plentiful white star flowers in spring. Very hardy; useful for shady dry positions. Prune lightly.	80cm–1.5m	90cm–1.5m	Temp S. tr	•		•		•	•		L
Phebalium phylicifolium	Small rounded alpine shrub, fine dense foliage, profuse display of cream star flowers in summer. Will grow successfully if root system remains cool and moist.	30cm–1m	50cm–1m	Temp	•				•	•		L
Phebalium squamulosum	Small to medium compact shrub, fine to elliptical foliage, massed cream or yellow star flowers in spring. Several forms. Prune lightly.	30cm–3m	60cm–2.5m	Temp S. tr	•		•		•	•	•	L
Philotheca salsolifolia	Dwarf to small shrub, fine foliage, pink to mauve star flowers in spring. Requires dry rocky conditions. Prune lightly after flowering.	30cm–1m	20–80cm	Temp S. ar	•		•		•	•		L
Phyla nodiflora	Tightly matting plant, small leaves, pink clover-like flowers in summer. Excellent substitute for lawn. Hard-wearing, self-layering, soil-binder.	prostrate	2–5m	Temp S. tr S. ar	•		•		•			H
Pileanthus filifolius	Small slender upright shrub, fine leaves, showy magenta open flowers spring–summer. Sand mound or container plant. Prune lightly after flowering.	50cm–1m	30–60cm	W. te S. ar	•		•		•	•		L
Pileanthus peduncularis Copper Cups	Small rounded shrub, crowded linear foliage, massed orange or orange-red open flowers with dark centres in spring. Sand mound or container.	60cm–1m	60cm–1m	W. te S. ar	•		•		•	•		L
Pimelea ferruginea	Dwarf to small compact shrub, neat crowded foliage, massed pompom flowers of pale to rose pink spring–early summer. Hardy. Prune after flowering.	30cm–1m	50cm–1.2m	Temp S. tr	•		•		•	•	1	L
Pimelea ferruginea 'Bonne Petite'	Small compact shrub, neat crowded foliage, deep pink pompom flowers in spring. Prune after flowering.	60cm–1m	60–90cm	Temp S. tr	•		•		•	•	1	L

Moss-encrusted basalt boulders
edge a set of timber and gravel
steps which dramatically link hard
surfaces at different levels. Privacy
and seclusion for the timber seat
are provided by the soft, low,
screening plants.

A squared section of granite serv
as a structural change of level, a
as paving. The solid timber step
blends well with the lichen-cove
rocks, providing a firm edge for †
paving. *Dampiera linearis* is the
sole plant in this bold detail,
suckering wherever a pocket of s
is available.

A longer slope is best treated by
curving steps across the contour.
The space between the risers
slopes gradually and is filled
inexpensively with packed
sawdust, topped lightly with
coarse sand. Few rocks are used;
bordering plants direct movement
along the pathway.

						np — temperate L — light

Legend (top):

np — temperate   L — light
te — warm temperate   H — heavy
p — tropical   N — nectar-feeding
r — sub-tropical   S — seed-eating
r — semi-arid   F — fruit-eating

Name	Description	Height	Width	Climatic zones	moist, well drained	wet	dry	dry limy	full sun	filtered sun	coastal regions	frosty regions	soil	bird attraction
elea ferruginea 'genta Mist'	Small compact shrub, neat crowded foliage, large bright magenta pompom flowers with white centres in spring. Prune after flowering.	60cm–1m	60–90cm	Temp S.tr	•		•		•	•		1	L	
elea filiformis	Dainty trailing dwarf plant, tiny leaves, pink-and-white pompom flowers spring–summer. Container or basket plant.	prostrate	30–60cm	Temp S.tr	•		•		•	•			L	
elea humilis	Dwarf suckering plant, neat grey-green foliage, creamy white pompom flowers in spring. Container or rockery plant. Light pruning beneficial.	10–30cm	10–50cm	Temp S.tr	•		•		•	•			L	
elea imbricata	Tiny mounding shrub, small grey-green foliage, deep pink pompom flowers spring–summer–autumn. Container plant. Prune after flowering.	20–40cm	30–60cm	Temp S.tr	•		•		•				L	
elea linifolia	Open fine-stemmed dwarf shrub, sparse grey-green foliage, nodding heads of white pink-tinged pompom flowers spring–early summer. Prune lightly.	30–60cm	15–30cm	Temp S.tr	•		•		•	•			L	
elea nivea	Small upright shrub, felted stems, shiny round leaves felted beneath, perfumed white pink-tinged pompom flowers spring–early summer. Prune lightly.	80cm–1.5m	60cm–1.2m	Temp S.tr	•				•	•			L	
elea rosea	Fine-stemmed open dwarf shrub, sparse foliage, large pink or white mop-head flowers in spring. Very showy. Prune lightly after flowering.	40–60cm	20–30cm	Temp S.tr	•				•	•			L	
elea spectabilis	Small shrub, grey-green foliage, large heads of pink or white flowers in spring. Grows best in deep sand or container. Prune lightly after flowering.	50–80cm	20–50cm	W.te S.ar	•		•		•	•			L	
elea sylvestris	Small erect shrub, neat foliage, white or pink (occasionally yellow) heads of bracted flowers winter–spring–summer. Container plant. Prune lightly.	1.2–1.5m	80cm–1m	W.te S.ar	•		•		•	•			L	
elea treyvaudii	Small compact shrub, crisp pale green foliage, numerous heads of creamy white pompom flowers in spring. Regular pruning beneficial.	40–80cm	20–80cm	Temp S.tr	•				•	•			L	
osporum llyreoides	Small weeping tree, linear leaves, perfumed creamy yellow flowers spring–summer, followed by orange berries. Attractive, hardy in dry areas.	4–8m	2.5–5m	W.te S.ar Arid	•		•	•	•	•			H	N S
osporum olutum	Large shrub, attractive shiny foliage, scented yellow flowers spring–early summer, followed by orange or red berries.	3–6m	2–5m	Temp Trop S.tr	•				•	•		1	L	N S

		Height	Width	Climatic zones	moist, well drained	wet	dry	dry limy	full sun	filtered sun	coastal regions	frosty regions
Temp — temperate L — light W. te — warm temperate H — heavy Trop — tropical N — nectar-feeding S. tr — sub-tropical S — seed-eating S. ar — semi-arid F — fruit-eating												
Pittosporum rhombifolium	Large shrub or medium tree, toothed rhomboidal leaves, dense racemes of perfumed creamy white flowers in summer, followed by orange berries.	4–20m	3–9m	Temp Trop S.tr	•				•	•		L
Pittosporum undulatum	Large spreading shrub or small tree, glossy foliage, perfumed creamy yellow flowers in spring, orange berries. Fast-growing, hardy, useful screening shrub.	4–8m	3–7m	Temp Trop S.tr	•		•		•	•	2	L
Platytheca juniperina	Upright dwarf shrub, fine rigid foliage, showy purple bell flowers all year. Container plant. Occasional tip pruning required.	30–90cm	10–30cm	Temp	•				•	•		L
Platytheca verticillata	Rounded dwarf shrub, very fine foliage, showy purple bell flowers all year. Container plant. Occasional tip pruning required.	30–60cm	20–60cm	Temp	•				•	•		L
Poa australis	Dense tufting grass, fine blue-green foliage, wispy open seed heads. Such plants provide contrast in landscapes, particularly when grown in drifts.	15–30cm	60cm–1m	Temp S.tr	•		•		•	•		H
Podocarpus elatus	Tall spreading conifer, long pointed leaves, edible blue-black plum-like fruit on female plants in autumn. Handsome shade tree; also tub plant while young.	6–15m	3–12m	Temp Trop S.tr	•				•	•		L
Polyscias elegans Celerywood	Tall slender shrub or elegant tree, canopy of pinnate foliage, small flowers spring–summer; blue-black seeds in large panicles in autumn, attractive to birds.	4–15m	1.5–6m	Temp Trop S.tr	•				•	•		L
Pomaderris andromedifolia	Small to medium upright shrub, small soft grey-green foliage with some orange-red leaves always present, creamy flowers in spring.	1–2m	60cm–1m	Temp S.tr	•		•		•	•		L
Pomaderris ferruginea	Medium to large erect shrub, soft hairy leaves, large heads of yellow flowers in spring. Attractive shrub for semi-shaded sites.	2.5–3m	2–2.5m	Temp S.tr	•		•		•	•		L
Pomaderris lanigera	Medium to large erect shrub, soft woolly leaves, heads of yellow flowers in spring. Attractive foliage contrast for semi-shaded sites.	2.5–3m	1.8–2.5m	Temp S.tr	•		•		•	•		L
Pomaderris obcordata	Compact dwarf shrub, small crowded leaves, dainty pink-and-white clustered flowers in spring. Container plant. Prune lightly after flowering.	30–60cm	60cm	Temp S.tr	•		•		•	•		L
Pratia pedunculata	Layering matting plant, tiny leaves, perfumed blue or white star flowers spring–summer. Ideal for soil binding, path edges and beside pools.	prostrate	1–2m	Temp Trop S.tr	•	•			•	•		L

np — temperate L — light
te — warm temperate H — heavy
p — tropical N — nectar-feeding
* — sub-tropical S — seed-eating
r — semi-arid F — fruit-eating

		Height	Width	Climatic zones	Soil types				full sun	filtered sun	coastal regions	frosty regions	bird attraction
					moist, well drained	wet	dry	dry limy					
tia purpurescens	Suckering vigorous matting plant, tiny leaves, mauve flowers summer–autumn. Useful for binding large areas of open moist soil.	prostrate	2–4m	Temp Trop. S.tr	•	•			•	•			L
naya fraseri	Dainty light climber, slightly hairy leaves, dark blue star flowers in summer. Very showy; useful for covering small sections of wall or up posts.	climber	light	Temp S.tr	•		•			•			L
stanthera ▪alathoides	Dwarf to small shrub, fine dense aromatic foliage; red, orange or yellow tubular flowers most of the year. Light tip pruning recommended.	30–80cm	20–60cm	Temp S.ar	•		•		•	•			L
stanthera baxteri , sericea	Small upright shrub, woolly white stems, soft fine silvery foliage, pale lavender flowers in spring. Very hardy, distinctive landscape plant. Tip prune.	80cm–1.2m	60cm–1m	Temp S.tr Arid S.ar	•		•		•	•			L
stanthera eata	Low spreading alpine shrub, crowded glossy aromatic leaves, massed white to pale mauve flowers late spring–summer. Light pruning recommended.	30–60cm	1–2m	Temp S.tr	•				•	•			H
stanthera ▪ticulata	Low spreading shrub, dense aromatic foliage, showy purple flowers in spring. Hardy and attractive. Regular pruning recommended.	30–50cm	80cm–1.2m	Temp S.tr	•		•		•	•			L
stanthera incana	Small bushy shrub, woolly pale green aromatic foliage, lavender flower spikes in spring. Very hardy. Regular pruning recommended.	1–1.5m	1–1.5m	Temp S.tr	•		•		•	•		2	L
stanthera anthos torian Christmas ush	Medium to large slender shrub, aromatic toothed foliage, showy purple-spotted white or pink flowers spring–summer.	2–6m	1.2–4m	Temp S.tr	•				•	•			L
stanthera gnifica	Small shrub, lanceolate foliage; pale mauve flowers in spring, each surrounded by a large purple bract-like calyx. Must have open sandy or gravelly soils.	30–80cm	40cm–1m	W.te S.ar	•		•		•				
stanthera lissifolia	Medium to large shrub, rounded aromatic leaves, pink or lilac flowers spring–summer. Well suited to cool shaded areas. Regular pruning recommended.	1.5–3m	1.2–2.5m	Temp S.tr	•				•	•			H
stanthera nivea induta	Upright medium shrub, narrow silver-grey foliage, blue-purple flowers in spring. Hardy and adaptable; foliage contrast. Regular pruning recommended.	2–2.5m	1.5–2m	Temp S.tr	•		•		•	•			L
stanthera lifolia	Medium to large shrub, dense aromatic foliage, massed mauve-purple flowers in spring. Excellent screening plant. Regular pruning recommended.	2–4m	1.2–3m	Temp S.tr	•		•		•	•		2	L

		Height	Width	Climatic zones	Soil types							
					moist, well drained	wet	dry	dry limy	full sun	filtered sun	coastal regions	frosty regions
Prostanthera 'Poorinda Ballerina'	Upright medium shrub, glossy crowded foliage, massed white flowers spring–early summer. Hardy, showy, useful screening plant. Requires regular pruning.	1.5–2.5m	1–2m	Temp S. tr	•		•		•	•		L
Prostanthera rotundifolia	Small to medium shrub, dense rounded aromatic leaves, massed mauve-purple or pink flowers in spring. Several forms. Regular pruning recommended.	1.5–2.5m	1–2.2m	Temp S. tr	•				•	•	2	L
Prostanthera saxicola var. *montana*	Low spreading shrub, crisp crowded foliage, blue-spotted white flowers spring–summer. Showy rockery plant. Light pruning recommended.	10–30cm	80cm–1.2m	Temp	•				•	•		L
Prostanthera violacea	Small rounded shrub, tiny aromatic leaves, lavender flowers in spring. Very dainty. Light tip pruning recommended.	60cm–1m	60cm–1m	Temp S. tr	•		•		•	•		L
Prostanthera walteri	Low spreading shrub, shiny leaves, unusual blue-green flowers spring–summer. Tolerates tough dry conditions and does well in shade. Prune.	20–60cm	1–2m	Temp	•		•		•	•		H
Pseudanthus pimeleoides	Small erect shrub, fine foliage, dainty clusters of white flowers spring–summer. Container plant. Light tip pruning beneficial.	30cm–1m	30–60cm	Temp S. tr S. ar	•				•	•		L
Pultenaea gunnii Eggs-and-bacon	Small open shrub, tiny crowded leaves, orange-and-yellow pea flowers in spring. Ideal for planting among other fine-foliaged small plants. Tip prune.	50cm–1m	40cm–1m	Temp S. tr	•		•		•	•		L
Pultenaea humilis	Prostrate to dwarf shrub, soft hairy foliage, golden orange pea flowers in spring. Rockery plant. Tip pruning recommended.	prostrate–60cm	60cm–1m	Temp	•		•		•	•		L
Pultenaea pedunculata	Dense carpeting groundcover, fine crowded foliage; massed yellow, golden, red or pink pea flowers in spring. Hardy in shady dry areas. Tip prune.	prostrate	1–3m	Temp S. tr S. ar	•		•		•	•		L
Pultenaea polifolia var. *mucronata*	Trailing or cascading plant, fine foliage, orange-yellow pea flowers spring–summer. Very showy; suitable for container, rockery, bank or wall. Tip prune.	10–15cm	60cm–1m	Temp S. tr	•				•	•		L
Ranunculus graniticola	Rosette of prettily lobed leaves; shiny yellow buttercup flowers on short stems in summer, also sporadic. Self-sows readily. Container plant.	5cm	10cm	Temp	•	•			•	•		H
Regelia ciliata	Small to medium spreading shrub, hairy grey-green ovate leaves, mauve brush flowers most of the year. Regular pruning recommended.	1–1.3m	1–2m	Temp S. ar	•		•		•	•		L

Temp — temperate L — light
W. te — warm temperate H — heavy
Trop — tropical N — nectar-feeding
S. tr — sub-tropical S — seed-eating
S. ar — semi-arid F — fruit-eating

		Height	Width	Climatic zones	Soil types				full sun	filtered sun	coastal regions	frosty regions	bird attraction
					moist, well drained	wet	dry	dry limy					

Legend:
- mp — temperate
- te — warm temperate
- ip — tropical
- r — sub-tropical
- ar — semi-arid

- L — light
- H — heavy
- N — nectar-feeding
- S — seed-eating
- F — fruit-eating

Name	Description	Height	Width	Climatic zones	moist, well drained	wet	dry	dry limy	full sun	filtered sun	coastal regions	frosty regions	bird attraction
gelia inops	Small to medium upright shrub, few branches, small ovate leaves, mauve-pink brush flowers in clusters spring–summer. Prune regularly.	1.5–2m	1–2m	Temp S.ar	•		•		•	•		L	N
gelia gacephala	Medium to large shrub, many branches, neat ovate foliage, red-purple brush flowers in summer. Regular pruning recommended.	2–4m	2–3m	Temp S.ar	•		•		•	•			N
gelia velutina	Small to medium shrub, silvery ovate leaves crowded neatly along stems, large bright red to crimson brush flowers in spring. Rarely flowers in eastern States.	1–3m	1–2m	Temp S.ar	•		•		•	•	1		N
stio tetraphyllus	Small clump of emerald green reed-like foliage, long plumes of bronze flowers and seed capsules spring–summer. Beautiful, especially beside pools.	1–1.2m	60cm–1m	Temp S.tr	•	•			•	•		L	
stio tetraphyllus . meiostachys	Dwarf clump, often curly emerald green new growth, bronze flowers and seed capsules spring–summer. Attractive pool or creek-side plant.	60cm	60cm	Temp S.tr	•	•			•	•			
agodia nescens	Spreading groundcover; silvery foliage, occasionally spiny; small flowers most of the year. Especially useful in dry conditions. Prune regularly.	60–75cm	1–1.5m	Temp S.tr	•		•	•	•	•		L	
ododendron hae	Small shrub, large ovate glossy leaves, brilliant waxy pink-red bell flowers in dramatic clusters summer–autumn. Container plant.	60cm–1m	60cm	Temp Trop S.tr	•					•			N
inocarpus erculatus	Upright medium shrub, very dark narrow foliage, masses of waxy white open-petalled flowers in spring. Attractive screening plant. Regular pruning beneficial.	2–3.5m	2–3m	Temp S.tr	•				•	•		L	
ingia manniifolia	Low wiry-stemmed spreading mound, crowded dark crinkled foliage, massed dainty pink-and-white flowers cover plant in spring. Prune regularly.	60cm	1–1.5m	Temp S.tr	•				•	•	2	L	
ingia kempeana	Small to medium shrub, soft grey-green foliage, a profusion of rich yellow flowers in spring. Very showy. Regular pruning recommended.	1–2m	1–2m	W.te S.ar	•		•		•	•		L	
ingia pannosa	Spreading medium shrub, velvety soft grey-green crinkly-edged foliage, showy profusion of pink-and-white flowers in spring. Prune lightly.	2–3m	2–2.5m	Temp	•				•	•		L	
aevola aemula	Herbaceous dwarf plant, soft broad leaves at base but sparse along stems, blue-mauve fan flowers spring–summer–late autumn. Rockery or container.	30–60cm	30–60cm	Temp S.tr	•				•	•			

		Height	Width	Climatic zones	Soil types				full sun	filtered sun	coastal regions	frosty regions
					moist, well drained	wet	dry	dry limy				
Temp — temperate	L — light											
W. te — warm temperate	H — heavy											
Trop — tropical	N — nectar-feeding											
S. tr — sub-tropical	S — seed-eating											
S. ar — semi-arid	F — fruit-eating											
Scaevola albida	Low loosely spreading plant, small leaves along stems; white, blue or pink fan flowers spring–summer. Regular pruning beneficial.	30–60cm	60cm–1m	Temp S. tr	•				•	•		
Scaevola hookeri	Tightly ground-hugging mat which roots at leaf nodes; flat lobed leaves, pale mauve fan flowers in summer. Drapes attractively over walls and banks.	prostrate	1–2m	Temp S. tr	•				•	•		H
Scaevola 'Mauve Clusters'	Very dense mat, crowded bright green fleshy leaves, massed vivid mauve fragrant fan flowers spring–summer. A more open form is also commonly grown.	prostrate	1–1.5m	Temp S. tr	•				•	•		L
Scaevola microphylla	Dwarf mound, tiny grey-green leaves, profusion of dainty mauve fan flowers spring–summer. Container or basket plant. Prune lightly.	10–30cm	60cm–1m	Temp S. tr	•				•	•		
Scaevola ramosissima	Light trailing herb, slender stems with few leaves, large lavender or pink fan flowers spring–summer. Rockery or container plant. Tip prune lightly.	10–30cm	60cm–1m	Temp S. tr	•		•		•	•		L
Scaevola striata	Suckering herb, soft hairy foliage; very large bright mauve fan flowers most of the year, especially spring. Rockery or container plant. Tip prune lightly.	15cm	60cm–1m	Temp	•				•	•		
Schefflera actinophylla Umbrella Tree	Small to medium multi-trunked rainforest tree, large elliptical leaflets in spreading umbrella formation, prominent spikes of red flowers spring–summer.	5–7m	2–4m	W. te Trop S. tr	•				•	•		
Scleranthus biflorus	Emerald green mossy mound, spreading slowly; tiny cream twin-flowered stems dot plant in summer. Very desirable landscape or container specimen.	10cm	60cm–1m	Temp S. tr	•				•	•		H
Sloanea australis Maiden's Blush	Large multi-trunked rainforest shrub or large tree, attractive foliage with pink new growth, white flowers in spring, decorative capsules. Handsome.	8–20m	5–10m	W. te Trop S. tr	•					•		
Sollya heterophylla	Climber, smooth broad light green foliage; loose clusters of blue, pink or white bell flowers spring–summer. May also form a small shrub. Very hardy.	climber	medium	Temp S. tr	•				•	•	2	L
Sollya parviflora	Climber, wiry stems, fine narrow foliage, clusters of blue bell flowers spring–summer. Hardy and attractive.	climber	medium	Temp S. tr	•		•		•			L
Sowerbaea juncea Vanilla Lily	Tuft of rush-like foliage; many slender stems bearing clusters of sweetly fragrant soft lilac lily flowers in spring. Container plant.	30cm	30cm	Temp S. tr	•				•	•		L

		Height	Width	Climatic zones	Soil types				full sun	filtered sun	coastal regions	frosty regions	bird attraction
					moist, well drained	wet	dry	dry limy					
ohaerolobium mineum	Sprawling or erect dwarf shrub, leafless stems; long spikes of vivid orange, scarlet or deep crimson pea flowers in spring. Ideal for sand mound.	30–60cm	30–60cm	Temp S. ar	•		•		•	•		L	
oyridium cinereum	Dwarf mound of tiny crowded grey-green soft leaves, small silvery flowers, surrounded by white leafy bracts, spring–summer. Rockery plant.	15cm	60cm–1m	Temp S. tr	•				•	•		L	
oyridium arvifolium ustraflora mbus'	Spreading carpet, dark green and silver crinkled leaves; fragrant white flowers surrounded by silver floral leaves spring–summer–autumn.	15cm	60cm–1m	Temp S. tr	•		•		•	•	1	L	
enocarpus lignus crub Beefwood	Variable large rainforest shrub or large tree, glossy green leaves, rounded heads of creamy green flowers in summer. Does well in moist shaded sites.	10–30m	6–15m	Temp Trop S. tr	•				•	•		L	S
enocarpus nuatus re-wheel Tree	Medium to large columnar tree, glossy entire or lobed foliage, glowing scarlet flowers spring–summer. Excellent tub plant; spectacular parkland tree.	8–20m	5–10m	Temp Trop S. tr	•				•	•			N
ipa teretifolia	Fine grass clump, tall slender beige flower plumes spring–summer. Attractive contrast in the landscape.	60cm–1m	30–60cm	Temp S. tr	•		•		•	•		H	
ylidium lbiferum igger-plant	Tiny matting plant, crowded minute leaves, terminal clusters of apricot to deep pink 'butterfly' flowers spring–summer. Rockery or container.	10cm	30–60cm	Temp S. ar	•		•		•	•		L	
ylidium aminifolium ass-leaved rigger-plant	Short tuft of narrow foliage, long stems bearing spikes of pale pink to deep cyclamen pink 'butterfly' flowers spring–summer. Container or rockery plant.	10–15cm	30cm	Temp S. tr	•		•		•	•		H	
ylidium boliferum ampians Trigger-ant	Tiny grey rosette, short grey stems bearing several creamy pink 'butterfly' flowers in spring. Container plant.	5cm	10cm	Temp	•	•			•	•		L	
ylidium athulatum p. lehmannianum	Tiny mound of crowded spathulate leaves, many slender stems bearing numerous cream 'butterfly' flowers in spring. Container plant.	10cm	10–30cm	Temp	•				•	•			
ypandra espitosa	Small clump of fine grey strap foliage, slender stems bearing loose clusters of vivid blue or white star flowers in spring. Container plant.	30–45cm	30–45cm	Temp S. tr	•				•	•		L	
ypandra glauca	Loose clump of many stems, each closely sheathed with foliage; showy clusters of vivid blue star flowers spring–early summer.	60cm–1m	1–1.5m	Temp S. tr	•		•		•	•		H	

Legend:

emp — temperate
te — warm temperate
op — tropical
tr — sub-tropical
ar — semi-arid

L — light
H — heavy
N — nectar-feeding
S — seed-eating
F — fruit-eating

		Height	Width	Climatic zones	moist, well drained	wet	dry	dry limy	full sun	filtered sun	coastal regions	frosty regions

Legend:
Temp — temperate
W. te — warm temperate
Trop — tropical
S. tr — sub-tropical
S. ar — semi-arid

L — light
H — heavy
N — nectar-feeding
S — seed-eating
F — fruit-eating

Name	Description	Height	Width	Climatic zones	moist, well drained	wet	dry	dry limy	full sun	filtered sun	coastal regions	frosty regions
Styphelia adscendens	Prostrate or dwarf shrub, crowded silver-grey pointed leaves; pale yellow fringed tubular flowers winter–spring. Container or rockery plant.	10–30cm	30–60cm	Temp S. ar	•		•		•	•		L
Styphelia tubiflora	Loose-stemmed dwarf shrub, stiff pointed leaves, long slender bright red tubular flowers autumn–winter–spring. Tip pruning beneficial.	30–60cm	30–60cm	Temp S. tr	•				•	•		L
Swainsona galegifolia Darling Pea	Small open shrub, pinnate foliage; sprays of large pea flowers in spring, mostly mauve-pink, also white or red. Prune old stems in late winter.	60cm–1m	60cm–1m	W. te S. ar	•		•		•			L
Swainsona greyana	Small shrub; pinnate foliage, woolly white beneath; large pink pea flowers in spring. Prune old stems in late winter.	60cm–1m	60cm–1m	W. te S. ar	•		•		•			L
Symphionema montanum	Compact dwarf shrub, dainty divided foliage, showy spikes of cream flowers in spring. Attractive in container or raised bed. Prune lightly after flowering.	60cm	60cm	Temp S. tr	•					•		L
Syzygium cormiflorum White Apple	Medium rainforest tree of variable habit; glossy foliage; profuse cream flowers, loved by lorikeets, on trunk or branches in winter; large white fruit.	8–10m	3–5m	W. te Trop S. tr	•				•	•		
Syzygium hodgkinsoniae Red Lilly Pilly	Large rainforest shrub, glossy foliage, fragrant cream flowers in winter, large scarlet fruit. Rare, endangered in natural habitat; easily grown in container.	3–4m	3–4m	W. te Trop S. tr	•					•		L
Syzygium luehmannii Riberry	Large rainforest shrub or tree; dense weeping foliage, vivid pink new growth twice a year; fluffy white flowers spring–summer, many scarlet-pink fruit.	5–30m	4–15m	W. te Trop S. tr	•				•	•	1	L
Syzygium moorei Rose Apple	Tall rainforest tree, glossy leaves, spectacular clusters of watermelon pink fluffy flowers cover branches in summer; large white edible flavourless fruit.	8–20m	4–9m	W te Trop S. tr	•				•	•		L
Syzygium oleosum Blue Lilly Pilly	Small rainforest tree; shiny elliptical leaves, aromatic when crushed; fluffy white flowers in winter, edible juicy blue-pink fruit.	5–6m	3–5m	W. te Trop S. tr	•				•	•		L
Syzygium paniculatum Magenta Lilly Pilly	Small to medium rainforest tree, glossy foliage, fluffy white flowers summer–autumn, edible scarlet fruit.	6–10m	4–8m	W. te Trop S. tr	•				•	•		L
Syzygium wilsonii Powderpuff Lilly Pilly	Medium to large rainforest shrub with weeping habit, bronze-pink new growth, clusters of fluffy crimson flowers in spring, white fruit. Attractive container plant.	2–3m	2–3.5m	W. te Trop S. tr	•	•				•		

		Height	Width	Climatic zones	Soil types								
					moist, well drained	wet	dry	dry limy	full sun	filtered sun	coastal regions	frosty regions	bird attraction
comanthe hillii	Rainforest twining liane, shiny pinnate foliage, profuse large pink tubular flowers in spring. Hardy in warm climates.	climber	vigorous	W. te Trop S. tr	•					•			
opea oreades	Medium shrub or pyramidal small tree, large purplish grey leaves; flat clusters of dusky crimson flowers in spring, very attractive to honeyeaters.	2.5–8m	2–5m	Temp S. tr	•				•	•		L	N
opea eciosissima S.W. Waratah	Multi-stemmed medium shrub, slightly serrated broad grey-green foliage; huge scarlet flowers late spring–summer. Pruning promotes flowering.	2–3m	1–2m	Temp S. tr	•				•	•		L	N
opea truncata smanian Waratah	Small to medium multi-branched shrub, dark oblong leaves, clusters of scarlet flowers at ends of branches in summer.	2–3m	2–2.5m	Temp S. tr	•				•	•		L	N
mpletonia retusa	Small to medium shrub, grey-green soft foliage, very showy scarlet (occasionally yellow) pea flowers winter–early spring. Prune regularly.	1–2.5m	1–2m	Temp S. ar	•		•	•	•	•	1		N
ratheca uerifolia	Tufting dwarf plant, crowded stems, neat dark foliage, vivid deep pink bell flowers clustered on stems in spring. Container or rockery. Prune after flowering.	10–20cm	10–20cm	Temp S. tr	•		•		•	•		L	
ratheca ciliata ck-eyed Susan	Variable dwarf plant, small neat leaves; perfumed white, pale mauve or deep pink bell flowers spring–early summer. Container plant. Prune lightly.	15–40cm	20–50cm	Temp S. tr	•		•		•	•		L	
ratheca setigera	Dwarf shrub; almost leafless slender stems, crowded with large fragrant nodding pink bells in spring. Sand mound or container. Prune lightly.	30–60cm	15–40cm	Temp S. ar	•		•		•	•		L	
ratheca nocarpa	Upright slender few-stemmed plant, widely spaced small foliage, pink or mauve pendent bells in spring. Very graceful.	50cm–1.2m	10–30cm	Temp S. tr	•		•			•			
ratheca baphylla	Dwarf mound; numerous arching, almost leafless stems covered with fragrant delicate pink bells in spring. Container or raised bed.	10–30cm	50–90cm	Temp	•		•		•	•		L	
ratheca vmifolia centennial Belle'	Dwarf shrub, erect stems, neat crowded foliage; large clusters of mauve-pink fragrant bells most of year, especially spring and autumn. Container or rockery.	30–60cm	50–90cm	Temp S. tr	•		•		•	•		H	
omasia glutinosa	Small rounded shrub; dainty, unusually sticky foliage; nodding clusters of mauve-pink bells in spring. Long-lasting posy flower. Prune lightly after flowering.	60cm–1m	80cm–1m	Temp S. ar	•		•		•	•		L	

		Height	Width	Climatic zones	moist, well drained	wet	dry	dry limy	full sun	filtered sun	coastal regions	frosty regions
Thomasia grandiflora var. *angustifolia*	Small rounded shrub, narrow grey-green foliage; large open frilled pink bells late winter–spring. Spectacular in flower. Prune after flowering.	50–80cm	60cm–1m	Temp S. ar	•		•		•	•		L
Thomasia laxiflora	Small rounded shrub, soft decorative foliage; pendent clusters of dainty fragrant lavender bells late winter–spring. Prune lightly after flowering.	60cm–1.2m	90cm–1.2m	Temp S. tr S. ar	•		•		•	•		L
Thomasia macrocarpa	Spreading dwarf shrub, broad woolly grey foliage; deep mauve-pink open-petalled flowers late winter–spring, good for picking. Prune lightly after flowering.	30–60cm	60cm–1m	Temp S. ar	•		•		•	•		L
Thomasia pygmaea	Compact dwarf mound; freckled stems and leaves, covered with papery freckled mauve-pink bells in spring. Container plant; posy flower. Prune lightly.	10–30cm	40cm–1m	Temp S. tr S. ar	•		•		•	•		L
Thomasia rhyncocarpa	Small spreading shrub, bronze-green broad leaves, showy lavender spicy-fragrant open-petalled flowers in spring. Lovely cut flower. Prune after flowering.	60cm–1.4m	1–2m	Temp S. tr S. ar	•		•		•	•		L
Thryptomene baeckeacea	Small arching shrub, tiny heath-like foliage, profusion of dainty mauve-pink teatree-like flowers autumn–winter–spring. Container plant. Tip prune.	30cm–1m	60cm–1m	Temp S. tr S. ar	•		•		•			L
Thryptomene calycina Grampians Thryptomene	Upright to spreading medium shrub, crowded tiny leaves, massed display of pink-and-white flowers late winter–spring. Popular cut flower. Tip prune.	1–2m	1–2m	Temp	•				•	•	2	L
Thryptomene saxicola	Variable small shrub, fine arching branches, crowded heath-like foliage; pale to deep pink dainty flowers winter–spring, charming in posies. Tip prune regularly.	60cm–1m	1–1.5m	Temp S. tr S. ar	•				•		2	L
Thysanotus glaucus Fringed Lily	Tufting clump of erect tubular foliage, slender stems bearing clusters of delicate fringed mauve-pink 3-petalled flowers in spring. Sand mound or container.	10–20cm	5–15cm	Temp S. ar	•		•		•			L
Thysanotus multiflorus Fringed Lily	Tufting clump of tubular foliage, numerous stems bearing clusters of fringed pale mauve 3-petalled flowers in spring. Container or sand mound preferable.	15–30cm	10–20cm	Temp S. ar	•		•		•			L
Toona australis Red Cedar	Medium to large rainforest tree, canopy of glossy pinnate leaves, panicles of pale pink flowers in spring. Fast-growing shade tree, deciduous. Beautiful timber.	6–15m	2–7m	W. te Trop S. tr	•				•	•		L
Trachymene coerulea Rottnest Island Daisy	Annual herb, hairy lobed leaves, round pincushion flowerheads of soft blue-mauve in summer. Attractive cut flower. Sow seed in early spring.	30–60cm	30–60cm	Temp S. ar	•		•		•		1	

		Height	Width	Climatic zones	moist, well drained	wet	dry	dry limy	full sun	filtered sun	coastal regions	frosty regions	bird attraction
np — temperate te — warm temperate p — tropical r — sub-tropical ar — semi-arid	L — light H — heavy N — nectar-feeding S — seed-eating F — fruit-eating												
staniopsis laurina (n. Tristania rina) nooka ter Gum	Small to large tree, glossy dark green to reddish foliage, clusters of yellow flowers in spring. Handsome, hardy, excellent in wet soils.	5–15m	3.5–8m	Temp Trop S.tr	•	•			•	•		L	N
chocarpa laurina e Heath	Large shrub or small tree; shiny veined leaves, pink new growth; heads of small white flowers throughout the year, dark blue fruit.	5–6m	2–3m	Temp Trop S.tr	•				•	•		L	F
rticordia acerosa	Erect dwarf shrub, variable linear to elliptical leaves, massed clusters of tiny yellow feather-fringed flowers in spring. Sand mound or container. Tip prune.	30–60cm	20–40cm	Temp S.ar	•		•		•			L	
rticordia ysantha	Small erect shrub, tiny linear leaves; showy clusters of vivid gold-fringed flowers in spring, lasting well in posies. Tip prune after flowering.	60–90cm	30–60cm	Temp S.ar	•		•		•			L	
rticordia siflora	Small erect shrub, tiny leaves; heads of soft mauve to almost white feathery flowers spring–summer, attractive in posies. Tip prune after flowering.	60–90cm	40–80cm	Temp S.ar	•		•		•			L	
rticordia grandis	Small sparsely branched erect shrub, round grey stem-clasping leaves, scarlet feathery flowers in spring. Spectacular; sand mound or container.	60cm–1.2m	40cm–1m	W.te S.ar	•		•		•			L	
rticordia insignis	Small upright shrub, flat ovate leaves, white to purple-pink feathery flowers on long stalks in spring. Tip prune after flowering.	60cm–1.2m	90cm–1.2m	Temp S.ar	•		•		•			L	
rticordia chelliana	Dwarf shrub, linear grey leaves; profuse scarlet feathery flowers, each with a prominent style, spring–summer. Raised bed or container. Prune lightly.	30–60cm	40–60cm	Temp S.tr S.ar	•		•		•			L	
rticordia plumosa	Compact dwarf shrub, short linear grey leaves; profusion of musky pink feathery flowers in spring, excellent for picking. Container plant. Tip prune.	40–60cm	40–60cm	Temp S.ar	•		•		•			L	
ninaria juncea tive Broom	Large erect shrub, long fine pendulous leafless branchlets, golden pea flowers spring–summer. Attractive beside pools; tolerates seasonally wet soils.	3–5m	2–3m	Temp Trop S.tr	•	•			•	•	2	L	
la betonicifolia	Spreading dwarf clump of broad lanceolate leaves, numerous purple violets summer–autumn. Self-sows readily, though not invasive.	5–20cm	5–25cm	Temp S.tr	•				•	•		H	
la hederacea ive Violet	Creeping ivy-leaved plant spreading on runners, long-stemmed purple-and-white violets most of year. Ideal in basket, tub or among ferns.	prostrate	1–2m	Temp S.tr	•	•				•	2	L	

Temp — temperate
W. te — warm temperate
Trop — tropical
S. tr — sub-tropical
S. ar — semi-arid

L — light
H — heavy
N — nectar-feeding
S — seed-eating
F — fruit-eating

		Height	Width	Climatic zones	Soil types							
					moist, well drained	wet	dry	dry limy	full sun	filtered sun	coastal regions	frosty regions
Wahlenbergia gloriosa Alpine Bluebell	Clump of tiny crinkled leaves, vivid blue bells on long stems in summer. Prefers cool root-run among rocks, or in container.	prostrate	50cm–1m	Temp S. tr	•				•	•		H
Waterhousea floribunda (syn. *Eugenia ventenatii*)	Medium to tall tree, pendulous shiny foliage; fluffy white flowers in clusters in summer, followed by fleshy green fruit.	8–30m	3–12m	Temp Trop S. tr	•					•		L
Westringia fruticosa	Small to medium spreading shrub, crowded linear grey-green foliage, attractive white flowers most of year. Low hedge or screen. Prune regularly.	1–2m	1.5–2.5m	Temp S. tr	•		•		•	•	1	L
Westringia glabra	Spreading medium shrub, elliptical leaves, profuse soft mauve flowers (occasionally white) spring–summer. Hardy. Prune regularly.	1–2.5m	1–2m	Temp S. tr	•		•		•	•		L
Westringia longifolia	Upright to spreading medium shrub, filmy foliage, very attractive white or mauve flowers cover plant in spring. Hardy screening plant. Withstands heavy pruning.	2–3m	1.5–2.5m	Temp S. tr	•		•		•	•	2	L
Westringia 'Morning Light'	Small to medium compact shrub, crowded linear foliage of bright variegated creamy yellow, white flowers most of year. Foliage contrast. Prune regularly.	1–2m	1.5–2.5m	Temp S. tr	•		•		•	•	2	L
Westringia 'Wynyabbie Gem'	Compact medium shrub, soft grey linear foliage; dainty lilac flowers most of the year, especially spring. Useful for screening and hedges. Prune regularly.	1.5–2m	1.5–2m	Temp S. tr	•		•		•	•	2	L
Xanthorrhoea australis Grass Tree Blackboy	Slow-growing ancient plant, black trunk, dense grass-like foliage; long spike covered in minute white flowers, sporadic. Spectacular focal point.	30cm–2m	60cm–1m	Temp S. tr S. ar	•		•	•	•	•	2	H
Xanthorrhoea minor	Fine grassy clump, never with trunk; several tall stems may appear, each bearing a long spike of tiny white flowers, generally in spring.	30–60cm	30cm–1m	Temp S. tr	•		•		•	•	2	H
Xanthosia rotundifolia Southern Cross	Low spreading plant, firm rounded leaves, unusual diamond-shaped arrangement of creamy felted flowers in spring. Sand mound or container plant.	10–30cm	60cm–1m	W. te S. ar	•		•		•			L
Xylomelum angustifolium Woody Pear	Medium shrub or small tree, long simple leaves, massed spikes of creamy flowers in summer, decorative woody pear-shaped capsules.	2–5.5m	1.5–3m	Temp S. tr S. ar	•		•		•	•		L
Xylomelum pyriforme Woody Pear	Large shrub or small tree, open pendulous canopy, spikes of creamy flowers in spring, decorative large woody capsules.	2–5m	1.5–2.5m	Temp S. tr	•		•		•	•		L

Quick-Pick Mini-Lists

These mini-lists are designed to provide solutions to particular problem areas or answers to specific needs in your garden. It is important to cross-reference these species with their entries in the alphabetical Plant Selection List (pp. 30–156) to ensure that your choices are appropriate in terms of size and suitability for your conditions.

Australian Cottage Gardens

An Australian cottage garden is a new approach to an old, traditional English idea. Using the same principles of low walls, shaped beds and winding pathways of gravel or stone, together with plants chosen for their appropriate characteristics of compact habit, length of flowering period, and dainty structure, it is possible to achieve a cottage garden with a truly Australian quality.

Plants suitable for borders, middle rows and background structure are set out in the following lists. Attention must be paid to achieving a freely draining soil structure, and regular pruning of plants is essential.

Annuals are an important addition to such a garden, and a selection of species which are readily available (by seed) is also given. Sowing should generally take place during late autumn, winter or very early spring.

Annuals

Brachycome iberidifolia
Helipterum roseum
Helipterum manglesii
Trachymene coerulea

Front row

Baeckea ramosissima prostrate
Blandfordia nobilis
Brachycome angustifolia
Brachycome multifida
Brachycome multifida var. dilatata
Brachycome sp. Pilliga
Bulbine species
Calocephalus brownii

Celmisia asteliifolia
Conostylis bealiana
Correa reflexa var. nummulariifolia
Crowea exalata 'Austraflora Green Cape'
Cryptandra amara prostrate
Dampiera diversifolia
Dampiera trigona dwarf
Darwinia taxifolia ssp. macrolaena
Dichondra repens
Goodenia hederacea var. alpestris
Goodenia lanata
Grevillea depauperata
Helichrysum bracteatum 'Diamond Head'
Helichrysum ramosissimum
Helipterum anthemoides
Hemiandra pungens
Hibbertia humifusa
Hibbertia obtusifolia
Hibbertia pedunculata
Hibbertia perfoliata
Hibbertia serpyllifolia
Hibbertia vestita
Lechenaultia formosa — all forms
Mentha gracilis
Pratia pedunculata
Pultenaea pedunculata
Pultenea polifolia var. mucronata
Scaevola aemula
Scaevola 'Mauve Clusters'
Scaevola striata
Spyridium parvifolium 'Austraflora Nimbus'
Thomasia pygmaea

Second row

Actinotus helianthi
Anigozanthos — small species
Baeckea ramosissima
Baeckea virgata dwarf form
Boronia filifolia
Chamelaucium ciliatum
Commersonia pulchella
Conostylis candicans
Correa pulchella
Correa reflexa — small forms
Crowea exalata
Cryptandra amara
Cymbopogon ambiguus
Dampiera hederacea
Dampiera linearis
Dampiera rosmarinifolia
Dampiera teres
Dampiera trigona
Darwinia citriodora 'Austraflora Seaspray'
Diplarrena latifolia
Epacris impressa forms
Epacris longiflora
Epacris pulchella
Epacris reclinata

Eriostemon verrucosus double
Glischrocaryon behrii
Grevillea alpina — small forms
Grevillea 'Bonnie Prince Charlie'
Helichrysum apiculatum
Helichrysum baxteri
Hibbertia calycina
Hibbertia microphylla
Hibbertia stellaris
Hibbertia stricta
Lechenaultia biloba
Leucopogon virgatus
Micromyrtus ciliata
Orthrosanthus laxus
Patersonia occidentalis
Pimelea ferruginea — small forms
Pimelea humilis
Pimelea imbricata
Platytheca verticillata
Prostanthera aspalathoides
Pultenaea gunnii
Scaevola striata
Stypandra caespitosa
Tetratheca ciliata
Tetratheca thymifolia 'Bicentennial Belle'
Thryptomene baeckeacea
Thryptomene saxicola
Verticordia chrysantha
Verticordia mitchelliana

Third row

Anigozanthos — tall species
Astartea fascicularis
Astartea 'Winter Pink'
Asterolasia asteriscophora
Boronia megastigma
Boronia muelleri 'Sunset Serenade'
Boronia pinnata
Calytrix aurea
Calytrix tetragona
Chamelaucium sp. Walpole
Chorizema cordatum
Chorizema dicksonii
Crowea exalata tall
Crowea 'Poorinda Ecstasy'
Crowea saligna
Cryptandra scortechinii
Dampiera purpurea
Darwinia leiostyla
Darwinia oxylepis
Darwinia squarrosa
Dillwynia sericea
Diplarrena moroea
Eriostemon angustifolius ssp. montanus
Eriostemon australasius
Eriostemon verrucosus
Eutaxia cuneata
Grevillea brachystylis
Guichenotia macrantha

Helichrysum bracteatum — tall
   forms
Hypocalymma angustifolium
Lomandra longifolia
Orthrosanthos multiflorus
Phebalium lamprophyllum
Thryptomene saxicola

Climbers

Billardiera bicolor
Billardiera erubescens
Billardiera longiflora
Billardiera ringens
Billardiera scandens
Billardiera variifolia
Chorizema diversifolium
Clematis aristata
Hardenbergia violacea
Hardenbergia violacea 'Australflora
   Aspiration'
Hibbertia dentata
Jasminum suavissimum

Butterfly-Attracting Plants

The following genera contain many species which are attractive to butterflies. These colourful, quiet visitors add a further dimension to our gardens. Check with your nursery specialists for the species they stock.

Acacia
Actinotus
Albizzia
Aotus
Asterolasia
Bossiaea
Brachycome
Bursaria
Callicoma
Calytrix
Carpobrotus
Cassia
Celmisia
Cordyline
Cotula
Craspedia
Dampiera
Dianella
Dillwynia
Diplarrena
Epacris
Eutaxia
Farradaya
Glischrocaryon
Goodenia
Helichrysum
Helipterum
Helmholtzia
Hovea
Hoya
Hymenosporum
Indigofera
Jacksonia
Kunzea
Leptospermum
Lomandra
Mazus
Metrosideros
Olearia
Orthrosanthus
Parahebe
Patersonia
Pelargonium
Phyla
Pimelea
Pittosporum
Pomaderris
Pratia
Pultenaea
Restio
Rulingia
Scaevola
Sowerbaea
Spyridium
Sphaerolobium
Trachymene
Westringia

Climbers and Creepers

A useful group of plants which in many instances can provide exceptionally quick screening for privacy or cover for shade, whether you need a light twiner to cover a few square metres, or a vigorous liane to block out a 10 metre wall or fence.

Light

Agapetes meiniana
Billardiera bicolor
Billardiera bignoniacea
Billardiera cymosa
Billardiera drummondiana var.
   collina
Billardiera erubescens
Billardiera longiflora
Billardiera ringens
Billardiera scandens
Billardiera variifolia
Chorizema diversifolium
Clematis microphylla
Hardenbergia violacea
Hardenbergia violacea 'Australflora
   Aspiration'
Hibbertia dentata
Jasminum suavissimum
Pronaya fraseri

Medium

Clematis aristata
Clematis pubescens
Hardenbergia comptoniana
Hibbertia scandens
Hoya australis
Hoya macgillivrayii
Hoya nicholsoniae
Hoya rubida
Kennedia beckxiana
Kennedia coccinea
Sollya heterophylla
Sollya parviflora
Tecomanthe hillii

Vigorous

Cissus antarctica
Faradaya splendida
Hardenbergia violacea 'Happy
   Wanderer'
Ipomoea brasiliensis
Kennedia macrophylla
Kennedia nigricans
Kennedia retrorsa
Kennedia rubicunda
Lonchocarpus stipularis
Millettia megasperma
Neosepicaea jucunda
Pandorea jasminoides
Pandorea jasminoides 'Lady Di'
Pandorea pandorana
Pandorea pandorana 'Snowbells'

Containers

Native plants can be grown successfully in containers ranging in size from small terracotta or glazed pots to large sections of pipe. There is no limit to the range of plants you can use, but the following lists provide interesting combinations. Remember that nursery plants are grown in quality potting mix. To achieve the best results in a container, use a specialised container fertilising product such as Debco Acid Loving plant Mix or Terracotta and Tub Mixture. Because a containerised plant is under more stress than one planted in an open garden, you must ensure that a constant moisture level is maintained. This may be assisted by the inclusion of a water absorption aid such as Debco SaturAid. However, beware of over-watering, as soggy soil will be detrimental. Annual application of a top dressing such as Debco Jacket Flower and Shrub fertiliser will maintain healthy growth, and light pruning will encourage a compact habit and good flowering. It is best to prune either following flowering, or prior to the two major growing periods, spring and autumn.

Combinations for containers

Astroloma conostephioides
Styphelia adscendens

Baeckea ramosissima prostrate
Baeckea ramosissima upright

Baeckea ramosissima prostrate
Pomaderris obcordata

Boronia muelleri 'Sunset Serenade'
Dampiera diversifolia

Boronia serrulata
Pimelea humilis

Brachycome sp. Pilliga
Poa australis

Conostylis bealiana
Cryptandra scortechinii
Grevillea depauperata

Correa pulchella
Hibbertia obtusifolia

Crowea exalata
Hemiandra pungens white

Cryptandra amara
Dampiera linearis
Epacris reclinata

Dampiera diversifolia
Pratia pedunculata

Dampiera linearis
Eriostemon verrucosus double

Darwinia leiostyla
Goodenia hederacea var. alpestris

Epacris breviflora
Hibbertis obtusifolia

Epacris impressa — pink, white and red forms

Eriostemon verrucosus single
Pimelea filiformis

Goodenia hederacea var. alpestris
Grevillea pilulifera

Goodenia lanata
Helichrysum baxteri

Hibbertia pedunculata
Tetratheca ciliata white

Hibbertia vestita
Tetratheca thymifolia 'Bicentennial Belle'

Lechenaultia biloba
Lechenaultia formosa — various colour forms

Single container specimens of particular note

Acacia amblygona 'Australflora Winter Gold'
Acacia cultriformis 'Australflora Cascade'
Acacia glaucoptera
Actinodium — both species
Actinotus helianthi
Agapetes meiniana
Anigozanthos — all species
Astartea 'Winter Pink'
Astroloma — all species
Baeckea ramosissima
Baeckea virgata prostrate
Banksia dryandroides
Banksia spinulosa 'Australflora Birthday Candles' and many other species of Banksia
Beaufortia — all species
Blandfordia — all species
Boronia — all species
Brachycome — all species
Bulbine bulbosa
Calectasia cyanea
Calostemma purpureum
Callistemon citrinus 'Australflora Firebrand'
Callistemon pallidus 'Australflora Candle Glow'
Callistemon viminalis 'Captain Cook'
Calytrix — all species
Celmisia asteliifolia
Chamelaucium — all species
Clianthus formosus
Commersonia pulchella
Conostylis — all species

Correa — many species
Crowea — all species
Cryptandra — all species
Dampiera — all species
Darwinia — all species
Diplarrena — all species
Dryandra — all species
Elaeocarpus reticulatus
Epacris — all species
Eremophila — many small species
Eriostemon — all species
Eucalyptus — select small-growing species for large terracotta pipes
Eutaxia — all species
Glischrocaryon behrii
Goodenia — all species
Grevillea — many species
Guichenotia macrantha
Hakea myrtoides
Helichrysum — all species
Helipterum — all species
Hemiandra pungens
Hibbertia — all species
Hovea elliptica
Hovea pungens
Hovea trisperma
Hymenosporum flavum
Hypocalymma — all species
Isopogon — all species
Kunzea ericifolia
Kunzea parvifolia dwarf
Lechenaultia — all species
Leptospermum 'Copper Sheen'
Leptospermum scoparium — dwarf forms
Leucopogon virgatus
Lobelia trigonocaulis
Lomatia tinctoria
Micromyrtus — all species
Olearia teretifolia var. compacta
Orthrosanthos — all species
Patersonia — all species
Persoonia pinifolia
Phebalium lamprophyllum
Phebalium squamulosum
Pimelea — all species
Platytheca — all species
Pomaderris obcordatum
Pultenaea pedunculata
Pultenaea polifolia var. mucronata
Ranunculus — all species
Restio tetraphyllus
Rhododendron lochae
Rulingia hermanniifolia
Scaevola — all species
Scleranthus biflorus
Sowerbaea juncea
Spyridium cinereum
Spyridium parvifolium 'Australflora Nimbus'
Stylidium — all species
Stypandra caespitosa
Styphelia adscendens
Symphionema montanus
Tetratheca — all species
Thomasia — many small species
Thryptomene — all species
Thysanotus — all species
Verticordia — all species
Wahlenbergia gloriosa
Xanthorrhoea — all species
Xanthosia — all species

Cut Flowers

Traditional plants such as roses and carnations are mainly used for indoor decoration, but we have found that many native plants, from the finest *Epacris* to the boldest *Telopea*, are excellent, long-lasting cut flowers.

Actinodium sp. *nova*
Actinotus helianthi
Anigozanthos — all species
Astartea 'Winter Pink'
Baeckea densifolia
Baeckea virgata
Banksia — all species
Blandfordia nobilis
Boronia — all species
Calytrix alpestris
Calytrix tetragona
Ceratopetalum gummiferum
Chamelaucium — all species
Chorizema cordatum
Correa — all species
Crowea — all species
Darwinia — all species
Dryandra — all species
Epacris — all species
Eriostemon — all species
Eucalyptus caesia
Eucalyptus calophylla
Eucalyptus ficifolia
Eucalyptus forrestiana
Eucalyptus leucoxylon — all forms
Eucalyptus macrandra
Eucalyptus macrocarpa
Eucalyptus preissiana
Eucalyptus torquata
Eucalyptus 'Torwood'
Glischrocaryon behrii
Grevillea alpina — all forms
Grevillea banksii
Grevillea buxifolia
Grevillea depauperata
Grevillea 'Evelyn's Coronet'
Grevillea 'Ivanhoe'
Grevillea 'Robyn Gordon'
Grevillea trifida
Guichenotia macrantha
Hakea bucculenta
Hakea francisiana
Hakea laurina
Hakea multilineata
Helichrysum — all species
Helipterum — all species
Homoranthus darwinioides
Hypocalymma angustifolium
Hycocalymma cordifolium
Isopogon anemonifolius
Isopogon anethifolius
Isopogon dubius
Isopogon formosus
Jasminum suavissimum
Kunzea baxteri
Lambertia formosa
Lasiopetalum behrii
Melaleuca fulgens
Melaleuca lateritia
Melaleuca nesophila
Melaleuca steedmanii
Olearia — all species
Oreocallis — both species
Pennisetum alopecuroides
Persoonia pinifolia
Petrophile — all species
Phebalium — all species
Pimelea — all species
Platytheca — all species
Prostanthera — all species
Restio — all species
Scaevola — all species
Sollya heterophylla
Sowerbaea juncea
Stypandra glauca
Telopea — all species
Tetratheca — all species
Thomasia — all species
Thryptomene — all species
Verticordia — all species

Decorative Seed Capsules

Many of the traditional forms of floral decoration include seed capsules as a part of their structure. Numerous Australian plants have capsules and pods which are quite different from those conventionally used. They look very effective as Christmas tree decorations, as mobiles, in dried arrangements and as imaginative animal characters. The following genera provide a wide range of unusual capsules.

Acacia
Agathis
Araucaria
Banksia
Brachychiton
Callitris
Casuarina
Dodonaea
Dryandra
Eucalyptus
Flindersia
Grevillea
Hakea
Harpullia
Isopogon
Lambertia
Lomatia
Lysiphyllum
Pandorea
Petrophile
Sloanea
Telopea
Xanthorrhoea
Xylomelum

OPPOSITE PAGE:
Angophora costata is a visually dominant component of its natural habitat on the sandstones of New South Wales and Queensland. It is often multi-trunked, and the sloughings of last season's bark reveal the clean trunk beneath and cover the ground in a coloured carpet.

LEFT:
Blue *Dampiera*, red *Lechenaultia* and purple *Calytrix* bordering a tramped earth pathway in the dry Wimmera area of Victoria. The *Dampiera* and *Lechenaultia* will sucker into the path, further softening its edges.

BELOW:
Grevillea rosmarinifolia 'Rosy Posy' displays its value as indoor decoration. Hundreds of our native plants are being used successfully in this way, as well as in floral art and wedding bouquets.

RIGHT:
Tecomanthe hillii
'Australflora Island Belle'

A light to medium twining liane, with glossy foliage and spectacular clusters of waxy flowers in spring and summer. An elegant and exotic adornment for pergolas or walls, and a splash of colour in fern or rainforest gardens.

Grasses and Rush-Like Foliage

If you intend creating a heathland, or are looking for plants to grow in association with water or rocks, the following list suggests plants which provide a foil to traditional shrubs. These plants, used in conjunction with rock work or groupings of trunks such as those of *Casuarina torulosa*, add a note of natural simplicity, so often the key to successful Australian landscaping.

Grasses

Cymbopogon ambiguus
Dichanthium sericeum
Pennisetum alopecuroides
Poa australis
Stipa teretifolia

Rush-Like Foliage

Agrostocrinum scabrum
Anigozanthos — all species
Blandfordia grandiflora
Blandfordia nobilis
Bulbine bulbosa
Bulbine semibarbata
Calectasia cyanea
Calostemma purpureum
Celmisia asteliifolia
Conostylis — all species
Craspedia glauca
Craspedia globosa
Dianella intermedia
Dianella laevis
Dianella revoluta
Dianella tasmanica
Dichopogon strictus
Diplarrena latifolia
Diplarrena moroea
Doryanthes excelsa
Helmholtzia acorifolia
Helmhóltzia glaberrima
Macropidia fuliginosa
Orthrosanthus laxus
Orthrosanthus multiflorus
Patersonia longifolia
Patersonia occidentalis
Patersonia sericea
Restio tetraphyllus
Restio tetraphyllus ssp. *meiostachys*
Sowerbaea juncea
Stylidium graminifolium
Stypandra caespitosa
Stypandra glauca
Xanthorrhoea australis
Xanthorrhoea minor

Groundcovers

The term 'groundcover' is used loosely to describe plants which vary from prostrate carpets to mounding spreading shrubs which cover the soil completely with their branches and foliage. They must be hardy, as they are often used in broad landscapes to stablise the soil, and to give quick and attractive cover to otherwise large, bare expanses of ground. The plants listed are in two categories: the first covers species which spread to approximately 1 metre; the second, those spreading more than 1 metre.

Small, spreading to approximately 1 metre

Acacia aculeatissima
Acacia amblygona 'Australflora Winter Gold'
Acacia bidentata
Acacia cometes
Acacia gunnii
Acacia tayloriana
Acacia ulicifolia var. *brownei*
Astroloma humifusum
Astroloma epacridis
Baeckea ramosissima
Baeckea virgata prostrate
Banksia spinulosa 'Australflora Birthday Candles'
Brachycome angustifolia
Brachycome iberidifolia
Brachycome multifida
Brachycome multifida var. *dilatata*
Brachycome sp. Pilliga
Brachysema latifolium
Brachysema species
Callistemon sieberi 'Australflora Little Cobber'
Claytonia australasica
Conostylis aculeata
Conostylis seorsiflora
Conostylis setigera
Conostylis setosa
Correa decumbens
Crowea exalata 'Australflora Green Cape'
Cryptandra amara
Dampiera alata
Dampiera coronata
Dampiera diversifolia
Dampiera linearis
Dampiera trigona
Darwinia citriodora 'Australflora Seaspray'
Darwinia taxifolia ssp. *macrolaena*
Epacris longiflora
Eremaea violacea
Eremophila behriana
Eriostemon hybrid 'Decumbent'
Eutaxia microphylla
Frankenia pauciflora
Gastrolobium truncatum
Goodenia humilis

Goodenia lanata
Goodenia varia
Grevillea alpina Grampians low
Grevillea 'Australflora McDonald Park'
Grevillea australis
Grevillea 'Bonnie Prince Charlie'
Grevillea confertifolia
Grevillea depauperata
Grevillea diffusa
Grevillea lanigera prostrate
Grevillea lavandulacea Billywing cascading
Grevillea lavandulacea Billywing compact
Grevillea thyrsoides
Hakea lehmanniana
Hakea myrtoides
Helichrysum bracteatum 'Diamond Head'
Helichrysum ramosissimum
Helipterum anthemoides
Hemigenia sericea
Hibbertia humifusa
Hibbertia obtusifolia
Hibbertia pedunculata
Hibbertia perfoliata
Hibbertia serpyllifolia
Hibbertia vestita
Hibbertia virgata
Homoranthus flavescens
Isotoma fluviatilis
Kennedia microphylla
Kunzea ericifolia
Kunzea parvifolia dwarf
Mazus pumilio
Micromyrtus ciliata
Oxylobium tricuspidatum
Persoonia chamaepitys
Pimelea filiformis
Pimelea humilis
Pratia pedunculata
Prostanthera saxicola var. *montana*
Pultenaea humilis
Pultenaea polifolia var. *mucronata*
Scaevola aemula
Scaevola albida
Scaevola hookeri
Scaevola microphylla
Scaevola ramosissima
Scaevola 'Mauve Clusters'
Scaevola striata
Scleranthus biflorus
Spyridium cinereum
Spyridium parvifolium 'Australflora Nimbus'
Styphelia adscendens
Thomasia pygmaea
Viola hederacea
Xanthosia rotundifolia

Large, spreading to more than 1 metre

Acacia cultriformis 'Australflora Cascade'
Acacia farinosa
Acacia glandulicarpa
Acacia leptospermoides
Acacia pravissima 'Golden Carpet'

Actinostrobus acuminatus
Adenanthos meisneri
Aotus ericoides prostrate
Atriplex cinereum
Atriplex nummularia
Atriplex rhagodioides
Austromyrtus dulcis
Banksia blechnifolia
Banksia dryandroides
Banksia gardneri
Banksia integrifolia 'Australflora
   Roller Coaster'
Banksia petiolaris
Banksia repens
Banksia serrata 'Australflora Pygmy
   Possum'
Bauera rubioides — prostrate
   forms
Bossiaea cordigera
Brachysema sericeum black-red
Brachysema sericeum cream
Callistemon citrinus 'Australflora
   Firebrand'
Callistemon pallidus 'Australflora
   Candle Glow'
Callistemon viminalis 'Little John'
Calocephalus brownii
Calothamnus quadrifidus prostrate
Calystegia soldanella
Carpobrotus rossii
Clianthus formosus
Correa alba
Correa 'Pink Bells'
Correa reflexa
Correa reflexa var. nummulariifolia
Cotula coronopifolia
Cotula filicula
Dampiera lavandulacea
Dampiera rosmarinifolia
Dichondra repens
Dodonaea humifusa
Dryandra calophylla
Dryandra nivea
Dryandra tenuifolia
Eremophila biserrata
Eremophila bowmanii
Eremophila densifolia
Eremophila glabra
Eremophila lehmanniana
Eremophila macdonnellii
Eremophila maculata
Eremophila polyclada
Goodenia hederacea var. alpestris
Grevillea aquifolium prostrate
Grevillea 'Australflora Canterbury
   Gold'
Grevillea 'Australflora Copper
   Crest'
Grevillea 'Australflora Fanfare'
Grevillea 'Australflora Old Gold'
Grevillea banksii prostrate
Grevillea baueri
Grevillea bedggoodiana
Grevillea 'Bronze Rambler'
Grevillea 'Bush Carpet'
Grevillea crithmifolia prostrate
Grevillea curviloba
Grevillea diminuta
Grevillea floripendula
Grevillea gaudichaudii
Grevillea 'Grass Fire'
Grevillea ilicifolia

Grevillea 'Jolly Swagman'
Grevillea juniperina 'Molonglo'
Grevillea juniperina prostrate
Grevillea laurifolia
Grevillea microstegia
Grevillea nudiflora
Grevillea obtecta
Grevillea 'Pink Lady'
Grevillea 'Poorinda Royal Mantle'
Grevillea repens
Grevillea thelemanniana
Grevillea thelemanniana ssp.
   obtusifolia
Hardenbergia comptoniana
Hardenbergia violacea
Helichrysum apiculatum
Hemiandra pungens
Hibbertia scandens
Ipomoea brasiliensis
Kennedia beckxiana
Kennedia carinata
Kennedia coccinea
Kennedia eximea
Kennedia glabrata
Kennedia macrophylla
Kennedia nigricans
Kennedia prorepens
Kennedia prostrata
Kennedia retrorsa
Kennedia rubicunda
Kunzea pomifera
Leptospermum flavescens
   'Cardwell'
Leptospermum flavescens 'Pacific
   Beauty'
Leptospermum juniperinum
   'Horizontalis'
Lobelia trigonocaulis
Maireana brevifolia
Melaleuca hypericifolia 'Ulladulla
   Beacon'
Melaleuca incana 'Velvet Cushion'
Melaleuca violacea
Mentha gracilis
Myoporum debile
Myoporum ellipticum
Myoporum parvifolium
Phyla nodiflora
Prostanthera cuneata
Prostanthera denticulata
Prostanthera walteri
Rhagodia spinescens
Rulingia hermanniifolia

Hanging Baskets

Not everyone has the space to grow
plants in an open garden. If you live
in a flat or unit, where a balcony
provides the only scope for gardening
you can still develop an interesting
collection of plants in hanging
baskets. Plants in any container which
restricts root growth are under greater
stress than those in the garden. A
specialised mixture, such as Debco
Hanging Basket mixture provides
optimum growing conditions for
healthy plants in baskets.

Acacia amblygona 'Australflora
   Winter Gold'
Acacia cultriformis 'Australflora
   Cascade'
Acacia pravissima 'Golden Carpet'
Agapetes meiniana
Austromyrtus dulcis
Baeckea ramosissima
Billardiera cymosa
Billardiera longiflora
Billardiera scandens
Brachycome angustifolia
Brachycome multifida
Chorizema diversifolium
Correa — low-growing species
Crowea exalata 'Australflora Green
   Cape
Dampiera diversifolia
Dampiera linearis
Dampiera teres
Goodenia hederacea var. alpestris
Goodenia lanata
Grevillea australis
Grevillea depauperata
Hardenbergia comptoniana
Hardenbergia violacea
Helichrysum apiculatum
Helichrysum baxteri
Helichrysum bracteatum 'Diamond
   Head'
Helichrysum ramosissimum
Helipterum anthemoides
Hibbertia amplexicaulis
Hibbertia dentata
Hibbertia empetrifolia
Hibbertia pedunculata
Hibbertia perfoliata
Hoya australis
Hoya macgillivrayi
Hoya nicholsoniae
Hoya rubida
Kennedia coccinea
Kennedia glabrata
Kennedia microphylla
Kennedia prostrata
Lechenaultia biloba
Lechenaultia formosa
Lobelia trigonocaulis
Myoporum parvifolium
Pelargonium rodneyanum
Persoonia chamaepitys
Pimelea filiformis
Pimelea imbricata
Pronaya elegans
Pultenaea pedunculata

ltenaea polifolia var. *mucronata*
aevola aemula
aevola microphylla
aevola 'Mauve Clusters'
yridium cinereum
yridium parvifolium 'Austraflora Nimbus'
tratheca ciliata
tratheca thymifolia 'Bicentennial Belle'
omasia pygmaea
ola hederacea

Hedges and Screening

Plants are not used for hedges as much today as they were, but still there are many areas where this form of horticulture is appropriate. Car parks, school grounds, narrow median strips, and boundaries of private and rural properties are all areas where hedges can be utilised. Whether you want tall plants for privacy and screening, or windbreak; or shorter, simply to impede movement; prickly or soft, there are many to choose from.

Acacia anceps
Acacia argyrophylla
Acacia boormanii
Acacia brachybotrya
Acacia cultriformis
Acacia cyclops
Acacia decora
Acacia farinosa
Acacia glaucoptera
Acacia howittii
Acacia longifolia
Acacia myrtifolia
Acacia plicata
Acacia pravissima
Acacia sclerophylla
Acacia spathulifolia
Acacia truncata
Agonis flexuosa nana
Atriplex cinerea
Atriplex nummularia
Baeckea densifolia
Baeckea virgata
Banksia ericifolia
Banksia 'Giant Candles'
Banksia marginata
Banksia spinulosa
Bauera rubioides
Bauera sessiliflora
Boronia megastigma
Brachysema lanceolatum
Callistemon — most species
Calocephalus brownii
Calothamnus quadrifidus
Cassia artemisioides
Casuarina nana
Chamaelaucium uncinatum
Correa alba
Correa backhousiana
Correa glabra
Correa 'Mannii'
Correa 'Marian's Marvel'
Correa reflexa
Correa schlechtendalii
Crowea exalata tall
Crowea 'Poorinda Ecstasy'
Crowea saligna
Cryptandra scortechinii
Cuttsia viburnea
Darwinia citriodora
Diplolaena angustifolia
Diplolaena grandiflora
Diplolaena microcephala
Eremophila bowmanii
Eremophila glabra
Eremophila maculata

Eriostemon myoporoides
Eutaxia cuneata
Eutaxia obovata
Goodenia vernicosa
Graptophyllum excelsum
Grevillea — many species
Hakea nodosa
Hakea salicifolia
Hakea sericea
Hakea stenocarpa
Hakea suaveolens
Hibbertia cuneiformis
Howittia trilocularis
Hypocalymma cordifolium
Hypocalymma puniceum
Hypocalymma robustum
Kunzea ambigua
Kunzea baxteri
Lambertia ericifolia
Lambertia multiflora
Lasiopetalum behrii
Leptospermum coriaceum
Leptospermum flavescens 'Cardwell'
Leptospermum flavescens 'Pacific Beauty'
Leptospermum laevigatum
Leptospermum lanigerum
Leptospermum nitidum
Leptospermum scoparium var. *rotundifolium*
Leptospermum junipermum 'Horizontalis'
Maireana brevifolia
Melaleuca acerosa
Melaleuca armillaris
Melaleuca bracteata 'Golden Gem'
Melaleuca conothamnoides
Melaleuca cuneata
Melaleuca cuticularis
Melaleuca decussata
Melaleuca densa
Melaleuca diosmifolia
Melaleuca eleutherostachya
Melaleuca erubescens
Melaleuca glaberrima
Melaleuca huegelii
Melaleuca hypericifolia
Melaleuca incana
Melaleuca lateritia
Melaleuca laxiflora
Melaleuca micromera
Melaleuca nesophila
Melaleuca seriata
Melaleuca spathulata
Melaleuca striata
Melaleuca tamarascina
Melaleuca wilsonii
Metrosideros queenslandicus
Micromyrtus drummondii
Myoporum ellipticum
Olearia axillaris
Olearia iodochroa
Olearia teretifolia var. *compacta*
Persoonia pinifolia
Phebalium bilobum
Phebalium lamprophyllum
Phebalium squamulosum
Pimelea ferruginea
Pimelea imbricata
Pimelea nivea
Pomaderris andromedifolia

Prostanthera baxteri var. sericea
Prostanthera incana
Prostanthera nivea var. induta
Prostanthera ovalifolia
Prostanthera rotundifolia
Regelia velutina
Sollya heterophylla
Templetonia retusa
Thomasia rhyncocarpa
Thryptomene calycina
Thryptomene saxicola
Verticordia acerosa
Verticordia chrysantha
Verticordia mitchelliana
Westringia fruticosa
Westringia glabra
Westringia longifolia
Westringia 'Morning Light'
Westringia 'Wynyabbie Gem'

Narrow Areas

Narrow beds beside driveways, or between fenceline and residence, have their own particular planting problems. Soft, fine foliage, or an erect habit, and the ability to be pruned back, are attributes plants should possess for such positions.

Acacia beckleri
Acacia boormanii
Adenanthos obovata
Agrostocrinum scabrum
Anigozanthos — all species
Astartea 'Winter Pink'
Asterolasia asteriscophora
Austromyrtus lasioclada
Austromyrtus tenuifolia
Baeckea crenatifolia
Baeckea linifolia
Baeckea utilis
Baeckea virgata
Beaufortia decussata
Beaufortia sparsa
Beaufortia squarrosa
Blandfordia grandiflora
Blandfordia nobilis
Boronia deanei
Boronia denticulata
Boronia heterophylla
Boronia pinnata
Bossiaea dentata
Bossiaea linophylla
Bulbine bulbosa
Bulbine semibarbata
Callistemon viridiflorus
Callitris oblonga
Calytrix depressa
Calytrix flavescens
Calytrix tetragona
Casuarina humilis
Casuarina nana
Casuarina pusilla
Conostylis — all species
Cordyline petiolaris
Cordyline stricta
Cordyline terminalis
Correa aemula
Craspedia glauca
Craspedia globosa
Crowea exalata tall
Crowea saligna
Cryptandra scortechinii
Cuttsia viburnea
Cymbopogon ambiguus
Dampiera purpurea
Dianella — all species
Dichanthium sericeum
Diplarrena latifolia
Diplarrena moroea
Diplolaena angustifolia
Epacris — all species
Eriostemon australasius
Eriostemon myoporoides
Grevillea alpina Mt Ida
Grevillea alpina Mt Zero
Grevillea arenaria
Grevillea aspera
Grevillea 'Australflora Jubilee'
Grevillea brachystylis
Grevillea dielsiana

Grevillea endlicheriana
Grevillea iaspicula
Grevillea jephcottii
Grevillea occidentalis
Grevillea polybractea
Grevillea rosmarinifolia green
Grevillea sericea
Grevillea speciosa ssp. oleoides
Grevillea 'Winpara Gem'
Grevillea 'Winpara Gold'
Hakea conchifolia
Hakea cucculata
Hakea elliptica
Hakea obtusa
Hibbertia bracteata
Hibbertia cuneiformis
Hovea acutifolia
Hovea elliptica
Hymenosporum flavum
Isopogon anethifolius
Jacksonia scoparia
Kunzea parvifolia
Kunzea pauciflora
Kunzea pulchella
Kunzea recurva
Lagunaria patersonii
Lambertia multiflora
Leptospermum lanigerum upright
Leptospermum liversidgei
Leptospermum petersenii
Leptospermum squarrosum
Linospadix monostachyus
Lomandra longifolia
Lomatia silaifolia
Lomatia tinctoria
Melaleuca citrina
Melaleuca cuticularis
Melaleuca erubescens
Melaleuca lateritia
Melaleuca micromera
Melaleuca pentagona
Melaleuca seriata
Melaleuca spathulata
Melaleuca squamea
Olearia phlogopappa
Orthrosanthus laxus
Orthrosanthus multiflorus
Patersonia occidentalis
Patersonia sericea
Pennisetum alopecuroides
Persoonia pinifolia
Petrophile biloba
Petrophile fucifolia
Petrophile serruriae
Polyscias elegans
Pomaderris andromedifolia
Prostanthera baxteri var. sericea
Prostanthera nivea var. induta
Prostanthera ovalifolia
Prostanthera rotundifolia
Pseudanthus pimeleoides
Restio tetraphyllus
Stypandra caespitosa
Telopea speciosissima
Tetratheca stenocarpa
Tetratheca thymifolia 'Bicentennia Belle'
Verticordia chrysantha
Verticordia insignis

Perfumed and Aromatic Plants

Many native plants have perfumed flowers, aromatic foliage, or both. They provide a further sensory interest in your garden, and bring 'a bit of the bush' into your home environment. The foliage of a number of plants such as *Backhousia citriodora* and *Prostanthera* species (mints) increasingly are being used in the making of pot-pourri.

Flowers

Acacia — all species, but especially
A. *adunca*
A. *boormanii*
A. *cognata*
A. *cultriformis*
A. *dealbata*
A. *elata*
A. *fimbriata*
A. *genistifolia*
A. *leprosa*
A. *pravissima*
A. *retinodes*
A. *terminalis*
A. *truncata*
Angophora — all species
Archidendron grandiflorum
Banksia conferta
Banksia ericifolia
Banksia 'Giant Candles'
Banksia integrifolia
Banksia marginata
Banksia media
Banksia ornata
Banksia spinulosa
Boronia fraseri
Boronia heterophylla
Boronia megastigma
Boronia serrulata
Buckinghamia celsissima
Bursaria spinosa
Cassia odorata
Cuttsia viburnea
Dampiera diversifolia
Dichopogon strictus
Ehretia acuminata
Epacris impressa
Eucalyptus annulata
Eucalyptus dives 'Little Honey'
Eucalyptus eximia
Eucalyptus macrandra
Eucalyptus stellulata
Eucryphia lucida
Faradaya splendida
Goodia lotifolia
Grevillea australis
Grevillea confertifolia
Grevillea curviloba
Grevillea leucopteris
Grevillea obtecta
Grevillea vestita
Hakea sericea
Hakea suaveolens
Helmholtzia acorifolia

Helmholtzia glaberrima
Hoya australis
Hoya macgillivrayii
Hoya nicholsoniae
Hymenosporum flavum
Hypocalymna myrtifolium
Indigofera australis
Jasminum suavissimum
Jacksonia scoparia
Kunzea ambigua
Kunzea parvifolia
Kunzea pomifera
Lomandra longifolia
Melaleuca acuminata
Melaleuca ericifolia
Melaleuca huegelii
Melaleuca linariifolia
Melaleuca rhaphiophylla
Melaleuca squarrosa
Pandorea jasminoides
Pandorea jasminoides 'Lady Di'
Pimelea nivea
Pittosporum revolutum
Pittosporum undulatum
Pratia pedunculata
Sowerbaea juncea
Syzygium hodgkinsoniae
Thomasia rhyncocarpa

Foliage

Acacia cognata
Acacia howittii
Acacia leprosa
Backhousia citriodora
Baeckea — all species
Boronia — all species
Callistemon — most species
Calytrix — all species
Crowea exalata
Crowea 'Poorinda Ecstasy'
Crowea saligna
Cymbopogon ambiguus
Darwinia taxifolia ssp. *macrolaena*
Eriostemon myoporoides
Eucalyptus — most, especially
  E. *citriodora*
Homoranthus darwinioides
Kunzea — all species
Leptospermum flavescens
Leptospermum liversidgei
Leptospermum petersenii
Melaleuca alternifolia
Melaleuca bracteata
Melaleuca citrina
Melaleuca lateritia
Mentha gracilis
Micromyrtus ciliata
Phebalium lamprophyllum
Prostanthera — all species
Sollya heterophylla
Thryptomene saxicola

Pine Tree Underplanting

Much housing development has taken place on previously broad acres, where pine trees (often *Pinus radiata*) were planted decades ago to act as windbreaks. These now very large trees can present problems if you have only a limited space in which to develop a garden. If you have no intention of removing the pines and because of the massive root system you can only undertake minimum soil preparation, then unfortunately you limit the range of plants you can grow. The following plants will grow satisfactorily in such conditions, providing a little more attention than normal is given to watering, pruning and fertilising.

Acacia anceps
Acacia argyrophylla
Acacia ausfeldii
Acacia beckleri
Acacia boormanii
Acacia brachybotrya
Acacia cardiophylla
Acacia cultriformis
Acacia genistifolia
Acacia glaucoptera
Acacia implexa
Acacia iteaphylla
Acacia pravissima
Acacia pycnantha
Acacia rigens
Acacia rupicola
Acacia terminalis
Acacia truncata
Acacia ulicifolia
Acacia venulosa
Atriplex cinerea
Atriplex nummularia
Atriplex rhagodioides
Brachysema lanceolatum
Bursaria spinosa
Callitris columellaris
Callitris endlicheri
Callitris oblonga
Callitris preissii ssp. *verrucosa*
Callitris rhomboidea
Calothamnus quadrifidus
Calystegia soldanella
Carpobrotus rossii
Cassia artemisioides
Cassia brewsteri
Cassia nemophila
Cassia odorata
Casuarina distyla
Casuarina glauca
Casuarina humilis
Casuarina lehmanniana
Casuarina obesa
Casuarina verticillata
Dianella laevis
Dianella revoluta
Dryandra nobilis
Dryandra praemorsa
Dryandra sessilis

Eremophila bignoniiflora
Eremophila bowmanii
Eremophila calorhabdos
Eremophila decipiens
Eremophila densifolia
Eremophila divaricata
Eremophila glabra
Eremophila laanii
Eremophila latrobei
Eremophila maculata
Eremophila polyclada
Grevillea curviloba
Grevillea glabrata
Grevillea iaspicula
Grevillea olivacea
Grevillea phanerophlebia
Grevillea rosmarinifolia
Grevillea vestita
Grevillea willisii
Grevillea willisii ssp. pachylostyla
Hakea ambigua
Hakea costata
Hakea eriantha
Hakea hookerana
Hakea leucoptera
Hakea obtusa
Hakea oleifolia
Hakea prostrata
Hakea rostrata
Hakea sericea
Hakea suaveolens
Hakea trifurcata
Hakea varia
Hakea verrucosa
Hardenbergia violacea
Hardenbergia violacea 'Happy
  Wanderer'
Kennedia macrophylla
Kennedia nigricans
Kennedia retrorsa
Kennedia rubicunda
Kunzea ericoides
Kunzea pomifera
Lagunaria patersonii
Maireana brevifolia
Melaleuca acerosa
Melaleuca densa
Melaleuca diosmifolia
Melaleuca eleutherostachya
Melaleuca micromera
Melaleuca tamarascina
Myoporum acuminatum
Myoporum desertii
Myoporum ellipticum
Myoporum insulare
Myoporum parvifolium
Nuytsia floribunda
Persoonia pinifolia
Pittosporum undulatum
Pomaderris ferruginea
Pomaderris lanigera
Rhagodia spinescens
Templetonia retusa
Westringia fruticosa

Rainforest Plants

To those accustomed to the fine-
foliaged structure of plants from
drier regions, trees and shrubs from
warmer, northern rainforest areas
appear very exotic. Large lobed
leaves and leaves with striking vein
patterns and brilliant red, orange or
pink new growth are some of the
characteristics which recommend
their use as indoor and tubbed patio
specimens.

If grown indoors, plant into
containers of fertilised soil, such as
Debco Acid Loving Mix, containing
a water saturation aid such as Debco
SaturAid to ensure that constant
moisture is available. Regular visits
outside to the fresh air, in a position
sheltered from hot or cold winds,
and in filtered light are essential.
Foliage must be kept clean at all
times by sponging or gentle hosing.

It is worth developing a 'bank' of
plants, so that some are outside
resting while others are inside
decorating. A weekly changeover
will maintain good health and
vigorous growth, and almost
eliminate the results of the stress
imposed by living inside in artificial
light and atmosphere.

For outdoor growing it is wise to
select sites sheltered from frost and
winds. Well-prepared soil, rich in
compost or humus, and regular
summer moisture applied to soil and
occasionally to foliage will ensure
lush, vigorous growth.

You may wonder at, and even
query, the size variation given in our
chart for some trees deriving from
rainforest areas. The low light
conditions under the rainforest
canopy force trees to grow upward
until the canopy is penetrated, and
this results in mostly tall shafting
trunks with foliage concentrated
towards the top. However, the same
plants used in open parklands or in
street plantings respond differently.
Here it is usual for them to develop a
lower branching and spreading
habit, almost as if they are casting a
protective umbrella over their root-
runs to prevent drying out.

*These plants are recommended for
indoor use.

*Acmena australis
*Acmena smithii
Agapetes meiniana
Alectryon coriaceus
Alphitonia excelsa
Alphitonia petriei

*Alpinia caerulea
Amorphospermum whitei
*Anopterus macleayanus
*Araucaria bidwillii
*Araucaria heterophylla
*Archidendron grandiflorum
*Archirhodomyrtus beckleri
*Archontophoenix alexandrae
*Archontophoenix
  cunninghamiana
Argyrodendron actinophyllum
Athertonia diversifolia
Austromyrtus lasioclada
Austromyrtus tenuifolia
Backhousia citriodora
Backhousia myrtifolia
*Barklya syringifolia
*Boea hygroscopica
Brachychiton acerifolius
Brachychiton discolor
Buckinghamia celsissima
*Caldcluvia paniculosa
*Callitris macleayana
*Castanospermum australe
Cinnamomum oliveri
Commersonia bartramia
*Cordyline petiolaris
*Cordyline stricta
*Cordyline terminalis
Cryptocarya laevigata var. bowiei
Cupaniopsis anacardioides
Cuttsia viburnea
*Davidsonia pruriens
Diploglottis campbellii
Diploglottis cunninghamii
Ehretia acuminata
*Elattostachys nervosa
Endiandra pubens
Eugenia reinwardtiana
Euodia elleryana
Eupomatia laurina
Faradaya splendida
*Ficus benjamina
*Ficus rubiginosa variegated
*Geissois benthamii
Grevillea hilliana
Grevillea pinnatifida
Grevillea robusta
*Harpullia alata
Harpullia pendula
Helmholtzia acorifolia
Helmholtzia glaberrima
*Hicksbeachia pinnatifolia
*Hoya australis
*Hoya macgillivrayii
*Hoya nicholsoniae
*Hoya rubida
Jagera pseudorhus
Linospadix monostachyus
Lonchocarpus stipularis
Macadamia tetraphylla
Macaranga tanarius
*Mackinlaya macrosciadia
Melia azedarach
Metrosideros queenslandicus
Millettia megasperma
Nauclea orientalis
*Neolitsea dealbata
Neosepicaea jucunda
*Omalanthus populifolius
Oreocallis pinnata
Oreocallis wickhamii

Orites excelsa
Pittosporum rhombifolium
* Podocarpus elatus
Polyscias elegans
Rhododendron lochae
* Schefflera actinophylla
Sloanea australis
Stenocarpus salignus
Stenocarpus sinuatus
Syzygium cormiflorum
* Syzygium hodgkinsoniae
* Syzygium luehmannii
Syzygium moorei
Syzygium oleosum
* Syzygium paniculatum
* Syzygium wilsonii
Tecomanthe hillii
Toona australis
Trochocarpa laurina

Rigid Foliage

Many people ask for plants to restrict movement by both people and animals through specific areas of garden. By their very nature, rigid-foliaged plants quickly deter any who touch them. They also make safe nesting and perching habitats for birds, which are often subjected to unnatural predators such as cats.

Acacia bidentata
Acacia colletioides
Acacia genistifolia
Acacia gunnii
Acacia peuce
Acacia pulchella
Acacia riceana
Acacia rigens
Acacia rupicola
Acacia tetragonophylla
Acacia triptera
Acacia ulicifolia
Acacia verticillata
Acacia victoriae
Banksia ashbyi
Banksia audax
Banksia caleyi
Banksia candolleana
Banksia laevigata ssp. laevigata
Banksia lehmanniana
Banksia praemorsa
Banksia victoriae
Bursaria spinosa
Callistemon macropunctatus
Callistemon pachyphyllus
Callistemon rigidus
Dryandra ferruginea
Dryandra nobilis
Dryandra polycephala
Dryandra praemorsa
Dryandra quercifolia
Dryandra sessilis
Eremophila divaricata
Graptophyllum spinigerum
Grevillea acanthifolia
Grevillea aquifolium
Grevillea asparagoides
Greviliea 'Australflora Copper
    Crest'
Grevillea bipinnatifida
Grevillea 'Clearview David'
Grevillea confertifolia
Grevillea dielsiana
Grevillea glabrata
Grevillea huegelii
Grevillea insignis
Grevillea juniperina — all forms
Grevillea molyneuxii
Grevillea montis-cole
Grevillea 'Ned Kelly'
Grevillea phanerophlebia
Grevillea pilosa
Grevillea 'Pink Pearl'
Grevillea platypoda
Grevillea 'Poorinda Peter'
Grevillea rivularis
Grevillea 'Robyn Gordon'

Grevillea rosmarinifolia — all
    forms
Grevillea trifida
Grevillea tripartita
Grevillea 'White Wings'
Grevillea wickhamii
Grevillea willisii ssp. pachylostyla
Grevillea wilsonii
Hakea ambigua
Hakea baxteri
Hakea ceratophylla
Hakea corymbosa
Hakea costata
Hakea erinacea
Hakea gibbosa
Hakea leucoptera
Hakea lissocarpha
Hakea myrtoides
Hakea oleifolia
Hakea orthorrhyncha
Hakea platysperma
Hakea prostrata
Hakea purpurea
Hakea pycnoneura
Hakea rostrata
Hakea ruscifolia
Hakea sericea
Hakea suaveolens
Hakea teretifolia
Hakea undulata
Hakea varia
Hakea verrucosa
Hakea victoriae
Hovea pungens
Isopogon anethifolius
Isopogon ceratophyllus
Isopogon dubius
Isopogon formosus
Lambertia formosa
Leptospermum juniperinum
    'Horizontalis'
Mirbelia dilatata
Petrophile biloba
Petrophile fucifolia
Podocarpus elatus
Xanthorrhoea australis
Xanthorrhoea minor

Rockeries

A rockery is an attractive component of any garden, large or small. Choose plants which are in proportion to the size of your rockery; it is inappropriate to use large spreading plants in a small, confined area.

Acacia aculeatissima
Acacia amblygona 'Austraflora Winter Gold'
Acacia bidentata
Acacia tayloriana
Acacia ulicifolia var. *brownei*
Actinodium cunninghamii
Actinodium sp. *nova*
Actinotus helianthi
Agrostocrinum scabrum
Anigozanthos — many small forms
Aotus ericoides prostrate
Astroloma — all species
Baeckea — all dwarf species
Banksia spinulosa 'Austraflora Birthday Candles'
Bauera rubioides — prostrate forms
Beaufortia heterophylla

Beaufortia purpurea
Beaufortia schaueri
Blandfordia grandiflora
Blandfordia nobilis
Boea hygroscopica
Boronia anemonifolia
Boronia citriodora
Boronia filifolia
Boronia inornata
Boronia microphylla
Boronia muelleri 'Sunset Serenade'
Boronia serrulata
Brachycome — all species
Bulbine bulbosa
Bulbine semibarbata
Calectasia cyanea
Callistemon sieberi 'Austraflora Little Cobber'
Calytrix — many small species
Celmisia asteliifolia
Chorizema — many small species
Commersonia pulchella
Conostylis — all species
Correa reflexa
Craspedia glauca
Craspedia globosa
Crowea — all dwarf or small species
Cryptandra amara

Cryptandra scortechinii
Dampiera — all dwarf or small species
Darwinia — all species
Dillwynia sericea
Diplarrena latifolia
Diplarrena moroea
Dryandra nivea
Dryandra speciosa
Epacris — all species
Eremophila — many small species
Eriostemon — many small species
Eutaxia microphylla
Frankenia pauciflora
Gastrolobium truncatum
Gompholobium — all species
Goodenia — all species
Grevillea alpina —many small forms
Grevillea 'Austraflora McDonald Park'
Grevillea 'Bonnie Prince Charlie'
Grevillea brachystylis
Grevillea depauperata
Grevillea dryandrii
Grevillea lanigera prostrate
Grevillea lavandulacea — many small forms
Grevillea leptobotrys
Grevillea pilulifera
Guichenotia macrantha
Hakea myrtoides
Halgania cyanea
Halgania preissii
Helichrysum — many small species
Helipterum — all species
Hemiandra pungens
Hemigenia sericea
Hibbertia — all dwarf or small species
Homoranthus flavescens
Hovea chorizemifolia
Hovea heterophylla
Hovea pungens
Hovea trisperma
Hypocalymma —all species
Isotoma fluviatilis
Kennedia glabrata
Kennedia microphylla
Kennedia prostrata
Kunzea ericifolia
Kunzea parvifolia dwarf
Lechenaultia — all species
Leucopogon virgatus
Linum marginale
Mazus pumilio
Melaleuca incana 'Velvet Cushion'
Melaleuca scabra
Melaleuca thymifolia
Micromyrtus ciliata
Micromyrtus drummondii
Olearia ciliata
Olearia picridifolia
Olearia teretifolia var. *compacta*
Orthrosanthus laxus
Orthrosanthus multiflorus
Oxylobium tricuspidatum
Patersonia — all species
Pelargonium rodneyanum
Pennisetum alopecuroides
Pileanthus filiformis

Rockeries have great appeal. They are appropriate either as part of a large garden or as the chief landscaping feature of a small one.

The soil should be friable and should drain freely, while still retaining some moisture, because many rockery plants will only thrive under such conditions.

The choice of rocks and the skill with which they are positioned are all-important to the appearance and success of a rockery. Choose reasonably large rocks and place them together in sympathetic groups, perhaps with matching surfaces almost abutting. Broad, flat surfaces should be incorporated with more upright or rounded faces to create harmonious groupings. The incline of the rockery should be gentle not steep, and the rocks should be partly buried so that they suggest a natural outcrop.

Try to select rock of a soft, mellow colour that does not jar the senses. White limestone or red scoria boulders are difficult to use and often awkward in shape.

Choose plants which are in proportion to the size of your rockery. It is quite inappropriate to use large, spreading plants in a small confined area.

Finally, a word about mulching. Generally, a rockery looks its most attractive when finished off with a coarse sand topping. Choose sand in the same tones as the rocks to enhance the natural effect. However, if using organic mulch, select as fine a grade as possible, so that the small plants are not buried beneath a blanket of solid material.

Pileanthus peduncularis
Pimelea — all species
Platytheca juniperina
Platytheca verticillata
Poa australis
Pomaderris obcordata
Pratia pedunculata
Prostanthera saxicola var.
    montana
Pseudanthus pimeleoides
Pultenaea — all dwarf or small
    species
Ranunculus granaticola
Rulingia hermanniifolia
Scaevola — all dwarf species
Scleranthus biflorus
Sowerbaea juncea
Sphaerolobium vimineum
Spyridium cinereum
Spyridium parvifolium 'Australflora
    Nimbus'
Stylidium — all species
Stypandra caespitosa
Styphelia adscendens
Styphelia tubiflora
Tetratheca — all species
Thomasia — all dwarf or small
    species
Thryptomene baeckeacea
Thryptomene saxicola
Thysanotus glaucus
Thysanotus multiflorus
Trachymene coerulea
Verticordia — all species
Viola hederacea
Viola betonicifolia
Wahlenbergia gloriosa
Xanthosia rotundifolia

Seasonally Wet Sands

Many plants grow in low-lying
sandy areas which become
inundated after rain. However, these
areas usually maintain this state for
only short periods and either drain or
dry up. Because water moves freely
through sandy soils, carrying
oxygen with it, unlike clay soils,
they seldom become waterlogged
and sour. The following list includes
a wide range of different-sized
plants for these conditions.

Acacia elongata
Acacia melanoxylon
Acacia retinodes
Acacia verticillata
Actinodium cunninghamii
Actinodium sp. nova
Alocasia macrorrhiza
Anigozanthos flavidus
Anigozanthos viridis
Astartea fascicularis
Astartea 'Winter Pink'
Baeckea astarteoides
Baeckea crenatifolia
Baeckea densifolia
Baeckea linifolia
Baeckea utilis
Baeckea virgata
Banksia ericifolia
Banksia littoralis
Banksia oblongifolia
Banksia occidentalis
Banksia paludosa
Banksia paludosus
Banksia robur
Bauera rubioides
Bauera sessiliflora
Beaufortia decussata
Beaufortia orbifolia
Beaufortia sparsa
Blandfordia grandiflora
Blandfordia nobilis
Boea hygroscopica
Boronia crenulata
Boronia denticulata
Boronia megastigma
Boronia muelleri 'Sunset
    Serenade'
Calectasia cyanea
Callistemon — all species
Calytrix sullivanii
Casuarina cunninghamiana
Casuarina glauca
Casuarina obesa
Casuarina torulosa
Chorizema ilicifolium
Claytonia australasica
Clematis aristata
Correa aemula
Correa lawrenciana
Cotula coronopifolia
Cotula filicula
Epacris impressa
Epacris longiflora
Epacris microphylla
Epacris pulchella
Epacris reclinata

Eucalyptus bancroftii
Eucalyptus botryoides
Eucalyptus camaldulensis
Eucalyptus cephalocarpa
Eucalyptus cosmophylla
Eucalyptus crenulata
Eucalyptus elata
Eucalyptus ficifolia
Eucalyptus forrestiana
Eucalyptus intertexta
Eucalyptus kitsoniana
Eucalyptus largiflorens
Eucalyptus multicaulis
Eucalyptus occidentalis
Eucalyptus ovata
Eucalyptus spathulata
Eucalyptus stellulata
Eucalyptus tereticornis
Eucalyptus viminalis
Eucalyptus willisii
Eucryphia lucida
Eugenia —all species
Goodia lotifolia
Grevillea acanthifolia
Grevillea aquifolium
Grevillea 'Australflora Copper
    Crest'
Grevillea barklyana
Grevillea brachystylis
Grevillea confertifolia
Grevillea curviloba
Grevillea juniperina
Grevillea lavandulacea Billywing
    compact
Grevillea linearifolia
Grevillea molyneuxii
Grevillea mucronulata
Grevillea rivularis
Grevillea shiressii
Grevillea thelemanniana ssp.
    obtusifolia
Hakea lasianthoides
Hakea nodosa
Hakea salicifolia
Hakea stenocarpa
Helmholtzia acorifolia
Helmholtzia glaberrima
Hibbertia stellaris
Hovea elliptica
Hovea lanceolata
Howittia trilocularis
Hypocalymma angustifolium
Hypocalymma cordifolium
Indigofera australis
Isotoma fluviatalis
Jacksonia scoparia
Kunzea parvifolia
Lambertia inermis
Leptospermum — all species
Lobelia trigonocaulis
Mazus pumilio
Melaleuca — many are suitable for
    seasonal or periodic inundation
Mentha gracilis
Nothofagus cunninghamii
Pennisetum alopecuroides
Petrophile conifera
Phebalium lamprophyllum
Platytheca verticillata
Pratia pedunculata
Pratia purpurescens
Prostanthera lasianthos

Restio tetraphyllus
Sowerbaea juncea
Stypandra caespitosa
Thryptomene calycina
Thysanotus multiflorus
Tristaniopsis laurina
Viminaria juncea
Viola betonicifolia
Viola hederacea

Soil Binding

Steep clay banks and loose sandy areas of the landscape can be problematic and need specific attention. Clay banks can suffer from scouring and erosion, mainly by water action; and wind can play havoc with the stability of sandy soil, especially in open sites.

For Sandy Soil

Many of these plants have the added advantage of either layering or suckering.

Acacia sophorae
Acacia truncata
Actinostrobus acuminatus
Aotus ericoides prostrate
Atriplex cinerea
Atriplex nummularia
Atriplex rhagodioides
Austromyrtus dulcis
Banksia integrifolia 'Australflora Roller Coaster'
Banksia serrata 'Australflora Pygmy Possum'
Brachycome angustifolia
Brachycome multifida
Brachysema sericeum black-red
Brachysema sericeum cream
Calocephalus brownii
Calothamnus quadrifidus prostrate
Calystegia soldanella
Carpobrotus rossii
Casuarina muellerana
Claytonia australasica
Correa alba
Correa decumbens
Correa 'Pink Bells'
Correa reflexa var. *nummulariifolia*
Cymbopogon ambiguus
Dampiera diversifolia
Dampiera lanceolata
Dampiera lavandulacea
Dampiera rosmarinifolia
Dampiera stricta
Dodonaea humifusa
Dodonaea procumbens
Eucalyptus dielsii
Gastrolobium truncatum
Goodenia humilis
Grevillea thelemanniana
ssp. *thelemanniana*
Halgania preissii
Hibbertia scandens
Ipomoea brasiliensis
Isotoma fluviatalis
Kennedia nigricans
Kennedia rubicunda
Kunzea ambigua
Kunzea pomifera
Lasiopetalum macrophyllum
Maireana brevifolia
Mazus pumilio
Mentha gracilis
Muehlenbeckia adpressa
Myoporum ellipticum
Myoporum insulare
Myoporum parvifolium

Olearia axillaris
Pennisetum alopecuroides
Phyla nodiflora
Restio tetraphyllus
Rhagodia spinescens
Spyridium cinereum
Spyridium parvifolium 'Australflor Nimbus'

For Clay Loam Soil

These will impede water movement and provide stability through their root structures.

Acacia sophorae
Acacia truncata
Aotus ericoides prostrate
Banksia integrifolia 'Australflora Roller Coaster'
Banksia serrata 'Australflora Pygm Possum'
Bauera — all species
Brachycome angustifolia
Brachycome multifida
Brachysema sericeum black-red
Brachysema sericeum cream
Callistemon citrinus 'Australflora Firebrand'
Callistemon pallidus 'Australflora Candle Glow'
Calothamnus quadrifidus prostrat
Casuarina muellerana
Cotula coronopifolia
Cotula filicula
Cymbopogon ambiguus
Dampiera stricta
Dampiera teres
Dianella — all species
Dichanthium sericeum
Dichondra repens
Dodonaea humifusa
Gastrolobium truncatum
Goodenia hederacea var. *alpestris*
Goodenia humilis
Goodenia lanata
Grevillea aquifolium prostrate
Grevillea 'Australflora Canterbury Gold'
Grevillea 'Australflora Copper Crest'
Grevillea 'Australflora Fanfare'
Grevillea 'Australflora Old Gold'
Grevillea 'Bronze Rambler'
Grevillea curviloba
Grevillea diminuta
Grevillea x gaudichaudii
Grevillea juniperina prostrate
Grevillea thelemanniana
ssp. *obtusifolia*
Hardenbergia violacea
Hardenbergia violacea 'Happy Wanderer'
Helichrysum apiculatum
Hibbertia empetrifolia
Ipomoea brasiliensis
Isotoma fluviatalis
Kennedia eximia
Kennedia macrophylla
Kennedia nigricans
Kennedia prostrata
Kennedia retrorsa
Kennedia rubicunda

Kunzea ambigua
Kunzea ericoides
Kunzea pomifera
Lasiopetalum macrocarpum
Leptospermum flavescens 'Cardwell'
Leptospermum juniperum 'Horizontalis'
Maireana brevifolia
Melaleuca bracteata 'Golden Gem'
Melaleuca ericifolia
Mentha gracilis
Myoporum ellipticum
Myoporum insulare
Myoporum parvifolium
Olearia axillaris
Pennisetum alopecuroides
Pratia pedunculata
Pratia purpurescens
Pultenaea polifolia var. *mucronata*
Restio tetraphyllus
Scaevola hookeri
Scaevola 'Mauve Clusters'
Spyridium cinereum
Spyridium parvifolium 'Austraflora Nimbus'
Viola hederacea

Windbreaks

People on rural properties, particularly in exposed sites, have long been aware of the value of windbreaks and shelter-belts, and their benefits to stock. Now, in a fuel-conscious age, the cost savings on heating and cooling bills which can be achieved by the use of plants is widely realised.

The basic function of a windbreak is to slow down and filter the wind, rather than attempt to block it entirely, which generally results in severe turbulence on what is supposed to be the sheltered side. Therefore, shrubs and trees need to be selected and positioned to allow the wind to 'thread' through and between them. Double, perhaps even triple, lines of planting may be needed, allowing 3 to 4 metres between plants. Depending on spacing and available area, an upper and a lower storey of planting may be advisable.

Acacia adunca
Acacia argyrophylla
Acacia baileyana
Acacia boormanii
Acacia cognata
Acacia cyclops
Acacia elata
Acacia fimbriata
Acacia floribunda
Acacia howittii
Acacia iteaphylla
Acacia longifolia
Acacia melanoxylon
Acacia peuce
Acacia pravissima
Acacia prominens
Acacia saligna
Acacia sophorae
Acacia truncata
Actinostrobus pyramidalis
Agonis flexuosa
Albizia lophantha
Angophora costata
Banksia ericifolia
Banksia 'Giant Candles'
Banksia integrifolia
Banksia marginata
Banksia media
Banksia praemorsa
Banksia serrata
Banksia verticillata
Callistemon citrinus 'Splendens'
Callistemon 'Harkness'
Callistemon 'King's Park Special'
Callistemon macropunctatus
Callistemon pallidus
Callistemon salignus
Callistemon shiressii
Callistemon viminalis
Callitris columellaris
Callitris endlicheri

Callitris preissii ssp. *verrucosa*
Callitris rhomboidea
Casuarina distyla
Casuarina glauca
Casuarina littoralis
Casuarina nana
Casuarina obesa
Casuarina verticillata
Cupaniopsis anacardioides
Eremophila bignoniiflora
Eremophila polyclada
Eucalyptus albens
Eucalyptus angulosa
Eucalyptus burdettiana
Eucalyptus burracoppinensis
Eucalyptus cneorifolia
Eucalyptus conferruminata
Eucalyptus diversifolia
Eucalyptus incrassata
Eucalyptus lehmannii
Eucalyptus leucoxylon ssp. *megalocarpa*
Eucalyptus macrandra
Eucalyptus maculata
Eucalyptus melliodora
Eucalyptus oldfieldii
Eucalyptus platypus
Eucalyptus polyanthemos
Eucalyptus polybractea
Eucalyptus preissiana
Eucalyptus rugosa
Eucalyptus rupicola
Eucalyptus todtiana
Eucalyptus viridis
Grevillea — all large, shrubby species are very suitable
Hakea elliptica
Hakea eriantha
Hakea nodosa
Hakea oleifolia
Hakea petiolaris
Hakea salicifolia
Hakea suaveolens
Kunzea ambigua
Kunzea baxteri
Kunzea ericoides
Lagunaria patersonii
Lambertia inermis
Leptospermum flavescens
Leptospermum laevigatum
Leptospermum lanigerum
Leptospermum obovatum
Melaleuca acerosa
Melaleuca armillaris
Melaleuca bracteata
Melaleuca citrina
Melaleuca densa
Melaleuca diosmifolia
Melaleuca ericifolia
Melaleuca halmaturorum
Melaleuca hypericifolia
Melaleuca linariifolia
Melaleuca nesophila
Melaleuca styphelioides
Melaleuca tamarascina
Myoporum acuminatum
Myoporum desertii
Myoporum insulare
Pittosporum undulatum
Westringia fruticosa
Westringia longifolia
Westringia 'Wynyabbie Gem'

New and Recent Introductions

The following plants suitable for horticulture are now available to gardeners. The information about them is organised as in the Plant Selection List, the key to which is given on page 30.

Temp — temperate
W.te — warm temperate
Trop — tropical
S.tr — sub-tropical
S.ar — semi-arid

L — light
H — heavy
N — nectar-feeding
S — seed-eating
F — fruit-eating

		Height	Width	Climatic zones	moist, well drained	wet	dry	dry limy	full sun	filtered sun	coastal regions	frosty regions
Acacia baileyana prostrata	Ground-covering form of Cootamundra Wattle, grey-green foliage, brilliant yellow perfumed flowers in winter. Ideal for steep deep banks or bare ground.	30-50cm	2-5m	Temp S.tr S.ar	•		•		•	•	2	H
Acacia boormanii 'Olympic Gold'	Low branching, spreading shrub, lightly suckering; soft grey-green foliage covered with bright golden balls in late winter. Spectacular, adaptable.	1.2-1.8m	2-3.5m	Temp S.tr S.ar	•		•		•	•		H
Acacia caerulescens 'Buchan Blue'	Small to medium tree, lovely soft blue-grey foliage, pale lemon ball flowers in spring. Beautiful landscape tree, especially in groups.	7-9m	4-6m	Temp S.tr	•		•	•	•		2	L
Acacia cognata 'Australflora Mop Top'	Dwarf mounding form of large shrub, soft red-tipped foliage, pale lemon flowers in spring. Excellent soft low hedge or unusual container plant.	60-90cm	90cm-1.2m	Temp S.tr	•				•	•	2	L
Acacia cognata 'Green Mist'	Low mounding shrub, fine dense weeping light green foliage, sweetly fragrant; pale lemon flowers in early spring. Dramatic in large rockeries; hedging.	80cm-1m	2-3m	Temp S.tr	•				•	•	2	H
Acacia iteaphylla 'Parson's Cascade'	Vigorous cascading wattle, silver-grey foliage with plum new growth; showy golden flowers in winter. Tough, quick-growing groundcover for large areas.	40-60cm	2.5-4m	Temp S.tr S.ar	•		•		•	•	2	H
Acacia sp.aff. leprosa 'Red Wattle'	Medium shrub, weeping branches, curved slightly sticky foliage; spectacular crimson ball flowers in late winter-spring. A remarkable and sought-after rarity.	3-5m	2.5-3m	Temp S.tr	•				•	•		H
Acmena smithii 'Hedgemaster'	Dwarf compact shrub, dense glossy leaves; not known to flower. Selected for hedging, topiary and formal landscape purposes. Prune to shape.	20-30cm	15-25cm	Temp Trop S.tr	•	•			•	•		
Angophora costata 'Gumball'	Ball-shaped, multi-trunked small tree, dense foliage to the ground; not known to flower. Regular pruning produces red new growth winter-spring.	4-6m	3-4m	Temp Trop S.tr S.ar	•		•		•	•	1	L

Legend:

mp — temperate
e — warm temperate
— tropical
— sub-tropical
— semi-arid

L — light
H — heavy
N — nectar-feeding
S — seed-eating
F — fruit-eating

Name	Description	Height	Width	Climatic zones	moist, well drained	wet	dry	dry limy	full sun	filtered sun	coastal regions	frosty regions	bird attraction
gozanthos 'sh Gold'	Small plant, bright green strap foliage; massed bright yellow flowers on branched stems during spring and summer. Spectacular in mass plantings.	50-90cm	50cm	Temp S.tr S.ar	•		•		•	•	2	L	N
gozanthos 'sh Pearl'	Compact tuft, bright green foliage, showy massed bright pink flowers on branched stems all year round. Containers, rockeries, courtyards, path edges.	30-50cm	30cm	Temp S.tr S.ar	•		•		•	•	2	L	N
gozanthos 'yal Cheer'	Small tufting plant, grey-green leaves, bright red-and-green flowers on long stems, mainly spring and summer. Superb cut flower. Containers, rockeries, courtyards.	50cm-1m	50cm	Temp S.tr S.ar	•		•		•	•	2	L	N
hirhodomyrtus kleri 'se Myrtle'	Graceful small shrub, shiny leaves, shell-pink perfumed 'mini rose' flowers in spring-summer. Tasty jam made from red fruits. Compact, fruitful selection.	50cm-1.2m	65cm-1m	Temp Trop S.tr	•				•	•		L	
khousia anisata 'seed Tree'	Medium to large tree, large aniseed-perfumed leaves, showy white flowers in summer. Unusual aromatic shade tree.	6-12m	5-9m	Temp Trop S.tr	•				•	•		L	
ckea linifolia 'straflora Mini tle'	Tiny dense shrublet; fine bronze foliage, dainty starry white flowers cover plant in late summer-autumn. Container or small hedge. Prune lightly.	15-30cm	30-50cm	Temp S.tr	•	•			•	•	2	L	
ksia 'Australflora on Delicious'	Small compact shrub, fine light green foliage; buds lemon, opening to lemon-gold flowers, winter-spring. Hedge or low screen. Prune after flowering.	1-1.5m	1-1.5m	Temp Trop S.tr	•				•	•	2	H	N S
ksia 'ite Orange'	Large dense shrub with narrow toothed leaves; numerous large flowers, buds white opening to golden orange in autumn-winter. Spectacular.	3-8m	3-6m	Temp S.ar	•		•	•	•	•	2	H	N S
ksia coccinea 'ite Crimson'	Dense narrow medium shrub, toothed grey-green foliage; compact flowers of crimson and grey, spring. Spectacular cut flower. Dramatic container plant.	2.5-3.5m	1.5-2.5m	Temp S.ar	•		•		•	•	1	H	N S
ksia coccinea 'ite Flame'	Dense narrow medium shrub, toothed grey-green foliage, compact flowers of flame-orange and grey, winter. Superb cut flower, dramatic large container plant.	2.5-3.5m	1.5-2.5m	Temp S.ar	•		•		•	•	1	H	N S
ksia marginata 'straflora Bronzed sie'	Small shrub, grey-green foliage, numerous flowers; buds bronze, opening green to lemon in summer-autumn. Attractive focal or container plant. Prune spent flowers.	40-60cm	40-80cm	Temp S.tr S.ar	•				•	•	2	L	N S
ksia paludosa 'straflora Coastal e'	Low spreading shrub, stiff toothed leaves, lemon brushes in autumn-winter. Excellent cover for banks, loose sand. Prune spent flower heads.	45-75cm	1-1.2m	Temp S.tr S.ar	•				•	•	1	L	N S

			Height	Width	Climatic zones	Soil types						coastal regions	frosty regions
Temp—temperate W.te—warm temperate Trop—tropical S.tr—sub-tropical S.ar—semi-arid	L—light H—heavy N—nectar-feeding S—seed-eating F—fruit-eating					moist, well drained	wet	dry	dry limy	full sun	filtered sun		
Banksia serrata 'Austraflora Bush Possum'	Medium shrub, often spreading, decorative wrinkled trunk, serrated leaves, large fluffy silver-yellow flowers in summer-autumn. Prune spent flowers.	40cm-1.2m	80cm-1.5m	Temp Trop S.tr	•		•		•	•	1	L
Banksia spinulosa 'Honeypots'	Small shapely shrub, dense foliage, golden flowers with burgundy overtones, held above foliage, autumn-winter Single or group planting. Prune lightly.	60cm	1.2m	Temp S.tr	•		•		•	•	1	L
Bauera rubioides x sessiliflora 'Ruby Glow'	Compact small to medium shrub, small crowded foliage, showy magenta flowers most of year. Ideal for moist areas. Prune regularly.	1-2m	1.5-2.5m	Temp Trop S.tr	•	•			•	•	2	L
Boronia megastigma 'Royale'	Small compact shrub, fine crowded leaves, highly perfumed brown bells with yellow centres. Container or rockery plant. Prune after flowering.	20-30cm	25-35cm	Temp S.tr	•				•	•		L
Brachyscome 'Happy Face'	Rosette, small lobed leaves; bright cerise yellow-centred daisies on long stems, spring-summer-autumn. Cottage garden, container; extremely pretty.	30-50cm	50cm	Temp S.tr	•				•	•		
Brachyscome multifida (hybrids and forms)	Compact mound, finely divided foliage, many colours available: white, pink, blue, mauve or yellow, most of year. Prune regularly and lightly.	5-30cm	15-45cm	Temp Trop S.tr	•		•		•	•		L
Bracteantha 'Pink Sunrise'	Small spreading plant, dense green leaves, pink buds opening to showy cream everlasting flowers, held on stems above foliage. Prune after flowering.	30cm	60cm	Temp S.tr S.ar	•		•		•	•	1	L
Callistemon forresterae 'Austraflora Genoa Glory'	Medium upright to arching shrub, grey-green foliage, clusters of large lustrous purple-maroon brushes, autumn and spring. Prune after flowering.	1.5-2.5m	1-2.2m	Temp Trop S.tr	•	•			•	•	2	L
Callistemon viminalis 'Wildfire'	Medium compact weeping shrub, dense foliage, masses of flame-red brushes spring-summer. Ideal for screening in heavy wet soils.	1.5-2m	1-1.5m	Temp Trop S.tr	•	•			•	•	2	L
Calothamnus quadrifidus 'Austraflora Sand Groper'	Low mounding shrub, fine grey needle foliage, brilliant scarlet claw flowers spring-summer. Sturdy broad landscape plant. Prune to shape.	30-40cm	80cm-1.2m	Temp S.tr S.ar	•		•		•	•	1	L
Caryota rumphiana Fishtail Palm	Slender straight tree with once-divided leaves up to 4m long. Flowers purple and green, fruit blue and caustic to skin. Container or garden specimen.	10-18m	6-8m	Trop S.tr	•					•	2	L
Conostylis juncea	Tufting plant, rush foliage, furry yellow tubular flowers in winter. Beautiful container or rockery plant, especially in groups.	20-50cm	30-60cm	Temp S.tr S.ar	•				•	•		L

Legend	
p — temperate	L — light
⬦ — warm temperate	H — heavy
— tropical	N — nectar-feeding
— sub-tropical	S — seed-eating
— semi-arid	F — fruit-eating

Name	Description	Height	Width	Climatic zones	moist, well drained	wet	dry	dry limy	full sun	filtered sun	coastal regions	frosty regions	bird attraction
ea ...ex'	Erect narrow shrub, tight rounded leaves, numerous tubular lipstick-pink, yellow-tipped flowers late summer to winter. Neat container or border plant.	80cm-1m	40-60cm	Temp S.tr S.ar	•		•	•	•	•	1	L	N
mbia ...mer Beauty'	Small to medium tree, bronze-red new growth, massed vivid pink blossom summer-autumn. Grafted hybrid selection. Spectacular and reliable.	5-8m	4-7m	Temp Trop S.tr S.ar	•		•		•	•	1	L	N S
mbia ...mer Red'	Small to medium tree, bronze-red new growth, spectacular clusters of crimson flowers in summer-autumn. Grafted hybrid selection. Dramatic landscape feature.	5-8m	4-7m	Temp Trop S.tr S.ar	•		•		•	•	1	L	N S
um ...unculatum ...r or Swamp Lily	Handsome clumping plant, large strap leaves, showy white flowers in spring. Suitable indoors or warm coastal regions.	60cm-1m	30-60cm	Temp Trop S.tr	•		•		•	•	1		
vea exalata traflora ...equin'	Small arching shrub, fine aromatic foliage, festooned with multi-hued pink star flowers in late summer-autumn. Drought resistant. Prune after flowering.	30-45cm	80cm-1.2m	Temp S.tr S.ar	•		•		•	•	1	L	
vea exalata ...thern Stars'	Dwarf compact shrub, fine deep red foliage; profusion of pink star flowers autumn-winter. Rockeries, borders, containers. Prune lightly after flowering.	50-70cm	50-70cm	Temp S.tr S.ar	•		•		•	•	2	H	
honia ...pitosa ...aby Grass	Dense tussock, narrow leaves, cream seed heads on long stems, late spring-summer. Elegant landscape plant, especially when planted in groups.	20-50cm	30-60cm	Temp S.tr S.ar	•		•				2	H	S
ventia arenaria ...age Speedwell	Slender erect shrub, fine foliage, heads of bright violet-blue flowers in spring. Dainty container or cottage garden plant. Prune lightly.	50-80cm	30-80cm	Temp S.ar	•		•		•	•		L	
ventia perfoliata ...a Walling'	Dwarf compact shrub with stem-clasping leaves; sprays of ice-blue flowers held above foliage in late spring-summer. Cottage garden, container.	15-30cm	20-45cm	Temp	•				•	•		H	
es robinsoniana ...ding Lily	Clump, erect long strap leaves, delicate white 'iris' blooms in late spring. Lovely with ferns, pool edges, rainforest. Indigenous to Lord Howe Island.	80cm-1.2m	80cm-1m	Temp Trop S.tr	•					•	1		
poa dives ...Cane Grass	Tall slender grass, pale green stems and foliage, large loose flower plumes. Elegant, dramatic landscape plant; especially when backlit at night.	1-1.5m	40-60cm	Temp S.tr	•					•			S
ocarpus ...ulatus ...traflora Pink ...ls'	Ornamental small tree; multi-hued foliage, massed fringed pink bells in spring, followed by blue berries (non-poisonous). Special selection for garden or parkland.	5-8m	3-4m	Temp Trop S.tr	•		•		•	•	2	L	S

			Height	Width	Climatic zones	Soil types				full sun	filtered sun	coastal regions	frosty regions
						moist, well drained	wet	dry	dry limy				

Legend:
Temp — temperate
W.te — warm temperate
Trop — tropical
S.tr — sub-tropical
S.ar — semi-arid

L — light
H — heavy
N — nectar-feeding
S — seed-eating
F — fruit-eating

Name	Description	Height	Width	Climatic zones	moist, well drained	wet	dry	dry limy	full sun	filtered sun	coastal regions	frosty regions
Epilobium tasmanicum 'Edna Walling'	Dwarf cottage garden plant with soft shiny irregularly lobed leaves, numerous pink flowers in summer. Dainty container plant, or in mixed plantings.	15-25cm	20-30cm	Temp S.tr	•	•			•	•		H
Eriostemon 'Bournda Beauty'	Small bushy shrub, aromatic grey-green foliage; delicate pink buds, white waxy star flowers, peak flowering in winter-spring. Prune after flowering.	80cm-1m	80cm-1m	Temp S.tr S.ar	•		•		•	•	2	H
Eucalyptus tricarpa Blue Ironbark	Medium to large spreading tree, black hard furrowed bark, beautiful pendulous silver-blue foliage, cream or pale apricot flowers in threes, winter-spring. Handsome.	6-12m	5-10m	Temp S.tr S.ar	•		•		•	•	2	H
Eucalyptus leucoxylon 'Australflora Euky Dwarf'	Small graceful white-barked tree; fine dense foliage, massed crimson-pink blossom, occasionally cream, autumn-summer. Ideal small garden bird attractor, or street tree.	3-6m	3-5m	Temp S.tr S.ar	•		•	•	•	•	2	H
Eucalyptus pauciflora 'Australflora Little Snowman'	Small mallee or dwarf tree; open canopy above smooth creamy-white trunk, cream flowers in summer. Ideal small garden or street tree.	4-7m	3-4m	Temp S.tr	•				•	•		H
Eucryphia moorei 'Australflora Honeysweet'	Large shrub, soft pinnate foliage, masses of pearly nectar-rich flowers in early spring-late summer. Selected form of Victorian Leatherwood.	3-6m	1.5-2.5m	Temp Trop S.tr	•					•		L
Fieldia australis Fairies' Lanterns	Dainty epiphytic creeper, soft furry toothed foliage, long translucent cream bells summer-autumn, large succulent white berries. Combines well with ferns or rainforest.	climber	light	Temp Trop S.tr	•					•	2	
Goodenia ovata 'Australflora Coverup'	Dense layering groundcover; glossy waxy foliage, dainty yolk-yellow fan flowers most of year. A drought-resistant "mulch" for all landscapes. Prune lightly.	prostrate	1-1.5m	Temp S.tr S.ar	•		•	•	•	•	1	H
Goodenia ovata 'Australflora Lightenup'	Small variegated shrub, green and white or pale yellow leaves. Buttercup-yellow flowers in spring-summer. A light-coloured edging or tub plant. Prune lightly.	25-40cm	30-45cm	Temp S.tr S.ar	•		•	•	•	•	1	L
Grevillea 'Allyn Radiance'	Dense groundcover, small crowded leaves, fire engine red flowers perched on top of foliage, winter-spring-summer. Prune regularly.	10cm	60cm-1m	Temp S.tr S.ar	•				•	•	2	H
Grevillea 'Australflora Aussie Dawn'	Scrambling groundcover, finely divided bronze-tipped dark green leaves, multi-hued blue and pink flowers in summer-autumn. Sturdy broad landscape plant.	20-40cm	1-1.5m	Temp Trop S.tr	•					•	2	H
Grevillea 'Australflora Cherry Ripe'	Small compact lightly suckering shrub, soft grey foliage, cherry-pink flower bunches in winter-spring. Low hedging, containers or small gardens. Prune lightly.	30-40cm	30-50cm	Temp S.tr S.ar	•		•		•	•	2	H

Legend:

np—temperate	L—light
e—warm temperate	H—heavy
—tropical	N—nectar-feeding
—sub-tropical	S—seed-eating
—semi-arid	F—fruit-eating

Name	Description	Height	Width	Climatic zones	moist, well drained	wet	dry	dry limy	full sun	filtered sun	coastal regions	frosty regions	bird attraction
villea straflora non 'n Lime'	Low arching shrub, small pale green foliage, lime-yellow flower bunches most of year. Quick cover for broad landscape. Prune lightly.	30-50cm	1-1.2m	Temp S.tr S.ar	•		•		•	•	2	H	N
villea straflora Orange	Developed as an alternative to English Box. Small compact shrub, dense glossy leaves, orange flower bunches in summer-autumn-winter. Prune often to shape.	40-60cm	40-60cm	Temp S.tr S.ar	•		•		•		2	H	N
villea straflora gerine'	Spreading shrub; dense grey-green foliage, bright tangerine flower bunches most of year. Ideal for broad landscape cover and slopes. Prune to shape.	30-40cm	1-1.5m	Temp S.tr S.ar	•		•		•		2	H	N
villea den Yul Lo'	An open upright to spreading shrub, deeply divided grey foliage, bright yellow cylindrical flowers year-round. Dramatic as specimen or in groups.	3-4m	2.5-3m	Temp Trop S.tr	•				•	•	2	L	N S
villea ctar Delight'	Prostrate spreading groundcover, attractive lobed leaves with bronze new growth; large pink toothbrush flowers in summer. Useful on banks, open spaces. Trim regularly.	15cm	1.5-2m	Temp Trop S.tr	•				•	•	2	L	N
villea maxwellii	Small dense shrub, lacy divided foliage, large pendent orange to pink flowers in winter and spring. Strong landscape element.	30-50cm	1-1.8m	Temp S.tr S.ar	•		•		•		2	L	N
ea rrendong Beauty'	Low arching shrub, crowded grey-green foliage, intense cerise flowers borne in leaf axils winter-spring. Hardy and very attractive.	50cm-1m	1-2m	Temp S.tr S.ar	•		•		•		2	H	N
ea decurrens straflora Pink ds'	Slender weeping selection, needle leaves, branches festooned with fragrant musk-pink flowers in winter-spring. Beautiful habitat for small birds.	3-5m	1.5-2.5m	Temp S.tr S.ar	•		•		•	•	2	L	N S
denbergia ptoniana straflora Ultra et'	Medium climber or scrambler; glossy trifoliate leaves, long racemes of black-purple pea flowers in late spring. Use on verandas, walls, courtyards; prune lightly.	climber	medium	Temp S.tr S.ar	•		•		•	•	1	L	N S
denbergia acea shy Blue'	Small rounded shrub, blue-grey foliage, masses of blue-purple pea flowers, late winter-spring. Hedging or borders, large containers. Prune to shape.	50-60cm	50-60cm	Temp Trop S.tr S.ar	•		•		•	•	2	H	N S
denbergia acea e 'n Easy'	Elegant climber, smooth glossy leaves, massed lacy white flowers winter-spring; combine with H. 'Happy Wanderer' for dramatic effect. Prune after flowering.	climber or creeper	vigorous	Temp Trop S.tr S.ar	•		•		•	•	2	L	N S
denbergia acea ni Ha Ha'	Compact small shrub, small neat foliage, clustered deep violet pea flowers winter-spring. Neat border or path edge plant. Prune lightly after flowering.	50cm	1m	Temp S.tr S.ar	•		•		•	•	2	L	N S

Temp — temperate L — light
W.te — warm temperate H — heavy
Trop — tropical N — nectar-feeding
S.tr — sub-tropical S — seed-eating
S.ar — semi-arid F — fruit-eating

		Height	Width	Climatic zones	Soil types							
					moist, well drained	wet	dry	dry limy	full sun	filtered sun	coastal regions	frosty regions
Isopogon anemonifolius 'Australflora Little Drumsticks'	Small compact shrub, attractive divided foliage, showy masses of bright yellow flowerheads spring-summer. Container, rockery.	30-65cm	45-80cm	Temp S.tr S.ar	•		•		•	•	1	L
Isopogon anemonifolius 'Woorikee 2000'	Dwarf compact shrub, variously divided foliage with red tips; massed bright yellow flowers spring-summer. Dramatic container, rockery or small garden plant.	20-50cm	30-50cm	Temp S.tr S.ar	•		•		•	•	1	L
Kennedia nigricans 'Minstrels'	Vigorous climber or groundcover, large single or trifoliate leaves, startling black and white pea flowers spring-summer. Very hardy and useful cover.	climber, creeper	vigorous	Temp S.tr S.ar	•		•		•	•	2	L
Kennedia rubicunda 'Australflora Coral Carpet'	Scrambling climber or groundcover; fine trifoliate leaves, showy brick-red flowers in spring-summer. Suitable for banks, verandas, walls and fences.	climber, creeper	medium	Temp Trop S.tr	•		•		•	•	1	L
Kunzea pomifera 'Rivoli Bay'	Dense matting groundcover, bright green foliage, fluffy cream flowers in spring-summer. Selected for prolific fruiting; edible fresh or cooked.	prostrate	2-3m	Temp S.tr S.ar	•		•		•	•	2	H
Leptospermum liversidgei 'Mozzie Blocker'	Small graceful shrub, dense intensely aromatic foliage, pink flowers in summer. Plant as screen or container plant to keep mozzies at bay. Prune often.	1.5m	1.2m	Temp Trop S.tr	•	•			•	•	1	L
Leptospermum obovatum 'Australflora Lemon Pop'	Dwarf rounded shrub, tiny crowded lemon-scented leaves, covered in lime-white flowers in late spring-summer. Small garden accent, pathway hedge. Prune lightly.	45cm-1m	1-1.2m	Temp S.tr	•	•			•	•		L
Leptospermum rotundifolium x spectabile 'Rhiannon'	Small compact shrub, dense foliage, spectacular pink-mauve flowers with white stamens in spring. Container or low hedging; prune after flowering.	1.5m	1m	Temp Trop S.tr	•				•	•	2	L
Libertia paniculata Forest Lily	Small delicate lily, fine strap leaves, panicles of dainty white long-stemmed flowers spring-summer. Ideal for shady moist areas; with ferns. .	45-60cm	30-50cm	Temp Trop S.tr	•					•	2	
Licuala muelleri Fan Palm	Medium tree with beautiful circular fan-like leaves. Indoor or patio tub specimen, or shaded gardens in warmer climates.	6-10m	3-5m	Trop S.tr	•					•		L
Livistona decipiens Small Cabbage Palm	One of the smaller palms with deeply divided fan-like leaves. Useful for indoors or patio tubs, or growing in small tropical gardens.	4-7m	2-4m	Trop S.tr	•					•		L
Lobelia beaugleholei	Layering matting plant, small foliage, intense blue flowers spring-summer. Ideal for path edges, between paving stones; soil erosion control.	Prostrate	1-3m	Temp Trop S.tr	•	•			•	•		L

np—temperate	L—light
e—warm temperate	H—heavy
p—tropical	N—nectar-feeding
—sub-tropical	S—seed-eating
—semi-arid	F—fruit-eating

Name	Description	Height	Width	Climatic zones	Soil types: moist, well drained	wet	dry	dry limy	full sun	filtered sun	coastal regions	frosty regions	bird attraction
hostemon fertus y Bunter'	Small bushy tree, smooth bronze trunk, large leathery leaves, red new tips, white flowers in spring-summer. Useful for screening and hedging.	2-4m	2-3m	Temp Trop S.tr	•				•	•		L	
hrum hyssopifolia na Walling'	Small perennial herbaceous shrub, soft leaves, long magenta flowerheads summer-autumn. Charming cottage garden plant for wet areas.	60cm-1.2m	20-45cm	Temp S.tr	•	•			•	•		H	
laleuca nesophila tle Nessie'	Small to medium compact shrub, small rounded leaves, white bark, perfumed mauve ball flowers in summer. Recommended for windbreak. Prune to shape.	1.5-2.2m	2-2.5m	Temp Trop S.tr S.ar	•		•		•	•	1	L	N
laleuca gibbosa straflora Coverall'	Tiny, tangled suckering shrub; small aromatic leaves, deep mauve-pink flowers in spring-summer. Ornamental erosion control for wet areas and steep slopes.	30-50cm	40-60cm	Temp S.tr	•	•			•	•	2	H	N
laleuca linariifolia afoam'	Small to medium shrub, dense aromatic foliage, foamy white flowers in summer. Useful hedge, low windbreak. Prune after flowering.	1.5m	1.5m	Temp Trop S.tr	•	•			•	•	2	L	N
manbya manbyi ck Palm	A shapely slender palm with large divided leaves. Suitable as an indoor or patio tub specimen. Becomes a tall tree in the ground in warmer climates.	15-25m	5-7m	Trop S.tr	•				•	•	L	2	S
ndorea minoides uthern Belle'	Light climber or upright shrub; glossy pinnate leaves, profuse, large tubular pink flowers most of year. Elegant basket or container plant. Prune lightly.	90cm-1.2m	50-80cm	Temp Trop S.tr	•				•	•		L	
ysace lanceolata straflora Flower	Small suckering shrub, tiny rounded leaves, plum new growth, pink buds opening to white bouquets in spring-early summer. Containers, path edges.	10-20cm	40-60cm	Temp S.tr	•		•		•	•	1	L	
a labillardierei sock Grass	Small to large tussock with fine grey-green leaves; green to straw-coloured flower and seed heads slightly held above foliage. Attractive soil binder.	30-90cm	40cm-1m	Temp S.tr S.ar	•		•	•	•	•	1	H	S
yscias nbucifolius eberry Ash	Medium to large shrub, variously divided dark green leaves, tiny perfumed flowers in spring; blue fruit. Excellent 'designer' plant for ferneries or indoors.	1.5-4m	60cm-2m	Temp Trop S.tr	•					•		L	
tia pedunculata straflora Pink rs'	Creeping matting plant, tiny leaves, pink star flowers spring-summer. Suitable for soil binding, path and pool edges, and damp areas.	prostrate	1-2m	Temp Trop S.tr	•	•			•	•		L	
stanthera anthos lista Pink'	Medium shrub or small tree, aromatic foliage, large bunches of showy pink flowers in summer. Ideal screening plant; grows well with ferns.	3-5m	1.5-2m	Temp S.tr	•				•	•		L	

		Height	Width	Climatic zones	Soil types				full sun	filtered sun	coastal regions	frosty regions
	Temp — temperate · W.te — warm temperate · Trop — tropical · S.tr — sub-tropical · S.ar — semi-arid · L — light · H — heavy · N — nectar-feeding · S — seed-eating · F — fruit-eating				moist, well drained	wet	dry	dry limy				
Prostanthera lasianthos 'Mint Ice'	Medium shrub, variegated foliage, clusters of perfumed white flowers in summer. Suitable as light screen, especially in shaded areas. Prune lightly after flowering.	2-3m	1.2-2m	Temp S.tr	•				•	•		L
Prumnopitys ladei Lade's Pine	Medium to large rainforest shrub, bright green soft foliage arrayed in flat fans, attractive peeling brown bark. Container or sheltered courtyard.	3-6m	2.5-5m	Temp Trop S.tr	•					•		
Rhodanthe anthemoides 'Paper Baby' 'Paper Cascade' 'Paper Star'	Soft small shrubs, silvery foliage; wine-red buds, shiny white starry flowers spring-summer. Cottage garden, container, rockery. Prune lightly after flowering.	30-50cm	40-60cm	Temp S.tr	•				•	•		H
Rhododendron notiale Mt Bartle Frere Rhododendron	Small shrub, large glossy leaves, showy pink-red flowers in summer. Container plant, or combined with ferns. Similar to R. lochiae.	80cm-1.5m	1-1.5m	Temp Trop S.tr	•					•		
Scaevola aemula 'Blue Fandango'	Small upright shrub, soft light green leaves, blue-purple fan flowers in terminal clusters, spring-summer-autumn. Rockery or container plant. Prune lightly.	30-50cm	30-60cm	Temp S.tr	•				•	•	1	
Scaevola aemula 'Purple Fanfare'	Showy groundcover; bronze stems, dark leaves; purple fan flowers in terminal clusters, spring-summer-autumn. Rockery or container plant. Prune lightly.	20-30cm	60cm-1m	Temp S.tr	•				•	•	1	
Tecomanthe hillii 'Austraflora Island Belle'	Twining liane; glossy pinnate foliage, spectacular clusters of pink waxy flowers spring-summer. Courtyards, ferneries, large terracotta containers. Exotic, decorative. Selected cultivar.	climber	medium	Temp Trop S.tr	•					•	2	L
Telopea 'Shady Lady'	Handsome large shrub, broad leaves, numerous large red waratah flowers in spring. Showy specimen; lovely cut flower.	2-3m	1.5-2.5m	Temp Trop S.tr	•				•	•		L
Telopea speciosissima 'Dreaming'	Medium upright shrub, grey-green foliage, striking lipstick-pink flowers in spring. Spectacular when mass planted or in large container. Prune after flowering.	2-3m	1-2m	Temp S.tr	•				•	•		L
Telopea speciosissima 'Fire 'n Ice'	Medium upright shrub, glossy green foliage; deep red globular flowerheads touched with white. One of a number of recent choice selections.	2-3m	1-2m	Temp S.tr	•				•	•		L
Telopea speciosissima 'Wirrimbirra White'	Medium upright shrub, grey-green lobed leaves, large luminous white flowerheads in spring. Spectacular in groups; superb cut flower. Prune after flowering.	2-3m	1-2m	Temp S.tr	•				•	•		L
Telopea speciosissima x mongaensis 'Braidwood Brilliant'	Medium shrub, large grey-green leaves, brilliant red globular flowers in spring. Spectacular in courtyards, formal landscapes, large containers. Prune after flowering.	1.5-2m	1-2m	Temp S.tr	•				•	•		H

					Soil types								
		Height	Width	Climatic zones	moist, well drained	wet	dry	dry limy	full sun	filtered sun	coastal regions	frosty regions	bird attraction
mp—temperate L—light te—warm temperate H—heavy p—tropical N—nectar-feeding r—sub-tropical S—seed-eating r—semi-arid F—fruit-eating													
setum spicatum stle Grass	Shapely clump, dense erect grey-green leaves; flowering heads purplish, held well above foliage. Elegant pool-side or courtyard plant.	45-70cm	30-50cm	Temp S.tr	•				•	•		H	S
ahlenbergia stricta ebells	Tiny perennial herb, white or multi-petalled deep blue flowers spring-summer. Cottage garden, containers, rockeries. Suckers lightly.	20-40cm	30cm-1m	Temp S.tr S.ar	•		•		•	•		H	
estringia dna Walling'	Shapely medium shrub, small grey-green foliage, dainty lilac flowers along stems in winter-spring-summer. Formal hedging or specimen shrub. Prune lightly.	80cm-1.2m	80cm-1m	Temp S.tr S.ar	•		•		•	•	1	L	
estringia abra Cadabra'	Medium shrub, dense grey-green foliage, profuse violet-lilac flowers in winter-spring. Hedge, screen or shaped specimen. Prune after flowering.	1-1.5m	1.5-2m	Temp Trop S.tr S.ar	•		•		•	•	1	H	
estringia hite Rambler'	Spreading groundcover, small dense fleshy green leaves, white flowers in spring-summer. Soil binder. Prune regularly.	30cm	1m	Temp Trop S.tr	•		•		•	•	1		
ollemia nobilis ollemi Pine	Recently discovered spectacular large pine, with broad segmented fan-shaped leaves and unusual pimpled bark. A must for every Australian park.	10-30m	8-12m	Temp Trop S.tr	•					•			S
eria cytisioides nk Crystals'	Small compact shrub, aromatic foliage, starry pink flowers late winter-spring. Excellent low hedge or container plant. Prune lightly to shape.	80cm-1m	80cm-1m	Temp	•				•	•	2	L	

Changes to Botanical Names

The following list presents recent name changes that apply to plants this *Australflora A–Z*. The former name of a plant is given first; the recently changed or new name of that plant is listed below it.

Albizia lophantha
Paraserianthes lophantha

Alocasia macrorrhiza
Alocasia macrorrhizos

Alyogyne huegelii
Alyogyne pinoniana

Astroloma ciliatum
Astroloma foliosum

Baeckea crenatifolia
Babingtonia crenulata

Baeckea densifolia
Babingtonia densifolia

Baeckea virgata
Babingtonia pluriflora

Backhousia anisata
Anetholea anisata

Beaufortia heterophylla
Beaufortia cyrtodonta

Billardiera bicolor
Marianthus bicolor

Billardiera drummondiana
Marianthus drummondiana

Billardiera erubescens
Marianthus erubescens

Billardiera ringens
Marianthus ringens

Brachycome (all spp.)
Brachyscome (all spp.)

Brachycome sp. Pilliga
Brachyscome formosa

Brachysema lanceolatum
Brachysema celsianum

Brachysema sericeum (black)
Brachysema melanopetalum

Brachysema sericeum (red)
Brachysema minor

Calectasia cyanea has been split into two species:
C. cyanea (WA); **C. intermedia** (Vic and SA)

Callistemon 'Genoa River'
Callistemon forresterae

Callistemon macropunctatus
Callistemon rugulosus

Callistemon paludosus
Callistemon sieberi

Callistemon sieberi
Callistemon pityoides

Callistemon speciosus
Callistemon glaucus

Callitris columellaris
Callitris glaucophylla (some regions)

Calocephalus brownii
Leucophyta brownii

Cassia (all spp.)
Senna

Cassia nemophila
Senna artemisioides ssp. *filifolia*

Cassia odorata
Senna odorata

Casuarina cristata
Casuarina pauper (some regions)

Casuarina decaisneana
Allocasuarina decaisneana

Casuarina distyla
Alloasuarina distyla

Casuarina glauca
syn. *Casuarina obesa*

Casuarina humilis
Allocasuarina humilis

Casuarina inophloia
Allocasuarina inophloia

Casuarina lehmanniana
Allocasuarina lehmanniana

Casuarina littoralis
Allocasuarina littoralis

Casuarina muellerana
Allocasuarina muellerana

Casuarina nana
Allocasuarina nana

Casuarina paludosa
Allocasuarina paludosa

Casuarina pinaster
Allocasuarina pinaster

Casuarina pusilla
Allocasuarina pusilla

Casuarina torulosa
Allocasuraina torulosa

Casuarina verticillata
Allocasuarina verticillata

Claytonia australasica and *Montia australasica*
Neopaxia australasica

Clianthus formosus
Swainsona formosa

Correa schlectendalii
Correa glabra var. *turnbullii*

Cotula filicula
Leptinella filicula

Craspedia spp. (numerous new species now recognised)

Craspedia globosa
Pycnosorus globosus

Cryptandra scortechinii
Stenanthemum scortechinii

Dampiera linearis (purple)
Dampiera pedunculata

Danthonia caespitos
Austrodanthonia caespitosa

Dianella laevis
Dianella longifolia

Dichopogon strictus
Arthopodium strictum

Eriostemon angustifolius ssp. *montanus*
Philotheca angustifolia ssp. *montana*

Eriostemon 'Bournda Beauty'
Philotheca 'Bournda Beauty'

Eriostemon buxifolius
Philotheca buxifolia

Eriostemon myoporoides
Philotheca myoporoides

Eriostemon nodiflorus
Philotheca nodiflora

Eriostemon pungens
Philotheca pungens

Eriostemon spicatus
Philotheca spicata

Eriostemon verrucosus
Philotheca verrucosa

NB: *Eriostemon australasius* remains in *Eriostemon*

Eucalyptus alpina
Eucalyptus verrucata

Eucalyptus citriodora
Corymbia citriodora

Eucalyptus eximea
Corymbia eximea

Eucalyptus ficifolia
Corymbia ficifolia

Eucalyptus foelschiana
Corymbia foelschiana

Eucalyptus gummifera
Corymbia gummifera

Eucalyptus intermedia
Corymbia intermedia

Eucalyptus maculata
Corymbia maculata

Eucalyptus miniata
Corymbia miniata

Eucalyptus papuana
Corymbia paracolpica

Eucalyptus pauciflora 'pendula'
Eucalyptus lacrimans

Eucalyptus peltata
Corymbia peltata

Eucalyptus phoenicea
Corymbia phoenicea

Eucalyptus ptychocarpa
Corymbia ptychocarpa

Eucalyptus setosa
Corymbia setosa

Eucalyptus spathulata ssp.
grandiflora
Eucalyptus suggrandis

Eucalyptus tessellaris
Corymbia tessellaris

Eucalyptus torelliana
Corymbia torelliana

Euodia elleryana
Melicope elleryana

Grevillea glabrata
Grevillea manglesii

Grevillea paniculata (pink)
Grevillea levis

Grevillea speciosa ssp. dimorpha
(all forms)
Grevillea dimorpha

Grevillea speciosa ssp. oleoides
Grevillea oleoides

Grevillea thelemanniana (grey leaf)
Grevillea humifusa

Hakea sericea has now been split
into two species:
H. **sericea** SE Q to SE NSW (nat.
Anglesea, Vic); H. **decurrens**
SE NSW, Vic, Tas (nat. in SA)

Halgania preissiana
Halgania anagalloides var.
preissiana

Helichrysum apiculatum
Chrysocephalum apiculatum

Helichrysum argophyllum
Ozothamnus argophyllus

Helichrysum baxteri
Chrysocephalum baxteri

Helichrysum bracteatum
Bracteantha bracteata

Helichrysum obcordatum
Ozothamnus obcordatus

Helichrysum ramosissimum
Chrysocephalum apiculatum

Helichrysum semipapposum
Chrysocephalum semipapposum

Helichrysum viscosum
Bracteantha viscosa

Helichrysum obtusifolium
Argentipallium obtusifolium

Helipterum anthemoides
Rhodanthe anthemoides

Helipterum manglesii
Rhodanthe manglesii

Helipterum roseum
Rhodanthe chlorocephala ssp.
rosea

Hovea heterophylla
Hovea linearis

Hoya rubida (introduced)

Ipomoea brasiliensis
Ipomoea pes-caprae ssp
brasiliensis

Kunzea ericifolia
Kunzea muelleri

Leptospermum flavescens
Leptospermum polygalifolia

Leptospermum juniperinum
Leptospermum continentalis

Leptospermum juniperinum
'Horizontalis'
Leptospermum scoparium
'Austraflora Horizontalis'

Leptospermum lanigerum var.
macrocarpum
Leptospermum macrocarpum

Leptospermum nitidum
Leptospermum turbinatum

Leptospermum scoparium var.
rotundifolium
Leptospermum rotundifolium

Licuala muelleri
Licuala ramsayi

Lonchocarpus stipularis
Austrosteenisia stipularis

Mentha gracilis
Mentha diemenica

Metrosideros queenslandicus
Thaleropia queenslandica

Micromyrtus drummondii
Micromyrtus obovata

Milletia megasperma
Callerya megasperma

Myoporum debilis
Eremophila debilis

Myoporum deserti
Eremophila deserti

Myoporum ellipticum
Myoporum boninense ssp.
australe

Oreocallis pinnata
Alloxylon pinnatum

Oreocallis wickhamii
Alloxylon wickhamii and
A. **flammeum**

Oxylobium tricuspidatum
Gastrolobium pusillum

Parahebe perfoliata
Derwentia perfoliata

Phebalium bilobum
Leionema bilobum

Phebalium lamprophyllum
Leionema lamprophyllum

Phebalium phylicifolius
Leionema phylicifolium

Pittosporum rhombifolium
Auranticarpa rhombifolia

Pittosporum phillyreoides (WA only)
Pittosporum angustifolium (WA,
E Aust)

Platytheca verticillata
Platytheca galioides

Poa australis (name no longer
applicable)

Pratia pedunculata
Lobelia pedunculata

Pratia purpurescens
Lobelia purpurescens

Prosanthera baxteri var. sericea
Prosanthera sericea

Pultenaea polyfolia var. mucronata
Pultenaea polyfolia

Restio tetraphyllus ssp.
meiostachyus
Baloskion tetraphyllum ssp.
meiostachyum

Sollya parviflora
Sollya heterophylla (fine leaf)

Stipa teretifolia, Stipa stipoides
Austrostipa stipoides

Stypandra caespitosa
Thelionema caespitosa

Toona australis
Toona ciliata

Nurseries Stocking a Substantial Range of Australian Plants

Australian Capital Territory

Rodney's Nursery
24 Beltana Road
Pialligo 2609

New South Wales

Altra Nursery
5 Depot Road
Peakhurst 2210

Annangrove Grevilleas
98 Annangrove Road
Kenthurst 2156

Catt's Nurseries (Swanes)
237 Marsden Road
Carlingford 2118

Catt's Nurseries (Swanes)
80 Port Hacking Road
Sylvania 2224

Cranebrook Native Nursery
Cranebrook Road
Cranebrook 2750

Joylyn Native Nursery
5 Joylyn Road
Annangrove 2156

Kangarutha Nursery
Evans Hill
Tathra 2550

Longview Nursery
27–29 Great Western Highway
Wentworth Falls 2782

Peards Borella Road Nursery
Borella Road
Albury 2640

Swanes Nursery
490 Galston Road
Dural 2158

Sydney Wildflower Nursery
Veno Street
Heathcote 2233

The Wildflower Place
453 The Entrance Road
Erina Heights 2260

Wirrimbirra Native Nursery
Hume Highway
Bargo 2574

Northern Territory

Alice Springs Nursery
Ross Highway
Alice Springs 0871

Aussie Palms
Stuart Highway
Berrimah 0828

Inland Nurseries
14 Heley Crescent
Alice Springs 0871

Ironstone Lagoon Nursery
Lagoon Rd
Berrimah 0828

Weowna Native Plant Nursery
Humpty Doo 0836

Queensland

Fairhill Native Plants and Gardens
Fairhill Rd
Yandina 4561

Yuruga Nursery
Kennedy Highway
Walkamin 4872

South Australia

Benara Road Native Plant Nursery
Mount Gambier 5290

Brenton Tucker Native Plants and
Carawatha Gardens
off Placid Estates Road
Wellington East via Tailem Bend
5260

Kallinyalla Nursery
10 Shaen Street
Port Lincoln 5606

Nangula Native Plant Nursery
Mount Gambier Road
Millicent 5280

Nellie Nursery
46 Randell Street
Mannum 5283

Northside Native Plants
19 Diagonal Road
Cavan 5094

Southern Native Plant Nursery
Chalk Hill road
McLaren Vale 5171

oods and Forests Department
rsery
lair Recreation Park
lair 5052

smania

lans Garden Centre
5 Westbury Road
ospect 7250

rmony Garden Centre
0 South Arm Road
uderdale 7021

dina Nursery
art's Road
dina 7325

nts of Tasmania Nursery
Hall Street
dgeway 7054

dbreast Nurseries
dge Road
gana 7277

dbreast Nurseries
–40 Channel Highway
argate 7153

verview Nursery
Forth Road
n 7310

ctoria

erglades Nursery
estern Highway
urrenheip 3352

rdenworld
0 Springvale Road
eysborough 3173

anite Rock Nursery
Deptford Road
anite Rock 3875

owmaster Swan Hill
Nyah Road
an Hill 3585

Hall Native Nursery
urray Valley Highway
rrawonga 3730

ranga Native Nursery
3 Maroondah Highway
ngwood 3134

Lang's Native Plant Nursery
564 Eleventh Street
Mildura West 3500

Mildura Native Nursery
Cureton Avenue
(towards Apex Park)
Mildura 3500

Mt Cassel Native Plants
Lot 9, Wildflower Driver
Pomonal 3381

Old Pepper Tree Nursery
Pryors Road
Horsham 3400

Payntings Nursery
Somerville Street
Bendigo 3550

Pomonal Wildflower Nursery
Wildflower Drive
Pomonal 3381

Pretlove Cottage Nursery
41 Wentworth Street
Warrnambool 3280

Terraflora
South Gippsland Highway
Leongatha 3953

Treeplanters Nursery
530 Springvale Road
Springvale 3172

Wakiti Nurseries
Midland Highway
Shepparton East 3631

Western Australia

Carramar Coastal Nursery
885 Mandurah Road
Baldivis 6171

Colour Drop Garden Centre
2696 Albany Highway
Kelmscott 6111

Everbloom Garden Centre
665 Railway Terrace
Sawyers Valley 6074

Hunter Street Nursery
11 Hunter Street
Broome 6725

Kalgoorlie Garden Centre
393 Hannan Street
Kalgoorlie 6430

Lullfitz Nursery
Cnr Caporn and Honey Streets
Wanneroo 6065

Waldecks Kingsley
173 Wanneroo Road
Kingsley 6026

Waldecks Melville
116 North Lake Road
Melville 6156

Zanthorrea Nursery
155 Watsonia Road
Maida Vale 6057

Further Reading

Australian Plants

The Australian Daisy Study Group, *Australian Daisies For Gardens and Floral Art*, Lothian, Melbourne, 1987.

The Australian Plant Study Group, *Grow What Where*, Nelson, Melbourne, 1980.

——, Nelson, Melbourne, 1983.

——, *Grow What Tree*, Nelson, Melbourne, 1985.

——, *Grow What Small Plant*, Nelson, Melbourne, 1987.

Australian Plants, Quarterly Journal of The Society for Growing Australian Plants.

Brooker, M. I. H., and Kleinig, D. A., *Field Guide to Eucalypts*: vol. 1, *South-eastern Australia*, Inkata Press, Melbourne and Sydney, 1983; vol. 2, *South-western and Southern Australia*, Inkata Press, Melbourne and Sydney, 1990.

Brownlie, John, and Forrester, Sue, *The Beauty of Australian Wildflowers*, Viking O'Neil, Melbourne, 1987.

Cunningham, G. M., Mulham, W. E., Milthorpe, P. L., and Leigh, J. H., *Plants of Western New South Wales*, Soil Conservation Service of New South Wales, Sydney, 1981.

Elliot, Gwen, *Colour Your Garden with Australian Plants*, Hyland House, Melbourne, 1984.

Elliot, W. Rodger, and Jones, David, *Encyclopaedia of Australian Plants*, vols 1–5, Lothian, Melbourne, 1980–90.

Flora of Melbourne, Society for Growing Australian Plants Maroondah, Ringwood, 1991.

George, A. S., *The Banksia Book*, Kangaroo Press, Kenthurst, 1984.

Harmer, J., *Northern Australian Plants*, S.G.A.P., Sydney, 1975.

Jones, David L., *Palms in Australia*, Reed, Sydney, 1984.

——, *Ornamental Rainforest Plants in Australia*, Reed, Sydney, 1986.

Jones, David L., and Gray, B., *Australian Climbing Plants*, Reed, Sydney, 1977.

Kelly, Stan, *Eucalypts*, rev. edn, vols 1–2, Nelson, Melbourne, 1983.

Molyneux, Bill, *Bush Journeys*, Nelson, Melbourne, 1985.

Nicholson, Nan, and Nicholson, Hugh, *Australian Rainforest Plants*, Terania Rainforest Nursery, The Channon via Lismore, 1985.

Simmons, Marion, *Acacias of Australia*, Nelson, Melbourne, 1981.

Williams, Keith A. W., *Native Plants of Queensland*, vols 1–2, Keith A. W. Williams, Ipswich, 1979–84.

Wrigley, John W., and Fagg, Murray, *Australian Native Plants*, Collins, Sydney, 1979.

——, *Banksias, Waratahs and Grevilleas*, Collins, Sydney, 1989.

Landscape Design

Molyneux, Bill, *Grow Native*, Anne O'Donovan, Melbourne, 1980.

Molyneux, Bill, and Forrester, Sue, *Native Gardens in Miniature*, Kangaroo Press, Kenthurst, 1992.

Molyneux, Bill, and Macdonald, Ross, *Native Gardens: How to Create an Australian Landscape*, Kangaroo Press, Kenthurst, 1992.

Snape, Diana, *Australian Native Gardens: Putting Visions into Practice*, Lothian, Melbourne, 1992.

General Maintenance

Chapman, Bruce, Penman, David, and Hicks, Phillip, *The Garden Pest Book*, Nelson, Melbourne, 1985.

Elliot, W. Rodger, *Pruning: A Practical Guide*, Lothian, Melbourne, 1984.

Hockings, F. D., *Friends and Foes of Australian Gardens*, Reed, Sydney, 1983.

Plumridge, Jack, *How to Propagate Plants*, Lothian, Melbourne, 1976.

Acknowledgements

The authors would like to thank their many colleagues in the nursery and horticultural industry throughout Australia for their assistance with sourcing new material for this edition of *The Austraflora A-Z of Australian Plants*. In particular, thanks to Val Stajsic of National Herbarium, Melbourne, Victoria, for assistance in updating name changes.

Books by the Same Authors

Molyneux, Bill, *Bush Journeys*, Nelson, Melbourne 1983

Molyneux, Bill, *Grow Native*, Anne O'Donovan, Melbourne 1980

Molyneux, Bill, and Forrester, Sue, et al, *The Austraflora Handbook*, Montrose (numerous editions since 1973)

Molyneux, Bill, and Forrester, Sue, *Native Gardens in Miniature*, Kangaroo Press, Kenthurst 1992

Molyneux, Bill, and Macdonald, Ross, *Native Gardens: How to Create an Australian Landscape*, Kangaroo Press, Kenthurst 1992

Molyneux, Bill, and Forrester, Sue, *Emma's Journey*, Molyneux & Forrester, Melbourne 2001